The Art of Magic

THE ART OF MAGIC

BY
T. NELSON DOWNS

AUTHOR OF
MODERN COIN MANIPULATION

EDITED BY
JOHN NORTHERN HILLIARD

WITH 68 ILLUSTRATIONS

Published in 2011
By Houdini's Magic Shop
Las Vegas, NV 89118
USA
www.houdini.com

ISBN: 978-1-936759-07-1
Copyright 2011

All rights are reserved. No part of this publication may be reproduced, stored in a retrieval system or transmitted, in any form or by any means mechanical, photocopying, recording or otherwise, without prior written permission of Houdini's Magic Shop, Inc.

Printed in U. S.A

ORIGINAL PUBLICATION

THE DOWNS-EDWARDS COMPANY

ENTERED AT STATIONERS' HALL, LONDON. ENGLAND
PUBLISHED JANUARY. 1909

PUBLISHED BY
ARTHUR P. FELSMAN
3234 Harrison Street,
CHICAGO, ILLINOIS

T. NELSON DOWNS.

To Dr. Albert M. Wilson of Kansas City, Editor of "The Sphinx," Collector of Magical Literature, and Lover of the Oldest Art in the World, whose Generous Assistance and Words of Encouragement have helped the Author, Editor and Publishers over many difficulties, this Volumne is Dedicated

CONTENTS

PAGE

CHAPTER I.
Flourishes and Fancy Sleights with Cards 17

CHAPTER II.
Card Tricks with Unprepared Cards and Not Requiring Sleight of Hand 40

CHAPTER III.
Card Tricks Involving Sleight of Hand 52

CHAPTER IV.
Sleight of Hand with Cards (continued) 80

CHAPTER V.
Sleight of Hand with Cards (continued) 111

CHAPTER VI.
Card Tricks Based on a New and Original System of Locating a Chosen Card 142

CHAPTER VII.
Clairvoyance With Cards 165

CHAPTER VIII.
A Series of Card Tricks Based on a New and Original System 169

CHAPTER IX.
The Rising Cards 183

CONTENTS

CHAPTER X.
The Four Ace Trick 213

CHAPTER XI.
Card Tricks with Apparatus and in Combination with other Objects 224

CHAPTER XII.
Fancy Flourishes with Coins, Useful Sleights and Additions to the Miser's Dream 243

CHAPTER XIII.
Coin Tricks with and without Apparatus 251

CHAPTER XIV.
A Coin Act and a Coin Ladder 278

CHAPTER XV.
Tricks of the Trade 289

CHAPTER XVI.
Tricks with Eggs 294

CHAPTER XVII.
Tricks with Balls 305

CHAPTER XVIII.
Miscellaneous Tricks 319

THE ART OF MAGIC

INTRODUCTORY

For the purpose of this book it will be convenient to divide magic into three branches: manual dexterity, mental subtleties and the surprising results produced by a judicious and artistic blending of the second and third branches. There are other branches, to be sure; but they are of little interest to modern students of the magic art. A century ago, and, indeed, as late as Robert-Houdin's day, a general knowledge of the physical sciences was considered necessary to the equipment of the conjurer or magician; and the old writers on magic filled their pages with clumsy experiments in chemistry, physics, mechanics and mathematics. In order to be an original conjurer of the first magnitude, said Robert-Houdin, it is necessary to have more than a speaking acquaintance with the sciences, so as to apply their principles to the invention of illusions and stage tricks. Houdin himself utilized chemistry, optics and physics, while many of his greatest and most successful illusions were based on the then little known science of electricity. Things have changed since Houdin's day, however, and the art he practiced has taken many forward strides toward the goal of perfection.

The modern conjurer is little inclined to base his magical effects on the expedients of physical science, but rather places his reliance on neatness of manipulation, on ingenious and interesting patter, and on a dexterity which, in many cases, seems to have been raised to its Nth power. It was the "Father of Modern Conjuring" who laid down this admirable rule: "To succeed as a conjurer, three things are essential: first, dexterity; second, dexterity; and third, dexterity." Would not Robert-Houdin open his eyes in amazement could he return to earth and remark the advance made in dexterity and manipulation since his day? "I myself practiced palming long and perseveringly," he tells us in his monumental work on conjuring, "and acquired thereat

The Art of Magic

a very considerable degree of skill. I used to be able to palm two five-franc pieces at once, the hand nevertheless remaining as freely open as though it held nothing whatever." He is a very ordinary performer who, in this age, cannot conceal a dozen or fifteen coins in his hand, and pluck them singly from the palm to produce in a fan at the finger tips; and there are several specialists in coin manipulation who experience no difficulty in handling a larger number of coins, thinking nothing, for instance, of concealing from thirty-five to forty coins in the hand; and, what is even more remarkable, executing the pass with this unstable stack as easily and indectably as if they were handling three or four half-dollars.

Magic has undergone many changes in the last quarter of a century. The devotees of the art have gone from one extreme to the other; from the simplicity of the school of Frickell to the cumbersome stage setting of Anderson, and from Anderson to Frickell again. The last decade was devoted to manipulation and specialization. Kings and emperors and dukes and panjamdrums of cards and coins, monarchs of eggs and handkerchiefs, czars of cabbages and billiard balls sprung up like mushrooms. Magic degenerated into a mere juggling performance. Dexterity was paramount and the psychological side of the art neglected. Mind gave way to matter. The conjurer aimed at novelty rather than entertainment. He "worked in one," to employ the vernacular of the stage, and in most instances gave a silent act. Of course, there were exceptions. A few—a very few—performers presented a really artistic act with cards and coins; but as each clever performer had a host of bungling imitators the profession became overcrowded and vaudeville managers were "not in" when an engagement-seeking magician sent in his card.

The cause of the overwhelming craze for manipulation was the discovery of the backhand palm, a sleight that has done more to initiate outsiders into the mysteries of magic than all the empirical magicians who have exposed tricks for the delectation of their audiences. As an ornamental sleight or flourish the backhand palm with cards is an exquisite thing; but it is a frail

The Art of Magic

foundation on which to build a card act, as many vaudeville performers have done. This is so because there is not a performer living, no matter how skillful he may be in executing this particular sleight, who can operate near the front of a stage and succeed in mystifying his entire audience with the backhand manipulation of cards. The angle of visibility is against him, and dexterity counts for little when the performer is handicapped by a law of optics. The spectators on the extreme right, or on the extreme left, as the case may be, inevitably catch occasional glimpses of the cards; and thus not only is the illusion of the cards disappearing into thin air destroyed, but — and this is vastly more important — the illusion that magic is something more than mere rapidity of movement is destroyed. It should be more to the purpose of the magician that the mind of the spectator be deceived than his eye; but the modern prestidigitator does not seem to realize this important distinction. Restricted, therefore, to a few — very few — manipulative movements, the backhand palm with cards is a decidedly effective addition to a magical programme, and we should advise every magician to become proficient in the sleight. But do not make this manipulation a dominating feature of the programme.

What has been said regarding the backhand palm with cards applies more or less to all flourishes and ornamental sleights. The performer is earnestly advised to curb the very natural desire to exploit his dexterity, or, in plain language, to "show off," and to be sparing in exhibiting fancy movements. It is effective to introduce a flourish or ornamental sleight at odd moments between tricks, or while the assistant is performing some duty among the audience. Such little exhibitions of skill make a good impression on the audience, and as the movements are executed rapidly the spectators are both surprised and mystified. Many persons who do not remember a single trick or illusion of the late Alexander Herrmann's programme will descant enthusiastically on the artistic manner in which he "shuffled cards with one hand." A certain foreign conjurer, who disguises himself under the attractive title of L'Homme

The Art of Magic

Masque (of whom we shall have more to say) actually shuffles the cards with either the right or left hand; but it is an operation that demands a large and powerful hand. To cite another example of the value of fancy sleights, how much more attractive Mr. Kellar's programme would have been, had he executed occasional flourishes with the cards!

The magic of today, however, is not like the magic of yesterday. The art of deception, like other arts, advances with every swing of the pendulum. Happily the mania for manipulation has abated, and the conjurer of the day is ambitious to entertain and mystify his audiences rather than to present a mere juggling act. One of the signs of the times is the revival of apparatus — not the cumbersome contraptions of Anderson and his followers, but the neat and attractive small things that add picturesqueness to the stage or drawing-room setting and do not detract from the mystery of the programme. This is as it should be. The ideal conjuring performance is a happy combination of apparatus and sleight of hand.

As to the future of magic, we shall not venture a prediction. Our good friend Dr. Wilson looks forward to the day when electricity shall become the nimble assistant and obedient servant of the worker of wonders; when the mysterious fluid will relegate strings, threads, pistons and such adventitious aids to the limbo of the obsolete; when it will open and close doors in cabinets, the lids of boxes, the traps in tables; and when by means of the counteracting forces of the positive and negative electro-magnet a body will be suspended in space after the manner of the traditional levitation of the coffin of Mahomet at El Medinah. As a matter of fact, however, the coffin of the Prophet is not suspended in space; and, while we shall not take issue with Dr. Wilson's prediction, we believe that electricity is not reliable enough to act as the assistant to the modern magician, and also that when the positive and negative poles of an electro-magnet hold the human body in space some genius will have invented a machine capable of perpetual motion and some alchemist will have discovered the secret of transmitting the baser metals into

The Art of Magic

gold. In such an age of real wonders mere magic will not be tolerated.

But all this is beside the mark. What have we to do with the future? The present volume is designed to give an account of the latest novelties in the fascinating art of deception and the most up-to-date methods in the magic of cards, coins, handkerchiefs, eggs, billiard balls, and other accessories of the modern conjurer. The lion's share of the space is devoted to tricks with cards. Three reasons may be advanced for this preference: First, card conjuring is the most popular department of magic; second, a pack of cards is susceptible to more surprising effects than all the other accessories of the magician; third, it has been many years since an elaborate treatise on cards has appeared. The author hopes that in the following pages the reader, be he amateur or professional, will find much to entertain and instruct. The explanations will presuppose an acquaintance with the ordinary sleights of the conjurer. When the book was first planned a chapter was devoted to new sleights with cards and coins and other small objects; but in the actual working out of the volume it was found more practicable to explain each new sleight in the actual description of the trick in which the "move" was introduced. In the description of new and novel methods of performing old favorites, such as the Four Ace trick, the Rising Card trick, etc., it has been deemed expedient to include references to standard works of conjuring in which the particular trick may be found, thus making the volume a valuable book of reference. Our heartiest thanks are due for much friendly assistance from correspondents in all quarters of the globe; and if we have not given credit where credit is due, it is only because of the almost impossible task of fixing the parentage of a trick or illusion beyond reasonable doubt.

T. NELSON DOWNS,
Author.

J. NORTHERN HILLIARD,
Editor.

Buffalo, N. Y., October 1st, 1908.

CHAPTER I

FLOURISHES AND FANCY SLEIGHTS WITH CARDS.

The effects described in this chapter belong naturally to the juggling order of sleight of hand, albeit they are none the less interesting for all that. Considering the recent craze for manipulation it is rather surprising that writers on magic have not made more of a specialty of this fascinating branch of the conjurer's art. From the time of Robert-Houdin down to the present day the elucidators of the arts and artifices of the craft have contented themselves with describing such simple flourishes as springing the cards, throwing the cards, one-hand passes, and turning the cards over on a cloth-covered table. There are a score or more ornamental sleights, however, that have never been explained in a treatise on magic, and which may be made valuable, to the manipulator and the card magician. We say "valuable" advisedly; for we do not believe in carrying manipulation and mere juggling dexterity to excess as many modern performers have done. But we earnestly advise the student to devote a modicum of his leisure moments to the acquirement of a series of fancy sleights and flourishes; for a mastery of these difficult movements will assist him materially in becoming proficient in the sleights. There is no limit to the degree of dexterity that can be attained by practice. In magic, as in other professions or vocations, there is no royal road to proficiency. Excellence is attained only by long years of arduous endeavor. Practice and practice only will bring the desired results. And after the desired degree of dexterity is attained the student should not, in the vanity of his achievement, exhibit his dexterity and boast of the rapidity with which he can execute the various movements. It is not quickness of the hand that deceives the eye, as the spectators so fondly imagine. The modern conjurer

The Art of Magic

depends for success on a more adroit and more permanent foundation — psychology. The cunning hand works in harmony with the active mind, and by means of both mental and physical adroitness the spectators are deceived and mystified. The really expert performer, however, does not prattle of his dexterity. He lets art conceal art. This should be the motto of every earnest student and exponent of magic.

This is the first treatise on the magic art in which a serious attempt has been made to collect and explain the various fancy movements with cards, and the student will find a variety of manipulations that, at first trial, he will consider impossible of achievement; but we hasten to assure the neophyte that nothing herein described is either impossible or impracticable. With the necessary practice even the most difficult drop catches with cards will, in time, become easy of achievement. Before entering upon our explanations, however, it will not be out of place to say a word or two concerning a very important consideration in conjuring, namely:

THE CARDS. — For superior work in manipulation, or in the presentation of tricks, good cards are necessary. Cheap cards are clumsy and difficult to handle with finished effect. "The adept at sleight of hand should accustom himself to the use of every description of cards," was Professor Hoffman's advice in "Modern Magic." When, however, the choice of cards is open to the performer, this authority recommended the use of smaller and thinner cards. Furthermore, the student was advised to use a piquet pack of thirty-two cards (the twos, threes, fours, fives and sixes being removed), the "complete whist pack being too bulky for sleight of hand purposes." This advice seems rather absurd in this day; for the twentieth century conjurer prides himself on his ability to handle or manipulate any kind of card, and the "Juniors" and the "Tankervilles" are relegated to the limbo of the obsolete. While we believe in the facility to use any make or pattern of cards, it is our experience that there is one ideal card for conjuring purposes. We have

The Art of Magic

in mind the card known commonly as the "Angel Back," which meets all the demands of card conjuring. These cards are strong, flexible, and highly polished. The student who is not accustomed to handling "Angel Backs" will find them rather difficult to manipulate at the outset; but with patience and perseverance the difficulty will be overcome. These cards come in two colors, red and blue. We advise the amateur conjurer to select cards with blue backs, for the reason that when a card is palmed there is not so much danger of a keen-eyed spectator catching a glimpse of its polished back in case there is a slight opening between the fingers. For backhand manipulation a cheap, uncalendered card is more desirable. The pasteboard known as the "Steamboat, No. 999" is the best for this purpose. The card being soft and pliable does not "talk" as it is shuttled between the fingers.

The first flourish to be described is known in the vernacular of the card conjurer as

THE CARD FAN.

This is one of the elemental flourishes as well as one of the simplest, for which reason it is passing strange that but comparatively few performers accomplish the move with grace and artistic effect. The fan is made with a slight twisting movement of the fingers and thumb; but, simple as it is, the movement is almost impossible to describe on paper. With practice it is astonishing how wide a fan can be made with one movement of the fingers and thumb. There are some performers who can almost describe a circle with the cards. The fan is used to excellent advantage in a movement that is known as the "Vanish and Recovery." The cards are apparently placed in the left hand. In reality, however, they are palmed in the right. The right hand then produces the cards fanwise at the left elbow, or behind the right knee, while at the precise moment of production, the left hand is open and shown empty. The cards may also be produced from the inside of the coat, fanning them as they come into view. A good effect is produced by striking the skull with the left hand and immediately producing the cards from the nose, fanning them as usual. The fan method of production adds greatly to the effect, the fan leading the spectators to believe that it is impossible to conceal such a quantity of cards in the hand. It is also a good plan to produce cards from the backhand in a fan, the effect being that the performer actually plucks a half dozen or so cards out of the thin air. This move may be varied very effectively by producing the cards at the left heel.

While on the subject of the "Vanish and Recovery" it will not be out of place to describe a simple and artistic method of vanishing a deck of cards and reproducing it from the vest. There are many ways of vanishing a complete pack, including divers kinds of mechanical clips and pulls which the amateur performer will do well to eschew — the professional will not use such contraptions anyway, so the advice will be lost on him—but the following sleight of hand method is the most startling and illusive. Hold the pack in the right hand face downward, the thumb at the lower end, the second, third and little fingers at the upper end, and the first finger curled on top of the pack. Now exert a slight pressure on the cards with the fingers and thumb, which will bend the cards in this position The left hand is now extended palm upward, and the right hand is held so that the upper part of the pack just touches the fingers of the left hand at *exactly* the *first* joints. The lower end of the pack, which is held by the thumb, is raised about an inch above the left palm. The lower edges of the cards are now allowed to spring from the thumb, one by one, causing a sharp, crackling sound as they strike against the left palm. The instant the last card leaves the right thumb the left hand is quickly reversed, so that its back is toward the audience. The cards are really in the palm of the left hand. This method of palming is simplicity itself, because, if the directions for the ruffle have been implicitly followed, the pack will lie in the left hand in exact position for palming, so that it is only necessary to contract the fingers slightly as the

The Art of Magic

hand is turned over. All these separate movements have been described at length, but in actual practice they coalesce, the effect being that the left hand is reversed simultaneously with the riffling of the cards. The left hand is extended, back toward audience, the performer's eyes fixed intently on the back of the hand, the index finger of the right hand pointing at the extended left. Maintain this position for a moment. Then relax, smile pleasantly, and remark, "Oh, no! I would not deceive you in that way. The cards are really in the left hand." While speaking the left hand is slowly and deliberately turned over, and the cards are revealed. The pack is now retaken in the right hand, exactly as described in the first movement, except that the cards are not curved. You now endeavor to imitate the first movement of placing the pack, with a riffling noise, into the left hand. This, however, is what you really do: As the right hand with the cards almost touches the left palm, instead of riffling the cards into the left palm, the fingers of the left hand grasp the deck, the left thumb in the exact center of one side, while the opposite side is grasped by the second, third and fourth fingers, the second finger being exactly opposite the thumb, while the little finger is at the lower end. The first finger of the left hand is curled under the pack. This position is important. The fingers of the right hand do not relax their grip on the cards. It will be remembered that in the first movement the right thumb produced the riffling noise. This time the left thumb obtains the same effect by drawing its tip rapidly over the left-side edges of the cards, the left first finger, which is curled under the pack, acting as a fulcrum. Now, the instant the cards are riffled the right index finger (which is curled on top of deck) is straightened and the pack palmed in the right hand. If the directions are implicitly followed it will be found that when the first finger is straightened the pack is in the exact position for palming. The cards are, in fact, propelled briskly into the palm, and at the same instant the left hand is reversed and elevated as if containing the cards. Care must be taken to hold the left hand exactly

The Art of Magic

as at first, when the cards were actually palmed; and if the simulation is carried out (this effect should be practiced before a looking-glass) the illusion is perfect. The right hand may now grasp the lapel of the coat, or, better still, take the wand from under the left arm, and, touching the left hand, show that the cards have vanished. The cards may be reproduced in any manner the performer prefers — from the left elbow, from behind the right knee, from the left heel, or from a spectator's whiskers or nose. The reproduction, it is unnecessary to add, should be in the form of a fan. Perhaps the most artistic method of reproducing a pack of cards, however, is from the vest; and the effective and very simple sleight by which the cards are introduced under the garment has never been explained, to the best of our knowledge, in a treatise on magic. Hold the right hand against the abdomen and insert the thumb under the vest. Hold the thumb rigidly against the inside of vest and turn the hand over so that palm faces audience. The simple movement of turning the hand introduces the cards under the vest, from which they may be slowly produced, a few at a time.

The following is an effective vanish for a half dozen cards. The cards, which are first exhibited fanwise, are bunched together and held in the right hand, which makes a motion as if tossing the cards into the air, whereupon they vanish. The right hand is shown back and front, the fingers wide apart, and the cards are recovered back of the right knee. This effective sleight is accomplished by means of a minute piece of apparatus known as the "Excelsior Clip," which may be bought at any stationery store. This spring clip has two arms, one of them bent over in the form of a hook, and sharpened to a point, so that it can be hooked to any part of the clothing. The working of the sleight will now be clear. The cards are placed in a clip and fanned. The cards are then closed, and the right hand makes two up and down motions. When the hand goes down the second time the cards are hooked to the trousers back of the right knee. The hand of course must not hesitate an instant; it is immediately

The Art of Magic

brought up and the cards, apparently, are vanished in the upward movement. It makes an effective interlude in a card programme.

CARD BALANCING.

The reader undoubtedly is familiar with an old trick known as the balancing card, in which a pasteboard is made to stand upright on a table without any visible means of support. This effect is accomplished by the use of a very small and simple apparatus, a strip of tin or brass, an inch and a half in length, and five-eights of an inch in width, bent at a trifle less than a right angle — say about eighty-five degrees, its shorter arm being one-third of its length. On the outer surface of the long arm is spread a thin layer of conjurer's wax, and to the inner surface of the shorter arm is soldered a small piece of lead, about an eighth of an inch thick. This little feke is pressed against the card in the act of placing the card on the table and thus forms a prop, or foot, the little lump of lead acting as a counterpoise to the weight of the card. This is an old trick (although a very good one and seldom seen nowadays) and the reason for referring to it is to introduce a new effect, namely, the balancing of an entire pack of cards on the fingers of the left hand. This trick is hardly of sufficient importance to be performed by itself; but as an incident introduced in the course of some more pretentious illusion produces a very good effect and serves to keep an audience interested and on the qui vive. As a matter of fact, the success of a conjuring entertainment often depends upon the performer's ability in introducing minor tricks that suggest spontaneity. The following experiment is of this variety: Hold the pack in left hand and show both sides of the right hand so as to convince the audience that no mechanical device is employed. Then transfer the pack to the right hand in order to show that there is nothing concealed in the left hand. In returning the cards to the left hand insert little finger of left hand under three or four of the top cards. Once more show that the right hand is empty. Place

The Art of Magic

pack on tips of fingers of right hand at back, as shown in Fig. 1, and in executing this movement the cards above the little

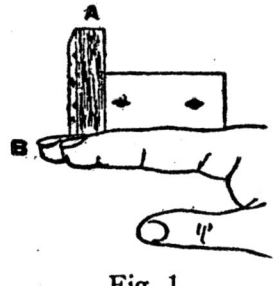

Fig. 1.

finger of the left hand are back-palmed into position between first and second fingers, as shown in at (B) in the illustration. This movement is completely covered by the left hand and the remainder of the cards. Do not prolong the effect, although some little time should be consumed in an effort to impress the spectators that the feat is extremely difficult to accomplish. In removing the pack all that is necessary is to relax the pressure on the backpalmed cards, allowing the pack (A) to fall on back of hand, the left hand immediately picking up the entire pack. If the performer desires he may hand the pack for examination, but a more effective method of proving that the cards are unprepared is

TO TEAR A PACK OF CARDS.

There is no deception about this spectacular feat, although a certain knack in holding the cards must be acquired. To tear a deck of fifty-two playing cards in twain requires a strong wrist and a powerful grip. There is just one way to hold the cards. The lower end of the pack, which must be carefully squared up, is laid across the ridge of the left palm exactly at the roots of the four fingers, the left thumb resting naturally on the lower left hand side of the pack. The four fingers are now closed tightly on the lower end of pack which has the effect of pressing the pack firmly against the left palm. The right hand now grasps the upper portion of the pack in exactly the same manner, only that the position is reversed, that is to say, the right thumb will be diametrically opposite the left thumb. These directions may seem a bit complicated, but they may be easily followed with a pack of cards in the hands. If the correct position is achieved it will be found that the cards are held as in a vise. Everything is now ready for the exhibition of strength. Twist the hands in opposite directions, the right hand turning to the right and the left hand to the left . Exert all your strength, and either your fingers or the deck will give way. At the outset you will find that the fingers cannot withstand the unusual strain, and for this reason it is wise to begin with thirty or thirty-five cards, gradually increasing the number until you can tear a whist pack. Cheap cards are easier to tear than the calendered variety, and a brand new pack is preferable to cards that are tough and leathery from much handling. It is related of the late Alexander Herrmann that after a private performance before the late Czar Nicholas II., his majesty, who was a very powerful man, undertook to show the magician a card feat that the latter could not imitate. He picked up a pack of cards and tore it into two pieces. "I am the only one in the world who can perform that feat," boastingly declared the Czar. Herrman said nothing, but, picking up one of the halves of the deck, calmly tore it in twain. This feat looks very difficult, but is really little more difficult than the tearing of a whole pack of cards. Were Nicholas alive he would doubtless be amazed to learn that some performers actually tear two complete decks of cards, while Sandow, so we have heard, can put three decks together and rip the unwieldy bunch asunder in the middle. An effective method of presenting this feat is to tear a new deck of cards, case, wrapper and all. This is not much more difficult than the tearing of a pack, but the effect is greatly enhanced.

The majority of spectators are skeptical about the ability of the amateur magician to tear a pack of cards. They are also prone to doubt the genuineness of the feat. They argue that the pack is spread in such a manner that the cards are torn one at a time. This explanation, of course, is absurd, but it is typical of the curious ideas sometimes conceived, by otherwise intelligent persons. The amateur performer will be repaid, therefore, by adding this feat to his repertory; for he will find in every company some individual who has seen Kellar tear a pack, or who has heard his wife's cousin's uncle tell of having seen the great Herrmann perform the feat. They are duly impressed, therefore, when the modest amateur successfully destroys his deck. There is a way of "faking" the pack so as to make the feat easier of accomplishment. The deck is screwed in a vise. A notch is filed in each side of the deck, exactly in the center. This cut will not be visible at a short distance. From our point of view, however, the magician who would take advantage of this subterfuge would use an "Electric," or string pack, in order to impress the audience with his dexterity.

THE FAN AND RUFFLE.

This movement is of the utmost simplicity, but its effect is out of all proportion to its intrinsic worth as a manipulatory movement. It may be used as a flourish or fancy sleight, or may be employed effectively as a false shuffle. The pack is held in the left hand, in the natural manner for dealing. The right hand is now brought to the top of the deck, and the left thumb spreads the cards in the form of a fan, the thumb and fingers of the right hand assisting in the movement. The right and left hands are then separated, each hand holding a half of the fan of cards, the faces of the cards toward the audience. The fan in the right hand is now brought directly in front of the cards in the left hand, so that the two fans touch. The performer now sweeps the fan of cards in the right hand briskly across the face of the cards fanned in the left, the cards giving forth a sharp, crackling sound. The instant the fan in the right hand is clear of the cards in the left hand the two packets are brought together and squared up. These separate movements, which are rather difficult to describe, coalesce, so to speak, in actual practice, and the rapidity with which they are done deceives the audience into the belief that an intricate movement has been accomplished. It is rather discouraging to the clever manipulator of cards to dis-

The Art of Magic

cover that his most elaborate movements, demanding ineffable skill and adroitness, should "fall flat," so to speak, whereas a simple movement like the fan and ruffle will elicit enthusiastic comment and admiration.

THE DOWNS FAN.

This is a bewildering move and is especially recommended as a brilliant opening to a series of front and back palm manipulations with cards. A good effect is also obtained by preceding this movement with the fan and ruffle just described. The effect of the flourish is as follows: The performer fans a pack of cards in his left hand (a movement, by the way that will not be accomplished without some practice). He shows that his right hand is empty, back and front, and then produces a fan of cards from behind the right knee. This is how the flourish is accomplished:

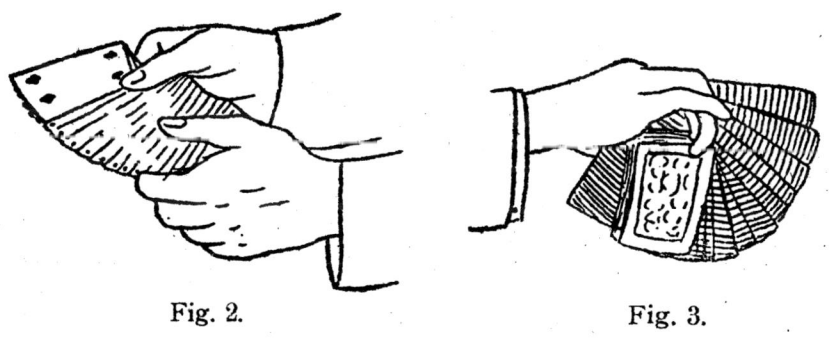

Fig. 2.   Fig. 3.

In the preliminary handling of the pack the performer palms a packet of cards in the right hand — a dozen cards is a good number for the experiment. He now fans the cards in the left hand, the right hand ostensibly assisting in the maneuver, Fig. 2, but in reality leaving the palmed packet behind the fan, securely gripped between the first and second fingers, Fig. 3. the cards are held, of course, so that the fan conceals the packet, Fig. 4. The proper position is to face the audience squarely, the left hand, palm outwards, hanging in a line with the left knee. The right hand is thrust straight out from the body, fingers wide apart, and shown back and front, so as to convince the audience that nothing can possibly be concealed in the hand. The performer now strikes the faces of the fan with the tips of the right fingers, and repeats the movement on the back of the fan. As the right hand fingers move back of the fan, the packet, which is gripped between the first and second fingers of the left hand, is

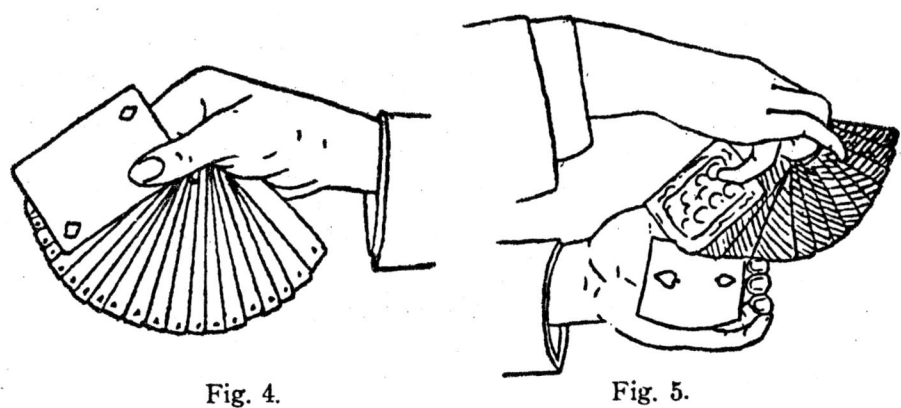

Fig. 4. Fig. 5.

palmed off in the right hand, Fig. 5. The instant the cards are palmed in the right hand, the left hand turns over so that the back of the fan is presented toward the audience. The right hand, containing the palmed cards, now strikes the back of the fan. Once more the face of the fan is exhibited to the audience and is held, face outward at the left knee. A slight wavy motion is made with the fan toward the right knee, and at the same moment the right hand produces, fanwise, the palmed cards from the right knee, the effect being that a portion of the cards in the left hand passed invisibly through the performer's knees and thence into his right hand. The movements may seem complicated on paper, but a few trials will enable the student to assume the proper positions of the body, hands and cards. It is the minute attention to details that is responsible for the beauty of this illusory effect.

SPRINGING THE CARDS.

This sleight, said Robert-Houdin, in his comprehensive volume on conjuring, is beyond question the most brilliant of all

The Art of Magic

the flourishes performed with a pack of cards. The "Father of Modern Magic" was acquainted with but one method of performing this fancy movement, however, and we suspect that the majority of his rivals in the conjuring art employed prepared cards to imitate the effect; for springing the cards requires a great deal of patient application before the knack is acquired. There are a number of methods of performing this flourish which are not commonly known to the magical fraternity, and which are here described for the first time in print. In the old method the cards are held in the right hand, between the tips of the second and third fingers at the top and the thumb at the bottom. The thumb and fingers are now brought slowly nearer together, so as to bend the cards slightly, when they will one by one, in quick succession, beginning with the bottom card, spring away from the pack. The left hand is held about a foot from the right, with the fingers slightly bent, so as to catch the flying cards. The following methods, however, are more effective:

FIRST METHOD — This is practically the reverse of the method just described. It is of the utmost importance that the student should understand at the outset the principle of holding the pack; for upon his accuracy in this matter depends his success in the series of the flourishes that follow. If the cards are held in the manner described for the old method the student will not be able to accomplish the new effects. The exact method of holding the pack is difficult to describe, but if the reader will follow the directions pack in hand he will soon acquire the knack. Extend the fingers and thumb of the right hand as far as possible, so that the hand is almost flat. The left hand now places the pack against the right hand exactly as follows: The middle of the top end of the pack is placed against the second joint of the second finger, while the corresponding part of the lower end is placed against the joint of the thumb. If the thumb and second finger are now brought slowly together, so as to bend the cards slightly, at the same time allowing the lower end of the cards to slip gradually to the very tip of the thumb, and the top end of the cards to slip to the tip of the second finger, the pack will describe a curve. As a result of the slipping movement each card is slightly separated from the other, the greatest space being at the center. Now, instead of bending the fingers so sharply that the cards will shoot into the air, as in the old method, the pressure of the tips of the thumb and second finger should be gently relaxed, which allows the cards to fall (beginning with the bottom card), and at the same moment the right hand describes a rapid sweep upward, the left hand following at a distance of ten or twelve inches. Just before making this upward sweep the right hand is held about waist high, the left hand, palm upward, just below the right. As a matter of fact, a half dozen cards actually fall from the right into the left hand before the right begins its upward sweep. After a little practice the student will be able to time the separation of the hands to a nicety. The hands should describe a sweep of at least two feet, and at the conclusion of the movement the left should be brought palm to palm with the right, the cards being instantly squared up. During the instant the cards are in the air there is a distance of about an eighth of an inch between each card, the effect being as if the performer were drawing out an accordion. This beautiful and striking effect cannot be duplicated by the old method of springing cards. We shall now describe a novel flourish which we are confident will be appreciated by the conjuring fraternity.

SECOND METHOD — This is more effective if anything than the flourish just described. The cards are held in exactly the same manner, but the position of the hand is different. Instead of the pack being held so that the bottom card faces the floor, as in the first method, the right wrist is turned slightly so that the right side of the pack is parallel with the floor. The left hand is held palm upward, and the lower side of the pack is allowed just to touch the extended fingers of the left. The cards are now allowed to escape one by one, beginning with the front card, and at the instant the first card is released the right hand moves upward in a straight line, to a distance of two feet or thirty inches, Fig. 6. The effect is that of a ribbon of cards. During

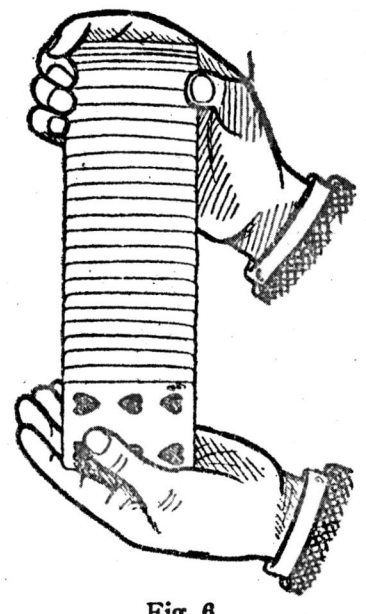

Fig. 6.

the operation the left hand, palm upward, remains absolutely stationary. When the right hand reaches its highest point, it remains in that position for a fraction of a moment; then, while the cards remain like a ribbon in the air, the right hand swoops down, gathering the cards in its descent, and the two hands come together with a sharp report, and the cards are squared. Perfection in this sleight, which may be attained with reasonable practice, consists in the ribbon of cards being unbroken, and in the cards falling evenly into the left hand, so that when the right palm strikes the left the cards are squared. The reader is advised to practice only the releasing movement at first, the right hand remaining stationary. As perfection is acquired in this important movement, the right hand may be raised a few inches during the operation, increasing the distance gradually. Particular stress is laid upon the necessity of the right hand moving upward

The Art of Magic

in a perfectly straight line. Otherwise the ribbon of cards will not be even, which detracts from the effect. Instead of holding the thumb and second finger of the right hand at the exact center of the two ends of the pack, as directed in the first method, the performer may find the flourish more easily acquired by placing the second finger at the upper right corner of the pack and the thumb at the corresponding upper left corner. This is a mere detail, however, and the student is advised to experiment with both positions, and to adopt the method that gives the best results.

THIRD METHOD — This is a variation of the second method. The effect is the same, but instead of the cards being held endways between the thumb and second finger of the right hand, the pack is held sideways, so that in the upward movement the cards are ribboned lengthwise. As explained in the second method, the finger and thumb may grasp the pack at the middle or at the top. The author prefers the latter position. The student will find this variation much more difficult than the second method, as it requires assiduous practice to keep the ribbon from breaking. When this movement has been mastered the reader will be ready to try his hand at what the writers regard as the most sensational and difficult of all flourishes or fancy sleights with cards.

THE ONE HAND DROP.

FIRST METHOD — This spectacular effect may be described in a few words, but it will require many weeks of hard practice before it is mastered. The effect is shown in Fig. 7. Hold the cards in the manner described in the first method of springing the cards. Extend the arm in front of the body, straight from the shoulder. Now let the cards drop toward the floor, releasing them one at a time. The right hand moves slightly upward at the same time, say about five or six inches. When the last card has fallen the right hand descends swiftly, catching the cards in its downward movement, and, if the flourish has been perfectly executed, the last card — or what was the first card released — will be caught as it is about to touch the floor. The effect of this flourish is indescribable in words. There is a knack about releasing the cards that cannot be explained, but which will be acquired by practice. Failure will be the reward of the student for many weary days, and when about to give up in despair the knack will suddenly be attained. It is not possible for even the most expert performer to catch all the cards every time. From personal experience the writer can say that on an average the flourish is

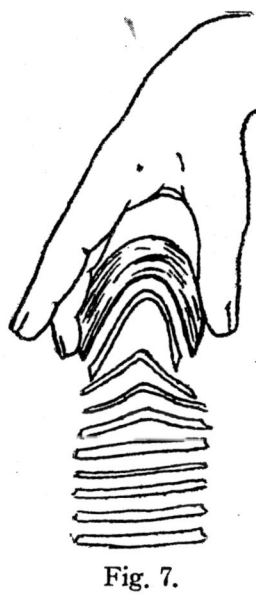

Fig. 7.

executed perfectly once out of three times. As a rule the performer is successful in the first attempt. If this is the happy result during a public performance, it is the part of wisdom for the performer to rest on his laurels and resist the temptation to show his skill a second time. If, however, he is sufficiently expert in this kind of manipulation he may respond to the encore with the

SECOND METHOD — In this method the pack is held with the lower side parallel to the floor, as described in the second method for springing the cards. The cards are dropped ribbonwise, the faces toward the audience.[1] The right hand catches the cards in much the same manner as described in the preceding sleight. This is even more brilliant in effect than the first method, and is correspondingly more difficult.

THE CARDS ON THE ARM.

A favorite flourish with expert card manipulators is running the cards up the arm, from the finger tips to the elbow, and, by a slight contraction of the fingers of the left hand, causing the cards to turn over. It is an effective sleight, and not difficult of execution, although some little practice is necessary before the cards can be spread neatly and evenly along the arm. It is rather surprising, considering the popularity of this pretty sleight, that it has not been explained in any work of magic known to the writer. The secret of the successful execution of this sleight is in holding the cards. The pack is bent slightly downward by the thumb and second finger of the right hand, the thumb at the lower end and the second finger at the upper end. Extend the left arm and hand, either palm upward or downward, as the performer may elect. Beginning at the very tips of the fingers of the left hand, the cards in the right hand are released, one at a time, the right hand at the same time sweeping up the left arm. It is important to remember that the cards are released by the fingers only. This maneuvre will leave the cards spread from the tips of the left fingers to the elbow, or even beyond it. As a matter of fact the first card or two should overlap the left fingers about an inch. Now by quickly contracting the two middle fingers toward the palm, the whole row of cards will be reversed in a spectacular fashion. There are several ways of terminating this flourish. One popular method consists in simply dropping the left arm to the side, the result being that the cards fall neatly into the left palm. Other performers reverse the cards in such a manner that instead of falling on the arm they drop into the right hand, which is held for this purpose just under the left elbow. In order to secure this effect, the left forearm revolves slightly to the right at the very moment the cards are being reversed. This causes the cards to tumble like a water-fall into the right hand. The effect is pretty. Another effective method is as follows: Just as the cards, in the process of reversing, are about to fall on the arm, the right hand passing under the first falling card — that is, the card at the elbow, catches it on the extended right thumb. The right hand then sweeps toward the left palm, the result being that the cards are once more reversed and fall into the left hand, where they should be immediately squared, so that the flourish may be repeated if desired. Another very pretty finish is to catch the falling cards at the elbow, on the right thumb, as just described, when the left forearm is allowed to drop from under the bridge of cards, all of which are caught by a swift forward dart of the right hand. The fact that the cards are lapped makes this movement easy of accomplishment. It may not be out of place to describe a slight variation of this popular flourish. Instead of the cards being riffled on the left arm, they are spread on the wand, or cane, held in the left hand. One end of the stick is held in the palm of the left hand by the third and fourth fingers. The first and second fingers are extended, serving as an additional support. The cards are held in the same position as for spreading the cards on the arm, but the work of releasing them is done by the thumb instead of the fingers. Beginning at the inner end of the wand, the first three or four cards slipped by the thumb are gripped by the left thumb pressing them against the stick. It is now a simple matter to lap the cards to the end of the wand. The flourish may be terminated in two ways, either by throwing the lapped cards into the air and catching them in the right hand, after the manner just explained, or the stick may be tilted slightly upward, when the cards will slip back into the left hand.

A SERIES OF FANCY FLOURISHES.

The following series of fancy flourishes with cards was originated by the author of this book, and this is the first time it has been explained in print. The series is really an adaptation of the riffle on the arm. Begin by riffling the cards on the left arm, as already described, throwing the lapped cards into the air and catching them in the right hand. Repeat by spreading the cards on the right arm, and catching the cards in the left hand. Now spread the cards on the back of the right forearm, which is held rigid. An upward movement is made with the right arm, the lapped cards are thrown into the air. Instead of catching them in the left hand, the right arm is drawn swiftly back and darts forward again, catching the cards before they have an opportunity to separate. In catching the cards the fingers and thumb of the right hand are extended in a V shape, and, as the cards are lapped, it follows that if the first card is caught a straightforward movement will gather in the rest of the cards. Spread the cards on the back of the right arm again. Toss them into the air, but instead of catching them, quickly turn the right forearm palm and wrist upward and allow the bridge of cards to fall on this side of the arm. A slight sinking movement of the forearm when the cards strike it will prevent them from being disarranged. Now contract the second and third fingers of the right hand which will turn over the whole line of cards, and the moment they fall reversed on the arm, throw the bridge of cards into the air and draw back the right arm, turning it over at the same time, and catch the cards as already described. These movements should follow one another quickly, the five being performed within the space of twenty seconds. This series of movements is more in the nature of juggling than conjuring, but it forms a brilliant interlude to a series of card tricks.

THE FLOWER OF CARDS.

The flourish bearing this rather Oriental title is contributed by a valued correspondent, the Yogi Girindrashekhar, of Calcutta, India, and the effect is really very pretty and startling to the uninitiated. You simply hold the pack between the finger and thumb of the right hand, give the hand a gentle shake, and the cards at once assume the shape of a spiked-shaped fan.

To produce this effect, divide the pack into two equal portions, and bend each half in opposite directions, so that when placed in position the cards will be "bridged," the opening

The Art of Magic

between the two halves being exaggerated. Now arrange the cards in pairs, one from the top and one from the bottom, and place these one above the other. In a complete pack there will be twenty-six such pairs, each having the appearance of a bridge. Now press the cards quite flat with the fingers and thumb and the pack will assume its normal appearance. Hold the deck as directed above and release the pressure. The cards, on account of their elasticity, will regain their curved form and arrange themselves fanwise, the flourish having all the hallmarks of a feat of genuine dexterity. In order to hand the cards for examination, bend them slightly backward and forward and give them a riffle shuffle, after which they will tell no tale.

THROWING CARDS.

This is one of the oldest of the ornamental sleights, and as every conjurer, even the veriest type, understands how to propel a card through the air (although the number of professional conjurers who can throw cards with accuracy and grace to any distance may be counted on the fingers of one hand) we should not refer to it except for the laudable purpose of acquainting the reader with a pretty variation of this sleight, the invention, we believe, of the celebrated French juggler and hand shadowist, M. Felicien Trewey, who makes a most mysterious card trick out of the flourish, an effect that will be described in due course in the department devoted to sleight of hand tricks with cards. Hold the pack in the left hand, as if for dealing, the thumb across the center of the top and the four fingers grasping the outer edge. Toss a card into the air, at any distance from ten to thirty feet, giving it a strong reverse twist, which cause the card, after it has exhausted its initial momentum, to return toward the performer. As the cards falls, revolving rapidly in its flight, separate the pack at the outer edge with the four fingers of the left hand, by simply pressing the fingers downward. This leaves a wedge-shaped opening into which the card is allowed to fall. As the left hand is held high in the air, and the wedge-shaped opening being toward the ceiling, the audience, of course, cannot see the break in the pack, and the sight of a card suddenly darting into the pack, like a homing pigeon into its eyrie, is pretty and effective. A skilled performer can propel a card at a surprising distance over the heads of his audience, and by reverse "english," so to speak, cause it to return to his hand. An effective variation is to throw a card high into the air, and, when it returns toward the performer, to seize a pair of scissors with the right hand and cut the whirling card in twain. Before throwing the card hold the scissors in the left hand, underneath the pack. Another pretty method is to toss the card into the air, and, when it returns, gracefully catch it between the thumb and first finger of the right hand. This may be followed by a more elaborate and more difficult flourish. Lay the pack on the table, taking two cards in the right hand, holding them as one. Now throw the double card into the air, giving it the reverse "english." The cards will remain together on their upward and outward movement, but the instant they begin their backward flight they will separate and whirl in different directions. With practice the performer will be able to catch one card in the right and the other in the left hand. The regulation method for throwing cards is to hold them lightly between the first and second fingers at the upper end. The hand should be curved toward the wrist and then straightened with a sudden jerk. In order to communicate a reverse movement to the card the hand is jerked back toward the performer at the precise moment the card leaves the tips of the first and second fingers. Knack rather than strength is the secret of the sleight.

CARDS FROM THE MOUTH.

This easy sleight has a stupendous effect upon the imagination of the average spectator, and it certainly is startling to see six cards pulled from the mouth, one after another. The production of any small object from the mouth, an egg or a billiard ball, is effective; but the mind cannot conceive how it is possible to conceal a playing card in the mouth, to say nothing of stowing away six pasteboards in that useful member of the physical economy of man. Six cards are used for the sleight. Vanish them in any manner that is most convenient. We prefer back-palming, reversing the hand so that the face of the cards are toward the palm. Now move the right hand toward the mouth. Quickly insert the end of cards in mouth. In removing the cards the uppermost one is first drawn off with the right hand assisted by the left hand which eventually secures the first three cards, as illustrated in Fig. 8. The second three cards are now

Fig. 8.

drawn off one by one and secured in the right hand in a similar manner. The general effect at the conclusion of the sleight is shown in the illustration. Drawing the cards down, one by one, gives the effect of actually pulling them from the interior of the mouth. If the head be slightly tilted back, and the mouth opened rather widely, the effect will be enhanced. We cannot urge too strongly the acquirement of this effective move. It can be introduced to advantage in the well-known trick of the cards passing up the sleeve and into the pocket of the performer.

CHAPTER II

CARD TRICKS WITH UNPREPARED CARDS AND NOT REQUIRING SLEIGHT OF HAND.

There are many excellent tricks with cards that require little or no dexterity of movement, but which, presented with appropriate patter, are as effective as many of the more elaborate effects demanding a mastery of sleight of hand. It is not always easy to determine the exact classification of a card trick; for the skillful performer, by introducing a pass or palm or false shuffle, will often transform a simple trick into a bewildering illusion. We shall begin this chapter by describing a number of new and novel methods of discovering a chosen card.

First Method.—This is subtle and indetectable. In offering the pack in the usual manner for a spectator to select a card, secretly keep count of a number of the top cards while you are spreading the pack from the left to the right hand. A good number to keep track of is ten. As soon as the spectator has made his selection, close up the pack, keeping the little finger between the ten cards and the remainder of the deck. Request the drawer to replace his card, lifting the packet of ten cards off the deck with the right hand, allowing the spectator to replace his card on top of the packet in the left hand. You now deliberately replace the packet of ten cards on top of the deck in left hand, squaring up the cards. The effect to the audience is that the drawn card is hopelessly lost in the pack. The performer knows, however, that it is the eleventh card. It is now essential to get possession of this eleventh card, or to reveal it in some magical manner. This is accomplished by means of the conventional, overhand shuffle, as follows: Hold the deck in the left palm, in the manner for the ordinary overhand shuffle, but a trifle more diagonally, so that the first finger from the second joint lies up against the outer end and the first joint of the little finger is slightly curled up against the bottom, with the thumb resting on the top, near the outer end, about the middle. This position is important, and we advise the student to acquire it at the outset, for the shuffle will prove very valuable at times to the magician, inasmuch as it can be used either for the purpose of discovering a drawn card or for a false shuffle. The drawn card is, you will remember, the eleventh from the top. The right hand seizes the pack at the ends between the thumb and second and third fingers, the first finger resting lightly on the upper side. Now in the process of shuffling you draw off one card at a time, the left thumb pressing lightly on the top card, the right hand making the shuffling movement. When ten cards have been drawn off in the manner described, you "jog" the eleventh, or selected, card. By "jog" is meant a card protruding from any part of the deck about a quarter of an inch. The "jog" is made in this case by simply shifting the right hand slightly toward the left wrist, when the card will protrude a little over the end of the left-hand packet and over the tip of the little finger. There should be no hesitation in making this "jog," but continue shuffling the remainder of the cards from the right hand onto the left-hand packet. When the shuffle is complete, the protruding card will mark the location of the drawn card. All that is necessary now is to cut the pack at the protruding card and shuffle off on top of left-hand packet, which leaves the drawn card at the bottom of the pack. It can now be discovered in any fashion the magician may desire. By continuing the ordinary shuffle the card may be brought to the top. It will be marked that this method of shuffling does away with the pass, for which reason it is a valuable variation to the conventional method of obtaining possession of a drawn card. This method may also be used as a false shuffle. By means of the "jog" the operator will experience no difficulty in keeping track of any number of cards that have been brought to the top of the deck.

SECOND METHOD—When the spectator returns his card to the pack, which is held fanwise, the lower right hand corner of the card is sharply bent between the second and third fingers of the right hand. As these fingers are under the pack this operation is not observed. The pack is squared and handed to a spectator for shuffling. When the deck is returned the conjurer can instantly discover the chosen card by glancing at the edge of the pack. This is a simple but often very useful method of discovering a card.

Third Method.—In the act of opening the pack for the reception of the drawn card, the fingers of the right hand draw the bottom card of the pack, which has been previously noted, to the right. Now, whenever the drawn card may be replaced, the performer merely breaks the pack at that spot. In closing up the pack this bottom, or key, card is on top of the drawn card, and the trick is concluded according to the fancy of the conjurer.

Fourth Method.—(To discover a card mentally selected). Allow pack to be shuffled by spectator and request him to deal four cards face upward on the table. As he does so the performer spreads them so that there is a space of at least six inches between each card. Ask a spectator to select mentally one of the cards, and if you follow the direction of his gaze you can, after a little practice, invariably hit upon the selected card. You should present this as a genuine mind-reading test, in which case you will have a legitimate excuse for failure. A performer may gracefully fail in a "mind-reading" experiment, but he must always succeed in a trick. In another part of this book will be described an elaboration of this simply effect, in which the contingency of failure is so carefully provided against that no matter what card is mentally chosen the performer will bring his trick to a successful conclusion.

Having discovered a chosen card, by one of the methods described, or by any method within the student's knowledge, it behooves him to produce the pasteboard in a magical manner. He would be a very lame performer who would simply take a card off the pack and hand it to a spectator with the remark, "Here's your card." There are a number of old and more or less effective methods of revealing a chosen card, all of which

The Art of Magic

are fully described in the familiar works on conjuring, such as the revolution, nailing a card to the wall, throwing the pack into the air and catching the chosen card, and knocking a pack out of a spectator's hand, he retaining the chosen card between the thumb and fingers. We shall describe one or two new methods of concluding a card trick and mention an improvement on one or two of the old methods. The first one we shall describe is an improvement on a very old trick, but which, nevertheless, is one of the most effective of the impromptu class of card effects.

FIRST METHOD.—In this method a chosen card is attached to the ceiling. As the reader is familiar with the old method of attaching a card to a door or wainscoting by means of a tack, we shall describe only the improved method. After the chosen card has been located by any of the foregoing methods, and brought on top of the pack, stick a small piece of chewing gum on the center of the card. Draw attention to the bottom card and ask if it is the card selected. The answer, of course, will be "no." Now take off the two top cards, holding them as one card. Repeat the same question, and the answer will also be in the negative. Replace the cards and toss the pack to the ceiling. The impact will force the gummed card against the ceiling, while the others will fall to the floor. Some little practice is necessary in order to throw the pack so that it will strike flat against the ceiling, while the others will fall to the floor. Use a sticky gum of the rubber variety.

SECOND METHOD.—This trick, which is known as "The Test of Nerve," is also an old standby, but as an impromptu it is more effective than many modern feats. The drawn card is brought to the top in any manner that the performer desires. Now request the drawer to hold the pack face upward, the thumb on the face of the pack at one end, the fingers below. The thumb must not project more than half an inch over the face of the cards, while the fingers, on the contrary, should have at least an inch of hold. Request the spectator to grip the cards tightly, and then give the pack a smart blow with the wand or hand. All the cards but one will fall to the ground, the one being the selected card, which, much to the surprise of the spectator, stares him in the face. The effect of this trick can be enhanced at least seventy-five per cent. by recourse to the expedient described in the first method, that of calling attention to the bottom card and then removing the two top cards, exhibiting them as one, and calling particular attention to the fact that neither the bottom nor the top card is the selected one. This little ruse completely baffles the "wise" person who thinks he knows all there is to know of the magic art, and in our own experience this subterfuge has on more than one occasion mystified exceptionally well-informed performers. "How was the card brought to the top of the pack?" they asked in surprise.

THIRD METHOD. — This in an effective and novel finish to a card trick, which will be new to most readers, as, to the best of our knowledge, it has never appeared in print. After the card has been brought to the top give the pack a shuffle, leaving the selected card the second from the top. Deal four cards face downward from the top onto the table in the manner illustrated in Fig. 9.

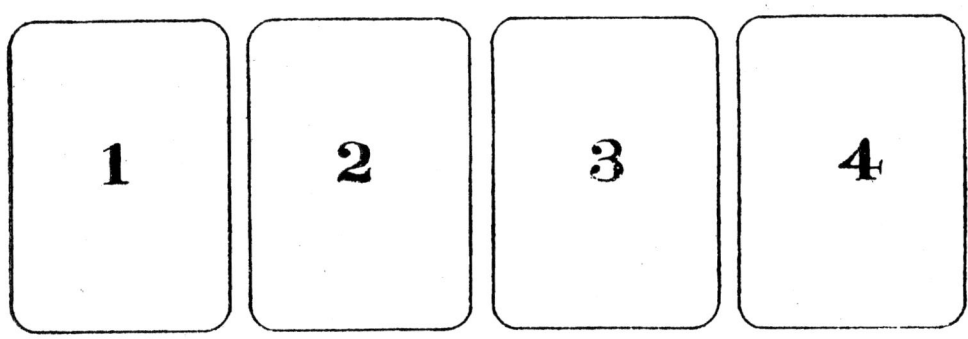

The cards are numbered to facilitate the task of explanation. The card at number "two" is, of course, the selected card. Hand the spectator an ordinary die, and ask him to throw it. Should it come up "one" or "four," request him to throw again in order to convince himself that the die is not loaded. If it comes up "two," you touch card number "one" with your wand or

The Art of Magic

finger, calling out "One." Then touch card number "two" with the wand, calling out "Two." This is the selected card, and with as much dramatic effect as possible turn the pasteboard over, or leave this duty to the person who drew the card. Should the spectator throw "three." the trick is brought to the same effective conclusion. In this case you begin to count from the right hand, at the card marked "four." Striking the cards "four," "three" and "two," counting "one," "two," "three," and the third card, which is marked "two" in the figure, is turned up. As the audience do not know what you are going to do, it is immaterial from which end you start counting. If the die turns up "five," you begin counting from the right hand card, as for "three," but when you have counted "four," which is card number "one," on the diagram, you start back, counting card number "two" as "five," which is the drawn card. Should the die turn "six," begin counting from the left hand card, or number "one." Count down to "four" and then return, counting card number "three" as "five," and card number "two" as "six." This is the drawn card. It will be seen that if "two," "three," "five" or "six" are thrown, and counting by the methods described, the drawn card, which should be always placed at number "two," will invariably beturned up. The only numbers that can fail are "one" and "four," and if either of these numbers is thrown it is only necessary to request the spectator to throw the die again in order to convince himself that it is not prepared in any way. Should "one" or "four" be thrown a second time the spectator will naturally conclude that the die is loaded," and will need no —urging to throw the die for a third time. This is a very effective trick and the reader is strongly advised to add it to his repertory. Of course, by means of sleight of hand, the effect of the trick may be greatly enhanced. That skillful conjurer, Mr. Adrian Plate, uses this artifice with decided effect in the four ace trick, which will be described in a special chapter devoted to this time-honored trick.

There are many other methods of reproducing a chosen card, but they are more or less familiar. Other methods will be

The Art of Magic

described in connection with more important tricks; but for the present it will be more profitable to describe a number of card experiments that do not call for any special dexterity of hand, but which, of course, can be greatly enhanced by the use of certain sleights, such as the pass or palm. One of the simplest, but also one of the most effective, is

THE REVERSED CARD:

There are several methods of working this pretty trick, but we shall confine ourselves to a description of the simplest and in our opinion the most perfect. Allow the pack to be thoroughly shuffled, and invite a spectator to select a card, and to mark it, if he desires. While the card is being noted and marked, slip the top card to the bottom of the pack so that it faces the rest om the cards, and turn over the pack. The cards are now face upward, with the exception of the top card, the back of which negatives any suspicion of the pack not being in the usual arrangement. Indeed no suspicion of trickery at this stage of the experiment ever enters the mind of the spectators. The performer holds the pack squared and requests the spectator to replace the chosen card. When this is done the performer slips the top card to bottom, at the same time turning over the pack which leaves the pack in statuo quo, with the exception of the selected card, which, unknown to the audience, is reversed in the pack. The performer may now shuffle the pack by means of the riffle or overhand shuffle. If he uses the latter method he must stand so that the audience can not see the back of the pack, a precaution that will at once be obvious to the reader. The performer now calls attention to the fact that the cards have been thoroughly shuffled, and that it is impossible for him to be acquainted with the whereabouts of the chosen card. With a sweep he spreads the cards in a line or semi-circle on the table, face downward, when the chosen card is revealed face upward. If desired the performer can begin the trick with the bottom card already facing the pack, in which case, of course, the preliminary shuffle is omitted. It is a simple matter to spread

The Art of Magic

the cards fanwise, when inviting spectator to draw a card, without showing the bottom card. The effect of the trick can be enhanced by allowing three spectators to draw cards, the three selected cards appearing reversed in different parts of the pack. The trick may also be accomplished without reversing the bottom card, but this method demands some expertness in sleight of hand. For sake of completeness it is described. Allow the pack to be shuffled, and when the card is returned, bring it to the top by means of the pass. If desired the card may be palmed and the pack handed out to be shuffled. Hold pack in left hand, the tips of the fingers pressing on the top card. The right hand now slightly lifts the top half of the pack, the left hand fingers pressing on the top card slides it off, and in the process the card is reversed as it enters the cut portion.

The PIANO TRICK:

Who invented this trick, or who gave it the queer title we do not know. We saw it first performed by Imro Fox, but he did not remember where it originated. It is a clever little trick, however, and, if well presented, very puzzling. A spectator is requested to place his finger tips on the table, in the usual position for playing a piano. The performer places two cards in each of the spaces between the fingers, one space excepted, in which he places one card only. As he places each pair between the fingers he says, slowly and distinctly, "Two cards — even." When he comes to the last space he puts in one card, saying, "One card—odd." This repetition impresses on the minds of the onlookers that an even number of cards are used, which is essential to the success of the experiment. The performer now proceeds to remove the cards, one pair at a time, accompanying the movements with such expressions as "always even;" "two more — even," and similar expressions. As he removes the pairs from the fingers he places the cards on the table in two heaps. When he comes to the one card he holds it in his own hand so that every one may see it. "Now," explains the conjurer, "we have two heaps containing an even number of

The Art of Magic

cards. I have one card in my hand. If I place this odd card on either of the two even packs it will make that pack odd, will it not?" The audience, appealed to in this manner, will always respond in the affirmative. "Now on which pack shall I place this odd card?" The card is placed on the packet indicated. "Will some one in the audience kindly hold this odd packet," continues the performer, handing the packet to a lady or gentleman. "I shall hold the even packet. My trick is this: I shall undertake to pass one card from my packet, which contains an even number of cards, to the odd packet held tightly by your representative. Ready! Hold tightly, sir. One, two, three! Did you feel the card as it struck the pack? No? Well sometimes the impact is imperceptible. But the card has arrived nevertheless. Will you count the cards in your packet? Wait a moment, sir. In the beginning you had the even packet, I believe? And now? (Spectator counts the cards), you hold the odd number, while I have the even number. (Performer counts the cards in his packet.) Isn't it wonderful?"

The secret of this trick is the essence of simplicity. There are seven pairs of cards, fourteen in all, placed between the spectator's fingers, and when these pairs are split into two packets, each packet is composed of seven cards; but the performer boldly announces that each packet is composed of an even number of cards, and if the patter, as described, has been used, the audience will never suspect the real condition of affairs. Consequently, it does not matter upon which packet the single card is placed. The result is the same in either case.

This is really an admirable impromptu trick and a valuable adjunct to any magician. We have added a little wrinkle, however, that makes the trick even more mystifying, and that is for the performer to count the cards in his packet. He counts the cards slowly in his hands, proving that there are eight in the packet, which agrees with his previous statement that both packets contain even cards, and the audience is more satisfied than ever that they hold the packet which the additional card has made odd. But, interposes the puzzled reader, the packet really contains seven cards. That is true. The performer makes what is known as a "false count." Although this stratagem comes naturally under the department of sleight of hand, it adds so much to the piano trick that we include it in this chapter. As this ruse will be frequently employed in other card tricks described in this book, the reader is advised to master it now. To make a false count the pack or packet is held as if to deal, and the cards are drawn off with the right thumb, one at a time, with a slight snapping noise as each card is removed, one snap being made with the right thumb on the edge of the other cards without removing one. If the cards are counted quickly and evenly, the keenest ear cannot distinguish the difference in sound and the sharpest eye cannot detect the subterfuge. The addition of this false count, as we have said, practically makes a new trick of the piano experiment; but in whichever way the trick is presented, the conjurer must impress upon the minds of his audience that the feat is one of pure sleight of hand. The spectators will believe then that the card has really passed from one packet to the other by means of some extraordinary movement on the part of the performer, and accordingly they will be loud in their praise of his dexterity.

THE TRANSPOSED CARDS:

One of the oldest and best of the non-sleight of hand tricks consists in dealing a row of ten or eleven cards face downward on the table and allowing a spectator to move as many as he wishes from one end to the other, the conjurer divining the number of cards thus transposed. As this feat is described in every book on card conjuring, and is so well known, it would be a waste of space to mention it except for a very brilliant adaptation of the trick, the invention, we believe, of Ziska. There are few better non-sleight of hand tricks in existence.

The performer allows a spectator to cut a pack of cards into two heaps. Now, while the performer's back is turned, the spectator is requested to transpose any number of cards from one packet to another, place the two packets together and square up the cards. The performer deals from the top of the pack about twenty cards, throwing them face downward on the table. He now requests different spectators to draw a card haphazard from this pile until four or five have been drawn. These cards are placed face downward on the table and a spectator is asked to select a card from them. The performer now asks the number of cards transposed, and after the spectator has replied, the selected card is turned over, and the number of its spots correspond to the number of cards transposed. Thus, if three cards were transposed, a three spot would be turned up.

The explanation is as follows: The pack is prearranged in this manner: On an ace, laid face downward place a deuce; on this a tray; on this a four; and so on to ten; and then jack, queen and king. These thirteen cards are on top of the pack. When the pack is cut the performer notes which packet contains the arranged cards. He now requests the audience to select one of the packets, forcing the ordinary packet by means of the familiar "your right or my left" equivoque. A spectator takes any number of cards up to ten from the selected packet and places them on the other packet, the performer turning his back while this is done. The two packets are now placed together, taking care that the packet on which the transposed cards were placed is uppermost. Now, no matter how many cards were placed upon the arranged packet, the fourteenth card from the top will always give the correct number, so that in dealing off the cards the performer must not lose sight of the fourteenth card. Deal off about twenty cards, throwing them carelessly on the table, but allowing the fourteenth card to be a trifle more exposed than the others. This will facilitate the choice of the card. If the twenty cards are properly arranged the chances are greatly in favor of the fourteenth card being drawn the very first time. If this happens, then, of course, the trick is ended, and all that remains is for the performer to ask how many cards were transposed, and to request the spectator to turn over the chosen card. If four or five persons draw cards, and the four teenth card does not happen to be among them, the performer remarks, "And I will draw one myself," selecting, of course, the desired cards. This one is placed among those selected and they are spread on the table, and the proper card forced in the manner familiar to conjurers. We suggest as a slight improvement on this part of the trick the use of the dice for determining the choice of the card, as already explained. This will add to the incomprehensibility of the trick. If desired, the magician may still change slightly the conclusion of the trick. Instead of throwing twenty cards face downward on the table he may deal sixteen cards on the table in four rows, four cards in a row. If the cards are dealt from left to right, the key card will, of course, be the second card in the fourth row. Request the audience to select two of the rows, either the inside or the outside. Whatever the choice may be pick up the two inside rows. Now ask the audience to select one of the remaining two rows, and whichever row is chosen, the magician, of course, picks up the top row, the one which does not contain the key card. There is now one row left, and the key card is discovered by means of the dice. As there are four rows the desired row may be forced by means om a loaded dice, which will always turn up four. In handing the dice to another spectator, to throw for the card, the loaded dice is exchanged for an ordinary one, similar in appearance. This exchange is absurdly simple, and as the spectators have the dice in their possession at the conclusion of the trick, and can examine it at their pleasure, the effect is extraordinary. The student of sleight of hand will, of course, enhance the effect of this trick by giving the cards a false shuffle.

CHAPTER III

CARD TRICKS INVOLVING SLEIGHT OF HAND.

In the last chapter a class of card tricks was described in which a knowledge of sleight of hand was not necessary, although it was suggested that even the simpler illusions of the card conjurer's art are enhanced by the judicious employment of the more or less familiar sleights. The feats described in this chapter demand a knowledge of sleight of hand, and practiced dexterity. The author assumes that the reader is familiar with the various passes, palms, forces, changes, false shuffles and other practical sleights that form the anatomy of card magic. As there are so many excellent works that exhaustively treat of this subject it would be a wrongful use of space to include descriptions of sleights familiar to the majority of readers. We should advise a careful study of Sach's "Sleight of Hand" and Professor Hoffman's admirable treatises on the art of magic, including his translation of Robert-Houdin's "Secrets of Conjuring and Magic," which is at once a grammar and a dictionary of the fascinating art of deception.

Without any further preliminary remarks, let us proceed with our description of actual tricks, choosing for the first number an effective sleight of hand experiment originated by the author of this book. Let us call it

THE TRANSFIXED PACK.

This is essentially an impromptu card trick, as any pack of cards may be used and no preparation is necessary. Invested with appropriate patter it is not beneath the dignity of the professional wizard.

EFFECT — Two cards are selected from a shuffled pack, returned to the deck, which is again shuffled by the spectators.

The Art of Magic

The pack is now wrapped in a sheet of paper and the packet held securely by a rubber band. The performer thrusts a paper knife through the packet of cards, and, upon investigation, the knife blade is found between the chosen cards.

TIME OCCUPIED: Three to five minutes.

REQUISITES AND PREPARATION: A pack of ordinary cards; a paperknife; a sheet of plain paper, about 8 by 6 inches; a pencil and a rubber band.

PRESENTATION OF TRICK — Hand an unprepared pack of cards to one of the spectators with the request that the cards be thoroughly shuffled and cut. While the deck is in spectator's possession allow him to draw a card, and while he is marking it take the deck and request a second spectator to select a card, which should also be marked. The drawn cards are returned to the pack, brought to the top by means of the pass, palmed, and the deck offered for shuffling. If the performer prefers, he may shuffle the pack himself, taking good care, of course, to keep the two drawn cards on the top. Whichever method he adopts, it is necessary that when this preliminary part of the trick is over, one of the selected cards shall be at the bottom of the pack and the other on the top.

Lay the pack on the table and bring forward the sheet of plain paper and the pencil. Allow the audience to examine the paper and request a spectator to write his or her name on it, or mark it in such a manner that it may readily be identified. Of course, there is no preparation about the paper, but the writing of the name is an excellent bit of misdirection; for while this is being done the performer picks up the cards, bends the whole pack downward over the first finger of the left hand and as quickly bends the top half of the deck upward. Now by making the pass the deck will be "bridged," and the chosen cards which, it will be remembered, were originally at the top and bottom of the pack, will now be the first cards of the upper and lower halves of the "bridge." Of course, it would not be magical to allow the audience to see this very noticeable "bridge." To obviate this the performer holds the pack between the first

The Art of Magic

finger and thumb of the right hand, near the center, and squeezes the cards so that the "bridge" is obliterated. Hold the pack in the air and call attention to the fact that it is impossible for any one to know the location of the drawn cards. Wrap the pack in the marked paper, and, when the cards are concealed in the folds, release the pressure of finger and thumb, which allows the "bridge" to spring back into shape. Turn down the ends of the paper and snap a rubber band lengthwise over the package. Call attention to the apparent fairness of the proceeding and remark that even if you knew in the first place what cards were drawn, it would be impossible to locate the cards now. While you are speaking hold the package in the right hand, and, running the left thumb nail lightly along the side locate the "bridge," marking the location by a slightly pressing on the paper. Address the audience somewhat as follows: "My trick is this: I shall endeavor to bring the two cards together in the pack, and this while the pack is securely wrapped in the marked paper. The operation is simple. I simply lay the package on my left palm (suiting the action to the word) and command the chosen cards to fly together. Presto! Pass! The cards have obeyed my command. What's that? I thought I heard some one remark that it is not much of a trick. Well I shall make it more difficult. I shall locate the two cards in the pack without removing the wrapper. Here is an ordinary paperknife (taking up a paperknife and exhibiting it). Now, watch me closely." The performer plunges the blade through the side of the package, at the point where it was marked by the thumb nail. The knife naturally enters the opening of the "bridge" and passes between the drawn cards. Bend the bundle sharply upward, which takes the "bridge" out of the cards, and hand the package to a spectator with the request that he remove the paper. While he is doing this ask for the names of the drawn cards. When the paper is removed the knife is found between the two marked cards.

CAUTION — With careful attention to detail there is not one chance in a thousand of failure in this experiment. The one

The Art of Magic

chance is in not making a wide enough "bridge," and for this reason a comparatively new pack is desirable, as new cards have the requisite spring. Enameled cards are the best.

SECOND METHOD — This is in some respects an improvement on a previous method. At the outset the sheet of paper is lying on the table, as is also the pack of cards, and the paper-knife. Offer the pack to be shuffled, and invite two spectators to select a card each. While they are marking their cards the performer replaces the pack on table, cutting it into two packets, as nearly equal as possible. Spreading one packet fanwise he requests a spectator to replace his card. This is brought to the top, palmed off, and the packet offered for shuffling. When the packet is returned the performer replaces the palmed card on top and lays the packet on the center of the sheet of paper on the table. In the act of placing the packet on table the performer slightly "bridges" it upward by contracting the fingers (at the upper end) and the thumb (at the lower end). The curve must not be too pronounced, and the packet must be so placed that the front edge squarely faces the audience. Properly placed, the keenest eye, at a distance of five or six feet, cannot detect the slight upward curve of the cards. The second selected card is now replaced in the remaining packet and brought to the top. After a shuffle the card is left at the bottom of packet. This packet is now "bridged" downward and placed on the first packet. The pack is now properly "bridged," and it only remains to wrap the pack in paper and bring the trick to the conclusion as already described.

EVERYWHERE AND NOWHERE.

This brilliant trick was the invention of the late Dr. Hofzinzer, of Vienna, who, at the perihelion of his fame, was regarded as the greatest card conjurer in the world. He originated many spectacular tricks with cards, the secrets of which have never been divulged. One of the most brilliant card effects in his repertory was entitled "Everywhere and Nowhere." In Hofzinzer's eloquent hands this experiment must have been

The Art of Magic

a veritable masterpiece of artistic card conjuring, and the modern magician will find it a decided addition to his accomplishments. It is an exceedingly difficult trick, calling for a mastery of a sleight to which the twentieth century conjurer pays little attention, namely, the change, a disposition that should be deprecated by every honest lover of the art, inasmuch as some of the most brilliant and startling effects in the whole range of card conjuring are accomplished by this expedient. We shall first describe the trick just as Dr. Hofzinzer performed it in Vienna, fifty odd years ago, and shall also give, word for word, the graceful and brilliant patter with which he clothed the experiment — patter devised for the paramount purpose of misleading the spectators at the critical points. We shall follow Hofzinzer's method with a revised or modernized version of the trick, introducing certain sleights and subterfuges unknown to the makers of magic in the Doctor's day.

EFFECT — From a pack of cards one is chosen, the drawer carefully noting it and replacing it in the pack, which is shuffled by the performer. The conjurer now announces that he can pick the chosen card from the pack of fifty-two cards, if he is allowed three chances. He proceeds with the trick by taking the top card and exhibiting it, but as this proves to be the wrong one it is laid on the table. The performer then exhibits the bottom card, which also proves to be the wrong card, and it, too, is laid on the table beside the first card.

Having exhausted two of the three chances, the performer makes his third choice from the center of the pack; but once more he fails to find the selected card. This third card is also deposited on the table beside the other two. The conjurer, of course, is embarrassed, and cannot explain his failure to the satisfaction of the spectators. However, in order that the time thus taken up shall not be wholly wasted, he will endeavor to bring the trick to some sort of conclusion. Accordingly, the conjurer requests a lady to select one of the cards from the three on the table. The magician announces that he will endeavor to change this card into the card originally chosen.

The Art of Magic

No matter which of the three cards is pointed out, the performer succeeds in changing it to the card that was selected in the first place, afterward laying it down upon the table. Another lady is now requested to say which of the three cards she would have chosen had she been given the opportunity. She points out either of the two remaining cards, and the performer takes it up and shows it also as the originally selected card. No other choice being possible, the magician picks up the third card and commands it to change in the same value and suit as the one chosen at the beginning of the experiment.

While holding this card in his hand the performer overhears, or pretends to overhear, a remark to the effect that he has been using a number of cards of exactly the same denomination. To prove the inaccuracy of this perfectly natural assertion the conjurer asks the spectators to glance from the card he is holding in the right hand to the card on the bottom of the pack. As this card happens to be similar to the one in the magician's hand, the audience naturally imagine that they have really detected the swindle; but they are cruelly deceived when, glancing back at the card held in the performer's right hand, they discover that it is entirely different from the card they saw there in the first instance. Placing this indifferent card upon the top of the pack the conjurer remarks that although the selected card is really on the bottom of the pack he has only to command it to pass and it will travel to the top of the pack. Raising the uppermost card the magician's command is seen to have been obeyed. The two cards on the table are now picked up, and they also have been mysteriously transformed into quite indifferent cards, which are placed amongst the others and the pack handed around for examination, when it is found to be without preparation and to contain but one of the cards that has taken such a prominent part in this really remarkable illusion.

TIME OCCUPIED: Eight to ten minutes.

REQUISITES AND PREPARATION: An ordinary pack of cards, with two extra cards of the same suit and denomination, say

The Art of Magic

the eight of hearts. Two of the eights must be placed on the top of the pack, the third eight being the last but one from the bottom.

PRESENTATION OF TRICK — Passing the two top cards to the center by means of the two-handed shift, one of the eight of hearts is forced on some unsuspecting individual; and while he is making a mental note of the card, another pass is made, which brings the cards back to their original position. The chosen card is now replaced in the center of the pack and by means of a false shuffle (this is Hofzinzer's own explanation) is brought to the top, the conjurer at the same time shuffling an indifferent card on the top of the two eights of hearts, which are now second and third from the top. In the shuffling care must be exercised not to disturb the third eight of hearts, which is last but one from the bottom of the pack. Suggest that perhaps the first card is the one selected by the gentleman, and remove the top card, which is, of course, the wrong one. While talking the top change must be executed, and supposed indifferent card (really one of the eight of hearts) is casually placed on the table as the first of the performer's three selections. At this point the performer must not neglect to remove the indifferent top card and place it anywhere in the center of the pack. Now ask whether the bottom card is the one selected, and on receiving a negative reply make what is known as the "slide" and lay the second eight of hearts on the table beside the first one.

Having had two out of his three chances without discovering the chosen card, the performer makes his third selection from the center of the pack. It will be remembered that the remaining eight of hearts was left at the top, but before making his last choice the conjurer shifts the eight to the center. Instead of removing one card, the eight must be taken out with a card underneath it, the two exactly fitting, and, therefore, appearing as one card. Exhibit this double card, and you will be informed that it is not the one selected by the spectator. In the act of laying this third and last choice on the table, the

The Art of Magic

bottom card must be slipped into the palm, and the eight of hearts laid by the side of the first two.

No matter which of the three cards is now chosen, that one, on being exhibited, will be the same as the card that was originally drawn. Before laying this card back on the table, it must be changed for the top card of the pack, and the indifferent card is laid back on the table — of course, face downward. The eight of hearts on the top of pack must now be palmed off and dropped on the servante or into some convenient pocket. Ask another lady to select one of the remaining two cards, which is also exhibited as the eight of hearts. This eight is then changed and left at the bottom of the pack, the indifferent card being placed on the table. Now the third card is picked up and is shown to be of the same denomination as the other two cards. The attention of the audience having been called to this third card, it must be adroitly top changed for an indifferent card, and the audience is directed to look at the card on the bottom of the pack, which appears to be same as the one they had just seen in the performer's right hand. The face of this latter card is now exhibited. Placing this indifferent card on the top of the pack, the cards are ruffled, and the eight of hearts on the bottom is commanded to travel to the top. This is shown to have been done by apparently picking off the uppermost card, although really the top card is drawn back, as in dealing seconds, and the eight of hearts drawn off and displayed. In turning the pack over to show that an indifferent card is on the bottom, the eight of hearts that was previously shown there must be palmed off and pocketed. The experiment is concluded by demonstrating ocularly that the two cards on the table are not the selected eights. The indifferent cards are returned to the pack, which is passed to the spectators for examination.

Such is the trick as performed by the celebrated Hofzinzer, and although it is not free from one or two minor faults, it is really one of the most brilliant of card tricks, deserving to rank in the same category as the "Cards up the Sleeve,"

The Art of Magic

the "Rising Cards" and the "Four Ace Trick." The reader who has followed each detail carefully will admit that in a trick of this kind, intricate in its movements, a greater or smaller effect will be obtained according to the manner in which it is presented. It is essentially a "talkee-talkee trick," and as the experiment formed the most striking one in its inventor's programme, there can be no better way of concluding Hofzinzer's own explanation than by translating into English the delightful and original patter with which the versatile Vienna conjurer surrounded the many intricate moves. Of course, this particular trick is more suitable for the drawing-room than the stage. Therefore, indulgent reader, kindly imagine yourself comfortably seated in your easiest arm chair listening to the suave magician as he begins:

"Ladies and gentlemen, card tricks, as you are well aware, are usually presented at a certain distance from the audience, many pinning their faith to the happy proverb that distance lends enchantment to the view.

"With this particular experiment, however, this proverb is not pertinent, and as magicians are commonly supposed to possess very contrary natures, I am going to perform this trick among you. Here I have an ordinary pack of cards. (Fan the cards and give them a false shuffle.) Would you, sir (make pass) select any one of them you please (forcing the eight of hearts). Thank you. (Make second pass, bringing pack back to its original condition.) After having looked at the card very carefully will you oblige by placing it back into the center of the pack, as near as you possibly can to the position from whence it came. (Card is replaced and by means of a false shuffle the eight is brought to top of pack and an indifferent card shuffled on top of the eight of hearts. This is according to the explanation offered by Hofzinzer, but it is a rather difficult move, and, in truth, the writer does not understand how this shuffle can be accomplished without disturbing the eight on top and the eight that is second from the bottom. A simpler and easier method would be to make the pass and have the

The Art of Magic

drawn eight of hearts returned on top of the eight of hearts in the pack, and then by means of the pass the two eights are brought to the top, when by means of an ordinary riffle shuffle the third eight will not be disturbed and an indifferent card can be left on top of the pack.)

"Thank you. Now, ladies and gentlemen, you have all noticed how fairly this preliminary detail has been conducted. Of course, it would be quite impossible for me to have any knowledge of the chosen card, and there is no method by which I can ascertain the exact position of it in the pack. However, to prove to any sceptic that the card is entirely lost, I will give the pack a thorough shuffle. (False shuffle.) Now it is commonly accepted that there are fifty-two cards in a complete pack, and as this is a complete pack the chances of selecting the chosen card by making a random pick are, as you will readily admit, very remote. However, by a curious and intricate mathematical calculation, I have materially reduced the number of chances, and I have the system now working so perfectly that out of three chances, at the very most, I can undertake to find the card this gentleman was kind enough to draw. To illustrate the invariability of this system, I will begin by asking the gentleman if this, the top card, is not the one he selected. (Exhibit top card.) Is it not? Very well, then, (making top change) I must place it on the table. It not being the top card perhaps it was the bottom one. Is this the card you selected, sir? (Holding up pack in left hand so that bottom card is visible.) No, not this one either, which is the second one of my chances, and which I shall also place on the table beside the first. (Performer, by means of the sleight known as the "slide," or "glide," places the eight of hearts, which was the second card from the bottom, on the table.) Now for my third and last chance of selecting the chosen card. This time I shall select a card from the center of the pack. (Make pass.) This must be yours, sir. (Exhibiting double card as one card) It is not? Then, for once, I regret to confess that my system has failed. However, so that the time we have ex-

The Art of Magic

pended on this experiment shall not be wasted, I shall place this card on the table (lying pack on table and making single hand change; that is to say, palming bottom card and laying the top card, the eight of hearts, on table) and trust to the power of the ladies to assist me.

"Ladies, you know, can often produce marvels by a single look. Therefore, why could they not exercise some wonderful influence over these cards? Madam, will you kindly determine which of these three cards lying here shall be the one selected originally by this gentleman. Thank you. I just raise the card, and it has changed to the eight of hearts. Is this your card, sir? It is. Then you see how well this lady has succeeded. I notice that this other lady here is anxious to exercise her power over the other two cards, so I shall ask her to name the one she would have chosen had she had the choice. This one? Then I shall merely raise the card, and you see it has also changed to the one originally selected.

"Now, a further choice is not possible, but, madam, if you had chosen this card (turning up the remaining card on table) it would also have turned out to be the one the gentleman chose at the beginning of the experiment. I beg your pardon, sir. You say that there are three eights of hearts in the pack? Oh, no. I assure you there is no such preparation about the cards, except that they possess some very peculiar properties.

"Kindly notice that I hold in my hands the eight of hearts. Now if you will allow your eyes to travel from my hand to the pack (here make top change for an indifferent card) you will see that the same eight of hearts is at the bottom of the pack. Of course, there are not two alike because the one in my hand is not really the eight of hearts (here you exhibit the indifferent card.) I place this indifferent card on the top of the pack and command the eight of hearts at the bottom to pass to the top. See how faithfully it obeys me, for it is here, (second deal and show eight of hearts) and no longer there (before showing bottom of pack palm off eight of hearts and get rid of it in a convenient pocket), and these two cards on the table are quite ordinary ones, (turning them over and replacing them in pack), and if any lady or gentleman will examine the pack they will find that there is absolutely no preparation about a single card."

The weak points, from the point of view of the modern conjurer, in this otherwise admirable trick are: First, Shuffling the drawn eight of hearts from the center of the deck to the top, at the beginning of the trick; second, dealing seconds in order to convince the audience that the eight of hearts has passed, as commanded, from the bottom to the top of the pack; third, palming off the eight of hearts left at the bottom of the deck after the second dealing just mentioned. In the new method of performing the trick, as devised by the author of this book, these impracticable maneuvers are obviated.

EVERYWHERE AND NOWHERE—NEW METHOD.

TIME OCCUPIED: About ten minutes.

REQUISITES AND PREPARATION—A pack of ordinary cards—instead of using the entire pack it will be found more convenient to work with about forty cards. In addition you must have three aces of diamonds and three cards covered with cloth of the same color as your table top. For the purpose of explanation it is assumed that the cloth-covered cards are the five of clubs, the ten of hearts, and the eight of spades. There is method in this order of the suits. It saves a good deal of mental work if the conjurer adheres invariably to the same order of suits in tricks where such arrangement is essential or in using pre-arranged packs. The simplest order is as follows: Clubs, hearts, spades, diamonds, which can never be forgotten if attention is paid to the mnemonic fact that the initial letters of the four suits spell "C-H-(a)-S-(e)-D." In using the three cloth-covered cards for this experiment, they are laid on the table, face downward, in this order, from left to right: Five of clubs, ten of hearts, and eight of spades. Under artificial light the cards are invisible. It is essential that you should remember the order of the cards. Before presenting the trick,

The Art of Magic

a slight arrangement of the pack is necessary. Place two of the three aces of diamonds on top of the pack, and on top of the aces lay the eight of spades, so that the order of the first three cards counting from the top is: Eight of spades, ace of diamonds, ace of diamonds. On the bottom of the deck place the third ace of diamonds; on the ace place the ten of hearts, and on this card lay the five of clubs. When this is done the order of the cards, counting from the bottom of the pack, will be: Five of clubs, ten of hearts and ace of diamonds. A pencil and a small piece of blank paper, or, preferably, a small pad, complete the preparations. With the table standing back several feet from the spectators, and on this table the three cloth-covered cards, the pre-arranged pack and the pad and pencil, the conjurer is in readiness to present this mystifying experiment.

PRESENTATION OF TRICK — Come forward with the pack of cards and request a spectator to draw a card, really forcing one of the two aces of diamonds. As the eight of spades is the top card, care must be taken not to allow it to be chosen. After the pass is made which brings the eight of spades and the two aces of diamonds to the center, a fan is made and the eight slid out of danger, so that when the spectator's fingers are about to close upon a card that card must be one of the two aces of diamonds. While the performer is impressing upon the spectator not to forget his card he inserts the little finger of left hand above the eight of spades and makes the pass, which restores the pack to its original arrangement, with the exception that one ace of diamonds has been removed. Make the pass once more, holding the little finger at the break. Request the spectator to replace his card, cutting the cards at the break and allowing him to replace the ace on the top card of the lower packet, which is the eight of spades. The bottom card of the top packet, which is held in the right hand, is the five of clubs. Now in the act of placing the two packets together, slightly fan the packet in right hand, which enables you, in sliding top packet on the lower, or left hand, packet, to insert little finger of left

DR. ALBERT M. WILSON.

The Art of Magic

hand above the five of clubs. After making the pass the arrangement of the cards, counting from the top, will be as follows: Five of clubs, ace of diamonds, eight of spades, ace of diamonds. The arrangement of the cards, counting from the bottom of the deck, will be: Ten of hearts, ace of diamonds. These directions may sound tolerably complicated, but if the different movements are followed with a pack of cards actually in the hands they will readily be comprehended.

As already explained, the performer announces that he can pick the chosen card out of the deck if he is allowed three chances. He accordingly turns up the top card (the five of clubs) and asks the spectator if it is the selected card. The answer is in the negative. "Very well," responds the performer. "That is one chance, and for the present I shall place this five of clubs on the table, so that I may not pick it out again by mistake." As he speaks the performer makes a half turn toward the table, during which he topchanges the five of clubs for the ace of diamonds. He now places this ace of diamonds on top of the cloth-covered five of clubs on the table. The audience sees only the one card, which they naturally think is the five of clubs, and even if there is any suspicion that the performer has changed the card, all that the conjurer has to do is to pick up the ace of diamonds and the cloth-covered five of clubs together and exhibit them as one card. This contremps, however, will seldom arise, for the spectators, not knowing what you are going to do, are not in the least suspicious at this stage of the proceedings.

For his second chance the performer chooses the bottom card, which is the ten of hearts. This also does not prove to be the right card, so the performer says that he will also place the ten of hearts on the table. By means of the "slide" he draws out the second card from the bottom, which, it will be remembered, is on ace of diamonds, and this ace is laid on the cloth-covered ten of hearts on the table. At this stage of the proceedings the pack is arranged as follows: From the top, the five of clubs, the eight of spades, and the ace of diamonds.

The Art of Magic

From the bottom, the ten of hearts. For his third and last chance the conjurer selects a card from the center of the pack. To do this, make the pass, which brings the lower packet on top, the little finger separating the ten of hearts from the five of clubs. The four desired cards are thus placed together. Spread the pack fanwise in the left hand, arranging the cards so that the ten of hearts, five of clubs, eight of spades and the ace of diamonds are more prominent than the rest, and also in such a manner that you may readily locate each of the four cards. After a moment of deliberation pick out the eight of spades, and, without showing its face, hand it to the spectator who drew the card, remarking confidently that your trick has succeeded. While he is looking at the card the performer slips his little finger in the opening of the fan left by the removal of the eight, closes the pack, and makes the pass. By this maneuver the ace of diamonds is brought to the top of the deck and the five of clubs and the ten of hearts to the bottom. By this time the spectator has more or less vigorously denied that the eight of spades is his card, and the performer, simulating embarrassment, takes the eight, and, in turning to place it on his table, deftly changes it for the ace of diamonds, which card he places on the cloth-covered eight of spades on the table. You now have three aces of diamonds on the table, each ace resting, unknown to the audience, on a cloth-covered card. The eight of spades, the five of clubs, and the ten of hearts, in this order, are on the bottom of the deck. You now lay deck on table, but before doing so bring these three cards to the top by means of the pass which, of course reverses their order, leaving the ten of hearts on the top of the deck. It is important to remember this. Explain how sorry you are that the experiment has failed, and picking up the ace of diamonds and the cloth-covered five of clubs together, holding them as one card, ask the spectator if he is certain that it is not his card. He, of course, replies in the negative, and the performer replaces the five of clubs on the table, at the same time pushing the top card, the ace of diamonds, to the front of table, which leaves the cloth-covered

The Art of Magic

five of clubs at the rear, where it is invisible. To the audience it appears as if you had simply laid the five of clubs on the table and pushed it forward. Repeat the same question and movements with the remaining two cards. Now, using Dr. Hofzinser's patter, request a lady to choose one of the three cards on the table. The middle one is invariably chosen. This is the ten of hearts, or rather, the audience suppose it to be. When the middle card is turned over the spectators will be bewildered at the transformation of the ten of hearts into the ace of diamonds, the card originally drawn. The performer apparently replaces the ace on the table, but in reality he bottom-changes it for the ten of hearts, which is laid on the table. Another spectator is invited to select one of the two remaining cards on the table, and by means of "your right or my left" equivoque the supposed five of clubs is forced. This card is lifted up, and it has also mysteriously changed into the ace of diamonds. While holding this ace of diamonds before the spectators the performer pretends to overhear a remark that he is using a number of cards of the same denomination. During this "patter" he deftly exchanges the ace for the top card of the pack, which is the five of clubs. He requests the spectators to glance from the ace of diamonds in his hand (really the five of clubs, the card, of course, being held with its back to the audience) to the card on the bottom of the deck, which is the ace of diamonds. The audience begin to laugh, inasmuch as they imagine that they have caught the performer, who turns the laugh on them when the supposed ace of diamonds in his hand is exhibited as the five of clubs. During the astonishment that follows, the performer, making a slight turn to the right, exchanges the five of clubs for the ace of diamonds on the top of the pack, leaving the five on the bottom. By this sleight the spectators are persuaded that the ace and five have again changed places. The ace of diamonds in the right hand is actually placed on the table, so that the spectators can see that no exchange has been made; but the card is really placed on the cloth-covered five of clubs. The last of the three cards on

The Art of Magic

the table, which the audience believes to be the eight of spades, is now taken up and likewise exhibited as the ace of diamonds. The ace is bottom-changed for the eight of spades, which is on the top of the deck, and it is this eight that is replaced on the table, although the spectators believe that it is the ace of diamonds. In reality the two aces of diamonds, with the five spot of clubs between them, are on the bottom of the deck. It is necessary to get rid of the two duplicate aces before concluding the trick. If the performer is expert enough he can palm them in the left hand and get rid of them in a convenient pocket. The majority of performers, however, will prefer to make the pass, bring the cards to the top, and palm them off in the right hand. In either case it is easier to palm the three cards rather than just the two aces; for as the five of clubs is between the two aces, it would necessitate too much fumbling in order to eliminate the five. After the duplicate aces are done away with, the trick is easily concluded. Draw attention to the fact that the three aces have been replaced on the table. Turn up first the cloth-covered five of clubs with the ace of diamonds on top, exhibiting them as one card. Draw attention to the fact that they did not see an ace of diamonds, that they only thought they did. Replace the double card on table, drawing away the ace of diamonds, as explained in the first part of the trick. Then turn up the ten of hearts and the eight of spades, which are both laid face downward on the ace of diamonds (which the spectators suppose is the five of clubs) and the three cards are replaced in the pack, which is shuffled and handed to the audience for examination. As the pack contains only one ace there is no danger in this proceeding.

CAUTION — This experiment should not fail in the hands of a performer tolerably proficient in the force and the top and bottom changes. The performer is earnestly cautioned against undue haste. The trick should be presented slowly and easily, and no attempt made to grace the experiment with fancy flourishes.

The Art of Magic

SUGGESTIONS — If the performer is accustomed to work with an assistant, it is not necessary to force a card in the beginning of the trick. For instance, the performer could have a card selected at random from an arranged pack, and by looking at the next card would instantly become acquainted with the drawn card, which information could be transmitted to the assistant by means of a specially arranged code, such as "Thank you," "Much obliged," "Very well," or a similar phrase. The ingenuity of the reader will supply a better code than can be arranged haphazard, inasmuch as each performer has his own peculiar habits, or tricks, of speech. The assistant arranges the required duplicates, as described, and places the arranged pack on the table, from which the performer picks it up in exchange for the first pack. If the conjurer is deft at exchanging packs he can bring the trick to a still more effective conclusion. In case the trick has been presented with the ace of diamonds as the selected card, have a duplicate pack made up of aces only. This pack is concealed about the person in such a manner that it may be readily secured. As many amateurs do not wear clothes with special pockets and other repositories, I shall describe a new method of exchanging packs, which can be performed with impunity right under the very noses of the audience. The pack consisting solely of aces of diamonds is in the right hand coat pocket underneath a moderately large silk handkerchief, with which during the course of his entertainment the conjurer is accustomed frequently to wipe his hands. Offer the pack, which you have been using, for examination; and while the spectators are investigating the cards, casually bring out the silk handkerchief, and with it the pack of cards, the deck, of course, being concealed by the folds of the handkerchief. Casually rub the palms with the handkerchief, and as you are about to take back the pack from the spectators the handkerchief is allowed to rest in the left hand, under the folds of which the pack of aces is palmed. Receive the pack from the spectators in the right hand, and then casually use the handkerchief again. During this motion the folds of the handkerchief

The Art of Magic

are allowed to fall over the pack in the right hand, which leaves the pack in the left hand in full view. The left hand continues to rub the handkerchief lightly over the right hand for two or three seconds, when the right hand replaces the handkerchief and cards in pocket. If the movements are made carelessly and without haste, the exchange is indetectable, as a trial before the mirror will convince the most skeptical reader.

Having exchanged packs the conjurer addresses the person who drew the ace of diamonds: "You appear to be fond of aces, sir. How many would you like?" What ever his reply may be you count off the number requested and ask him to blow on them. He does so and you hand him the packet of cards. While he is examining them palm off fifteen or twenty of the aces. Then ask him to blow again. "Ah, you blew rather strongly that time," you remark. "Too strongly, I'm afraid. You blew some of them out of my hand." Thrust your right hand into the breast of spectator's waistcoat and produce three or four aces, leaving the remainder inside. Palm some more from the pack and produce them from various parts of the spectator's clothes, dropping them to the floor so as to make them look as numerous as possible. You then say: "There really seems to be no end to the aces. Won't you kindly assist me? Take them out yourself." While he is taking the cards out of the waistcoat, palm in the right hand all the remaining aces. "Are you sure you have no more aces about you? No? That's strange. You blew rather hard, you know. I really think you must have some more about you." While saying this you stand on the spectator's right, and placing your right hand just below his eyes allow the cards to spring from the hand, the effect being exactly as if the stream of cards flowed from his nose.

REFERENCES—The reader, it is taken for granted, is familiar with the sleights employed in this trick, but if he is desirous of brushing up his knowledge of the various changes employed we recommend a study of "Modern Magic," pages 28 to 34, and of Sachs's "Sleight of hand," pages 108 to 112. The subject is also discussed in Mr Roterberg's "New Era Card Tricks,"

The Art of Magic

pages 17 to 29. The "slide," (glisser la carte) is described and illustrated in "Modern Magic" at page 36, and on page 37 of the same work is a description of springing the cards, which flourish is utilized at the conclusion of the trick just described. The force and the palm are also described at length in the books mentioned, which information is given for the benefit of the reader who may not be familiar with magical literature.

A trick rather similar in effect to Hofzinzer's "Everywhere and Nowhere," but differing largely in detail and execution, was invented a few years ago by the author of this book, and, therefore, it naturally follows the experiment just described. For want of a better name we shall refer to it as

THE GENERAL CARD—T. NELSON DOWN'S METHOD.

This is the title of one of the oldest tricks in magical literature, and is to be found in some of the earliest works on magic in the English and French language. It is described in Robert-Houdin's "Conjuring and Magic," page 245, under the title of "The Metamorphoses." Other references to this trick are as under:

"Sleight of Hand" (Sachs), page 119.
"Modern Magic" (Hoffmann), page 87.
"Tricks With Cards" (Hoffmann), page 120.
"New Era Card Tricks" (Roterberg), page 162.

The method pursued by Mr. Downs differs radically from the methods described by the authorities cited, and it is generally regarded by magicians as a brilliant piece of card artistry. To perform it successfully requires a high degree of manipulative ability, buttressed by unflinching nerve and audacity. It will repay all the study devoted to it, however, as it introduces some novel sleights and demands a mastery of the difficult art of second dealing, a sleight that has been sadly neglected by conjurers, and which can be used to great advantage in magic.

EFFECT—Any number of persons draw a card, and by a curious chance each card proves to be of the same suit and denomination. After showing each spectator his (or her) card, the performer places it on the table. The heap on the table is shown to consist of cards similar to the one drawn, say the five of clubs, and the performer then convinces the spectators that the pack contains nothing but fives of clubs. Finally the cards on the table are shown, and to the spectators' amazement not one of them is a five of clubs, and then the performer exhibits the remainder of the pack and there is not a single five of clubs among the cards.

TIME OCCUPIED—About eight minutes.

REQUISITES AND PREPARATION—An ordinary pack of cards.

PRESENTATION OF TRICK—In order to explain this brilliant trick in the simplest manner possible we shall describe it move for move exactly as performed by its inventor, numbering each move.

Fig. 10.

1. Performer hands pack to a spectator with the request that the cards be thoroughly shuffled and that the audience satisfy themselves that it is an ordinary deck of cards. When the cards are returned the performer spreads them on the table, face downward, and requests that one of the spectators select a card. Let us assume that the chosen card is the five of clubs. Any other card, of course, would answer the purpose just as well.

2. The chosen card is returned to the pack.

3. Chosen card is shifted to the bottom.

The Art of Magic

4. Take off the two bottom cards — the chosen card in front — holding the two cards so that they appear as one, as in Fig. 10.

5. A subtle sleight is now employed, which we may call the Downs change. The pack is in the left hand, face up, in exactly the same position for the regulation two-hand pass. The two cards in the right hand are now placed on the face of the pack, so that the double card overlaps the pack almost one-half as in Fig. 10. In this position the five of clubs* is held securely on the face of the pack by left thumb. The right first finger snaps that part of the five of clubs that extends over the edge of the pack, in order to draw especial attention to the card.

* By mistake the artist drew the ace of clubs instead of the five; otherwise the illustration faithfully represents the cards and the position of the hands.

To make the change, the right hand seizes the extended edge of the double card between the thumb and first finger—the thumb on top and the first finger underneath. The pack is now turned over, the movement being toward the body of the performer. Simultaneously with this movement of the left hand, the right thumb pushes the five of clubs towards the pack, the left thumb assisting in the work of imperceptibly pushing the card home, leaving the second card protruding from the bottom of the pack, and held between the thumb and first finger

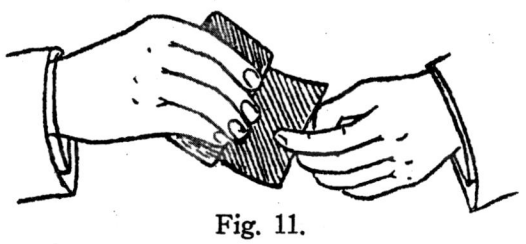

Fig. 11.

of the right hand, this time the thumb below and the first finger on top. The five of clubs is now on the bottom of the pack, and the card that the audience supposes to be the five of clubs is held face downward, in the right hand, as in Fig. 11. This

The Art of Magic

hand now drops the card, face downward, on the table. The cards in the left hand are, of course, held face downward. The change is now made. In "New Era Card Tricks" a variation of this sleight is described on page 87, although it is neither so subtle nor deceptive.

6. At this stage of the trick the five of clubs is on the bottom of pack, and a card, supposed by audience to be the five of clubs, lies face downward on the table. Make the shift, bringing the five of clubs to the middle, and force it on a second spectator, this time employing what is known as the single-hand force. For this purpose the cards are spread fan-wise, the five of clubs being so disposed as to show a little more surface than the others. This minute difference of surface catches the eye, and the chances are that the spectator will select the card so exposed.

7. While spectator is looking at the drawn card, the performer palms a card from the top of the pack.

8. The spectator replaces drawn card on top of pack, and immediately afterward the performer returns palmed card to the top of pack. The drawn card, the five of clubs, is now the second card.

9. The conjurer apparently picks up the top card, in reality picking up the two top cards, and holding them as one. For this purpose both cards are held slightly convexed toward the palm, the thumb at the lower end and the fingers at the upper end. The two cards are then replaced on top of the pack.

10. Performer now placed pack on the table, and with right hand takes off the top card, supposedly the five of clubs, and places it on the first card on the table. The spectators are convinced that there are two fives of clubs on the table. (Note: Adrian Plate's "Excelsior Change" can be used to good advantage instead of the move utilized by Mr. Downs. The "Excelsior Change" is described on page 22 of "New Era Card Tricks.")

The Art of Magic

11. The original five of clubs is on the top of the pack at this stage of the trick. Now give the deck a false shuffle, leaving the five on top.

12. Force the five of clubs on a third spectator, this time holding the pack behind the back. This force requires nerve and skill, but with practice is as sure as any other method.

13. Card received in right hand. Pack is held in left hand.

14. In turning toward table make the bottom change, that is, taking a card from the top of deck and leaving the five of clubs on the bottom: This change is described on page 28 of "Modern Magic," and will also be found in all other standard works on conjuring. The card in the right hand is thrown on the two cards lying on the table, and spectators believe that three fives of clubs are now on the table.

15. Give pack a false shuffle, leaving five of clubs on top of deck.

16. Force the five of clubs on a fourth spectator.

17. Card returned, and Downs change again made, as described in move No. 5. Four cards are now on the table, each one supposed to be a five of clubs.

18. Exhibit the bottom card of deck, which is the original five of clubs. Draw especial attention to the fact that it is the bottom card.

19. Shift, and show five of clubs as the top card of deck.

20. Shift the five to the center of pack, spread the cards fanwise, and, observing that it makes no difference from which spots, draw out the five of clubs from center of pack and exhibit to audience.

21. Carelessly waving the five spot of clubs in the right hand, as if wishing every one in the audience to see it, change it by means of top change ("Modern Magic," page 30) and place the indifferent card on table. There are now five cards on table, each supposed to be a five of clubs.

The Art of Magic

22. Give pack a false shuffle and force five of clubs on another spectator. While he is examining card, palm off top card of deck.

23. Have five of clubs returned on top of deck, replacing palmed card on top of the five. Deal top card on table, as described in moves 9 and 10. Six cards are now on table, each one supposed to be a five of clubs.

24. Turn up five spot of clubs on top of deck and throw it on the cards on table. This makes seven cards on the table. The audience is persuaded that each of the seven cards is a five spot of clubs, but in reality the top card only is a five spot of clubs. Place deck on table.

25. Pick up the packet of seven cards with the left hand. Show the top card, which is the five of clubs. In turning it face downward again shift it to the bottom, and exhibit bottom card as the five of clubs.

26. Insert little finger between the second and third cards from bottom and make the shift. This brings the five of clubs the second card from the top.

27. Show the two top cards as one, as described in move 9. Then place the top card, apparently the five spot, on the table.

28. Exhibit again the top card, which is really the five of clubs. Apparently place this five of clubs on table, but really deal seconds instead. (For directions for second dealing see Lang Neil's "The Modern Conjurer," page 59, and the "Expert at the Card Table," page 58.)

29. Repeat second dealing, showing the top card each time as the five of clubs. When the performer comes to the last two cards, shift and show last card as the five spot.

30. Palm off five of clubs and dispose of it in any manner that suits the time and occasion. Then show the cards on table, proving that there are no fives of clubs among them. Then exhibit the pack, proving that there is not a five of clubs in the deck. If this part of the trick is done with assurance and dex-

terity, the performer can convince the spectators (for the time being) that the five of clubs was not drawn in the first place, and that the whole experiment was nothing more or less than an optical illusion. Such is the effect in the hands of the inventor.

THE FLYING CARD.

The proper title for this trick should be "The Kinetoscope Card," but, obviously, such a name could not be used on a programme, as it might give a clue to the modus operandi. A trick, however, by any title will have the same effect; and this trick is really one of the subtlest and most mysterious in modern magic. We are indebted for the secret to the inventor who performs under the sobriquet of L'homme Masque, and who in private life is the Marquis d'Orighuala de Gago. He is one of the oldest and most expert magicians in France, and an especially expert manipulator of cards.

EFFECT — A spectator mentally selects a card. Without any sleight on the part of the performer the cards are handed to spectator to shuffle. When this is done the performer takes three cards out of another spectator's pocket, one of the three cards being the card mentally selected. The other two cards are the queen and jack of the same suit as the selected card, which is invariably the king of clubs.

TIME OCCUPIED — About four minutes.

REQUISITES AND PREPARATION — A pack of cards pre-arranged as follows: All the face cards, with the exception of the jack, queen and king of clubs and the king of spades, are placed at the rear of the pack. On the front of the pack are the spades, the ten spot being the first card. Following the spades are a few hearts and diamonds (no face cards or aces should be in this arrangement). Now arrange the next cards in this order: ten of clubs, nine of clubs, eight of clubs, king of spades, seven of clubs, six of clubs, five of clubs, four of clubs, three of clubs, two of clubs and ace of clubs. This arrangement is essential. Following these arranged cards place the rest of the red cards, indiscriminately, and last of all come the face cards. The jack, queen and king of clubs are utilized as follows: During some preceding experiment the performer in taking cards or any other object from a spectator's pocket has secretly introduced these cards into the pocket. Taking up the arranged pack he riffles the cards, the faces being toward the

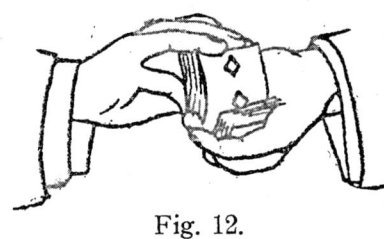

Fig. 12.

spectator in whose pocket he has planted the cards, asking him to think of one of the face cards. The method of forcing a card by the riffle is as follows: Hold the cards as in Fig. 12. The deck is in the left hand, thumb across top near inner end, and first and second fingers at side. Bring over the right hand and seize the deck with fingers at outer end and the thumb at the inner end, and hold so that the outer end of the cards may be sprung or riffled, the faces toward the spectator. Riffle the cards so that the only face card shown is the king of spades.

Here is where the deception comes in. The king of spades is the only face card in the front part of the deck, that is to say, in the part that is riffled; but owing to the peculiar arrangement of the cards (the king of spades in the midst of the clubs) the effect on the eye is kinetoscopic. In other words, it looks like the king of clubs. The cards must not be riffled hurriedly, as a slow riffle brings out the kinetoscopic effect better than a quick flourish. A few trials before the looking-glass will determine the exact amount of speed to use in riffling the cards. The trick is now done. The pack is shuffled so that the cards will not be in any particular order when the cards are subsequently examined. After the spectator has looked through the deck in vain for his card, ask him to feel in his pocket,

The Art of Magic

when to his utter bewilderment he will find the actual (?) card that he saw in the pack. L 'Homme Masque produces three cards, but this addition, in our opinion, does not enhance the effect of the experiment. To produce the three cards proceed as follows: After the spectator has shuffled the cards, request him to hold the pack tightly. Now ask him what card he mentally selected. "The king of clubs," you reply, after he has named the card. "A very good card for the purpose of our experiment. You cannot keep a king in the pack if he desires his liberty. I shouldn't be surprised if he has already left the pack and flown into your pocket. Perhaps he has taken the queen along, too. Where there are kings you generally find queens. Just for the sake of completeness let us send the jack to keep their majesties company. (Here you wave the wand over the pack). Will you kindly examine the pack and see if their majesties have departed, and also if the jack has obeyed my commands?" The three cards are subsequently found in the spectator's pocket.

CHAPTER IV
Sleight of Hand with Cards, continued.

THE PRINCESS CARD TRICK. (First Method.)

This trick is the invention of Mr. Henry Hardin, an American magician who has contributed many ingenious ideas to modern magic.

EFFECT—The performer exhibits four cards, held fanwise in the left hand, and requests a spectator mentally to select one of them. The performer takes one of the cards and deliberately places it in his pocket. Upon spreading the cards again the spectator's card is missing, and the performer draws the mentally selected card from his pocket.

TIME OCCUPIED—Two minutes.

REQUISITES AND PREPARATION—Four cards are arranged as follows: King of clubs, jack of hearts, jack of spades, and queen of diamonds. The order of the suits is the familiar C-H-(a)-S-(e)-D, or "chased," which has already been recommended, and which is of especial importance in this experiment. There is enough to remember in the magic of cards without burdening the memory with unnecessary orders or formulas. Behind the king of clubs, the top card of the packet, arrange these three cards: Queen of clubs, king of spades, and jack of diamonds. At the outset the seven cards can be on the top of the pack, the last named three cards, of course, on top of the king of clubs.

PRESENTATION OF TRICK—Give the pack a shuffle, taking care, of course, not to disturb the seven arranged cards on top. Rapidly count off these seven cards, in such a manner that the audience cannot see how many cards you take. Arrange the king of clubs, jack of hearts, jack of spades and queen of diamonds

The Art of Magic

fanwise in the left hand, keeping the three extra cards—the queen of clubs, king of spades and jack of diamonds—concealed behind the king of clubs. It does not matter in what order the suits of the three concealed cards are arranged. The proper method of holding the fan of cards is with the left side of the king (and the three concealed cards) pressed tightly in the crotch of the left thumb, the opposite edge being held by the tip of the first finger of the left hand. This will keep the cards from spreading and bringing the trick to a premature and disastrous conclusion. The other three cards of the fan are held between the tips of the left thumb and second and third fingers.

Turn your back to the spectators and hold the fan high above the head, the faces of the cards toward the audience, and request a spectator to think of one of the cards. When the choice has been made, square the cards, inserting the little finger between the king of clubs and the three cards back of it. Then you say: "I shall now place one of the cards in my pocket," and, suiting the action to the words, take the four cards you have just shown, and holding them as one card, place them in the pocket, leaving the three extra cards in your left hand. Ask the spectator to name his card. Let us suppose he chose the king of clubs. The performer replies, "The king of clubs? Ah, then I read your mind correctly; for I placed the king of clubs in my pocket. Let me show you first that the king has left the pack." The performer spreads the three cards, the queen of clubs, the king of spades and the jack of diamonds, on the table. He then produces the desired card from the pocket. As the order of the suits is known this part of the trick is a simple matter. The king of clubs is the first card, and as the packet is placed face down in the pocket all you have to do is to pick up the top card. If the chosen card is the jack of spades, the performer picks out the third card. A little practice is necessary in order to make the selection quickly, for there must be no fumbling in the pocket.

CAUTION—The spectator will never detect the substitution of the cards; for the ingenious arrangement of the suits tends

The Art of Magic

to confuse the mind. It is the part of wisdom, however, to hold the fan of cards so that only one person can make a selection; otherwise more than one person may remark a card. Consequently, when the three substitute cards are laid on the table the spectators may wonder at the disappearance of the cards they saw. With due attention to this minor detail there is no reason why the trick would fail.

THE PRINCESS CARD TRICK. (Second Method.)

In this form of the trick five cards are held in a fan, four of which are prepared as depicted in Fig. 13, which explains

Fig. 13.

Fig. 13.

the method of preparation better than a page of description. The fifth card, the king of spades, is unprepared. It is obvious, after a glance at the illustration, that the double cards may be arranged fanwise in the following order: Jack of clubs, queen of hearts, queen of spades, jack of diamonds. Now, by simply reversing the fan the order from left to right will be: Jack of spades, queen of diamonds, queen of spades, jack of hearts. In the actual performance of the trick you must have the following

The Art of Magic

unprepared cards in one of your pockets (preferably the trousers pocket), arranged in this order: Jack of clubs, queen of hearts, queen of spades and jack of diamonds. You are thus enabled to locate instantly any one of the four cards.

Hold the prepared cards and the unprepared king of spades in a fan. The order of the cards, from left to right is as follows: jack of clubs, queen of hearts, queen of spades, jack of diamonds and king of spades. Holding the fan aloft, as directed in the first method, request a spectator to think of one of the cards. The odds are somewhat in favor of his choosing the king of spades as that is the most prominent; but, whatever the

Fig. 13.

Fig. 13.

choice, square the cards, draw out the king of spades and thrust it into the pocket, announcing that it is the card the spectator thought of. Care must be exercised not to let any one see the face of the card. Now reverse the cards in your hand and again spread them in a fan, at the same time requesting the spectator to name his card. It is obvious that the card he chose is no longer visible. If he chose the king of spades, that card is in your pocket. If he names the jack of clubs, all you have to do is to show that the card is no longer in the fan in the left hand and then produce

The Art of Magic

the first of the four cards from your pocket. If the spectator names the queen of hearts, take out the second card; if the queen of spades, the third card; and if the jack of diamonds, the fourth card. For the reason already given do not allow two spectators to look at the fan at the beginning of the trick. The preparation of the cards requires delicate work. The pips must be inlaid perfectly, and the indices must be drawn with the proper inks. Neatly made the cards may be handed to a spectator without much fear that the preparation will be detected. If the reader cannot manufacture a satisfactory set he can purchase the cards from the dealers, or, better still, direct from the publisher of this book.

THE PRINCESS CARD TRICK.

This is the simplest as well as the best method of performing the trick, and, as any cards may be used, the most effective. In this method the effect is precisely the same—a card is mentally selected from four cards and subsequently is discovered in the performer's pocket.

The deck is shuffled and while in hands of audience four cards are drawn. One of these four cards is mentally chosen, and while this is being done the performer palms in the right hand three cards from deck, or he may get the cards from his pocket, where they were previously placed. We prefer this latter method. When the four cards are returned to the performer he places the palmed cards on top, squaring the packet so that the additional cards will not be noticed. The performer now slightly fans the four selected cards, directing the spectator to think intently of his card. As he fans the cards the performer notes their exact order. A little practice will enable one to remember the order of the four cards without the slightest difficulty. Announcing that you will pick out the card the spectator is thinking of, you remove one of the cards and put it in your pocket. At least that is what you apparently do. You really take the four selected cards, holding them as one card, and thrust them into the pocket, leaving the three indifferent cards in the left hand. Count these three cards, their backs, of course, being toward the audience, and replace them on the deck. When the spectator names his card, all the performer has to do is, remembering the order of the cards, to produce the proper card from the pocket. This can be done very quickly after a little practice.

THE TWENTY CARD TRICK.

A clever experiment in pure sleight of hand, which can be performed at any time and with any pack of cards.

EFFECT—The conjurer deals two packets of ten cards each, after which he lays the pack to one side. He now holds one packet in the right hand and the other in the left. One of these packets, chosen by the spectators and wrapped in a borrowed handkerchief, is given to some one in the audience to hold. Performer now passes three cards, one at a time from the packet in his one hand into the packet held by the spectator, counting the cards in his packet after the flight of each card.

TIME OCCUPIED—From three to five minutes, according to the amount of patter used.

REQUISITES AND PREPARATION—An ordinary pack of cards; no preparation.

PRESENTATION OF TRICK—Invite a spectator to shuffle a pack of cards, after which deal two packets of ten cards each on the table. Lay the pack to one side. Taking a packet in each hand, and holding the arms some distance apart, approach the audience and request a spectator to select either the right or the left packet. As you say this the hands naturally come together, and in that instant three cards are dropped from one packet onto the other. The best method of effecting this sleight, in our opinion, is as follows: The packets are held in the ordinary manner for dealing. While in this position the left thumb pushes the three top cards slightly over the end of the packet, where they are held separated from the remainder of the packet by the tips of the four fingers. Now, as the hands are brought together, the right hand is held a trifle lower than the left. The four fingers of the left hand are extended quickly, and this movement propels

The Art of Magic

the three cards from the top of the left packet onto the top of the right-hand packet. If the performer makes a slight turn of the body to the left as the hands approach, the movement will be facilitated. The success of the sleight, however, depends upon the natural method of bringing the hands together at the psychological moment of requesting the spectators to select one of the packets. Although the spectators are invited to exercise their own judgment, the packet in the right hand is actually forced, by the familiar "Your right or my left" equivoque. Request the spectator to throw a handkerchief over the chosen packet and to hold it securely. This packet has thirteen cards, while that in the performer's left hand has seven. "I am about to present an extraordinary experiment," says the performer. "The gentleman holds ten cards in the handkerchief. I hold ten cards in my own hand. I shall endeavor to pass a number of cards from the packet from my hand into the packet held by the gentleman. Now, watch me carefully; for here is where I am going to deceive you, if possible. One card, pass!" As he speaks the performer covers the packet with his right hand, and, apparently taking off a card, tosses it toward the packet held by the spectator. At the beginning of the throwing movement the right hand is held partially closed, as if actually containing a card; but at the conclusion of the throwing movement the hand is opened, showing the palm empty. Performed deliberately this movement is very deceptive. The effect on the audience is that the conjurer actually takes a card from the packet and causes it to disappear into thin air. "Did you feel anything, sir?" continues the performer. "I am sure that so far the experiment has been a success; for I observed a scarcely perceptible movement under the handkerchief as the card arrived. You should now hold eleven cards instead of ten, and there should be nine cards in my packet. Let us see if this is so."

The performer gives his cards a false count, as described in Chapter III, counting the seven cards as nine. Another card is passed in the same manner, and the seven cards in the left hand are counted as eight. A third card is passed, and, as there are seven cards in the packet, the cards may be handed to a spectator. The other packet is also counted and is found to contain thirteen cards, which, according to conjurer's logic, is adequate proof that the performer has passed three cards invisibly from one packet to the other.

CAUTION—There is no weak point in this experiment, and, given the requisite skill in false counting and in shifting the cards from one pocket to the other, there is no reason why the experiment should fail. It should be practiced, however.

CONCLUDING OBSERVATIONS AND SUGGESTIONS — If the reader finds any technical difficulty in shifting the cards from one packet to the other, there is an easier method of performing this part of the trick. If what is known as a "long card" be placed the fourth from the bottom in the right hand packet, the performer will experience no difficulty whatever in dropping three cards from the bottom of the right hand packet on the top of the packet held in the left hand. At the beginning the "long" card should be placed fourth from the top, when, after the cards are dealt face downward in two heaps of ten, this card will be fourth from the bottom of one of the packets. The disadvantage of this method is obvious; and, therefore, the student is advised to practice until he can shift the necessary cards from packet to packet by pure sleight of hand.

A COMEDY OF ERRORS.

This is more of a catch than a conjuring trick, but as it is really an ingenious arrangement, and also requires a certain deftness in execution, it is included in this chapter. The experiment is of especial value in an encounter with the disagreeable person who knows how all your tricks are done. He will fall a ready victim to this attractive snare.

EFFECT—The three of hearts and the three of diamonds change mysteriously to aces, and these aces then as mysteriously change back to three spots.

TIME OCCUPIED—Two or three minutes.

The Art of Magic

REQUISITES AND PREPARATION—Place the ace of hearts and the three of hearts on the bottom of the pack, the three being the first card and the ace the second. The ace of diamonds and the three of diamonds are placed on top, the ace being the top card and the three the second.

PRESENTATION OF THE TRICK—Hold the pack in both hands, the bottom card facing the audience. The pack should be held between the thumb and the first fingers at each end, the thumb on the back and the first fingers on the front of the pack, in such a position that the finger tips cover the outside spots of the three, making the three of hearts resemble the ace of the same suit. You call attention to the fact that the ace of hearts is on the bottom of the pack. As the indexes of the three spot are plainly visible the spectators will greet this confident announcement with a smile of derision, if not with a downright denial. The performer, however, pays no attention to the objections of the audience, verbal or otherwise, but continues: "I shall place this ace of hearts on the table," which, apparently, he does. In reality, however, he drops the pack to a horizontal position, "slips" the three of hearts, and really lays the next card, the ace of hearts, on the table. Inserting the little finger under the two top cards the performer makes a pass, bringing the ace and three of diamonds to the bottom of the pack, the three of diamonds being the bottom card. Repeat the patter and movements with the three and ace of diamonds. The spectators, of course, by this time are boisterously insisting that the two cards on the table are the three of hearts and the three of diamonds, and the performer is equally insistent that the two aces are on the table. After the spectators have been worked up to the proper pitch of excitement, the performer turns over the two cards, and there is an embarrassing moment of silence on the part of the spectators, in whose minds there dawns slowly the suspicion that they have been "sold." While all eyes are on the two aces, the performer makes the pass and brings the two three spots from the bottom of the deck to the top. Picking up the two aces, the performer exhibits them on all sides to the audience, and in

The Art of Magic

turning back toward the table deftly changes the aces for the two three spots, throwing the cards face downward on the table. The audience thinks, of course, that the cards on the table are the aces. "By the way," asks the conjurer, "what cards did you really think you saw"? He accompanies the words with a careless gesture in the direction of the cards on the table. "The three of hearts and the three of diamonds," answers the audience. "Well," replies the performer, " you were right. You really did see those cards." The performer turns up the two cards, and once more the spectators are obliged to confess that they have been duped.

CAUTION—We see no way by which this little catch can go wrong, even in the hands of a performer who is not very skillful in sleight of hand. The slip is the simplest of all sleights, and to change two cards at once is no more difficult than the change with one card. The fact that the audience are in a muddle most of the time gives the performer the necessary opportunity to accomplish the various movements.

CONCLUDING OBSERVATIONS AND SUGGESTIONS—If the performer is a good talker and is able to feign embarrassment he can work this simple feat up into a really brilliant and bewildering trick,—which illustrates the truth of the old conjuring maxim that it is not so much what you do but the way you do it.

THE SIAMESE ACES.

EFFECT—Two aces are removed from the pack, which is then cut into three packets. One of the aces is placed on the center packet, and while the performer is exhibiting the remaining ace, one of the spectators "maliciously" transfers a few cards from either of the outside packets to the top of the center heap. The performer, not noticing this disarrangement of the cards, places the second ace on top of the first heap. The third heap is now placed on top of the first, and the two on top of the middle heap, presumably on top of the first ace, although the spectators, who blithely imagine they are in a conspiracy against

The Art of Magic

the performer, know different. The cards are now dealt from the bottom, face upward, and the two aces come together.

TIME—Two or three minutes.

REQUISITES AND PREPARATION—An ordinary pack of cards; no preparation.

PRESENTATION OF TRICK—In taking out two aces—say the ace of clubs and the ace of hearts, glance secretly at the top card of the pack. For the purpose of explanation let us assume that this "key" card is the seven of spades. Now cut the pack into three heaps so that the top part of the pack will form the center heap. You must number the heaps in your mind from left to right, 1, 2, 3. The top card of the center heap is the seven of spades. Exhibit the ace of hearts, requesting the spectators to remember the card, and place it on the center heap. While you are exhibiting the second ace (the ace of clubs), move a little distance from the cards, and at this psychological moment a friend, who acts as your confederate (although the audience is not aware of the fact) transfers a few cards from either No. 1 or No. 3 to the top of the center heap. You are, apparently, oblivious of this maneuver, and place the ace of clubs on the No. 1 heap, concluding by placing No. 3 on No. 1 and these on the center heap. Inform the audience that you are about to illustrate for their benefit the surprising amount of affection that exists between cards of the same value. For instance, kings associate with kings, queens with queens, jacks with jacks, and aces with aces; of all cards, you declare, the aces are the most affectionate. Between them the bonds of sympathy are so strong that if they are separated only temporarily they will exert every effort to be reunited. This sympathy is especially strong between a red ace and black ace—between a club and a heart, a diamond and a spade. In fact, each pair may be likened to the Siamese twins, except that the bond is sentimental rather than material. "You will observe," adds the performer, "that the ace of clubs and the ace of hearts were placed in different parts of the deck but so strong is the affection between these aces that I have not the slightest doubt they are at this moment

The Art of Magic

reunited in some portion of the pack. Ah, you smile incredulously; but I assure you that what I say is literally true, and I am prepared to make my assertion good. Observe, pray, that I shall deal the cards one at a time on the table, and when I come to one of the aces, the other will be with it." The spectators, knowing that the cards have been disarranged, smile in expectation of the performer's discomfiture. The conjurer proceeds to deal the cards from the bottom, throwing them face upward on the table. When the "key" card turns up the performer knows that the next card is an ace. He slides this ace back with the third finger of the left hand, and keeps on dealing until the other ace appears, when he throws out the first ace. A flashlight picture of the audience at this moment would reveal an interesting study in chagrin.

The card sharper works the same effect in a slightly different manner. He saunters into a bar-room where, by previous arrangement, the bartender acts as his confederate. Inviting the habitues to step up and "liquidate," the affable stranger offers to amuse them with a little trick with cards. The bartender produces a pack, from which the affable stranger extracts two aces—say the two red ones. He then makes two heaps of the pack, and, showing both aces to the spectators, places one on top of each packet, after which he turns to one side and finishes his glass of beer. During which operation the bartender, after winking at the crowd, transfers five or six cards from one packet to the other. Having finished his drink the stranger proceeds with the trick by placing the two packets together. He calls attention to the fact that one ace is near the center of the pack and one on top. The spectators, however, know that this is not so; for the bartender's interference destroyed the arrangement. The stranger declares that he will deal the cards from the bottom so that the two aces will come out together; and adds that if the spectators detect him dealing the top card he will forfeit five dollars. Noticing the ill-concealed merriment among the habitues, the stranger becomes somewhat nettled. "What will you bet the two aces don't come out together?" he says, rather

The Art of Magic

angrily. There are always three or four "sports" who are willing to wager money on what they regard as a "sure thing," and the bartender obligingly holds the stakes. The trickster deals the cards, and, to the consternation of the "sports," the two aces come out together. Moral: Never bet at another man's game.

The trick is worked precisely as described in the three packet method. The trickster glances at the top card of the deck and this is used as the "key." The bartender watches the performer divide the pack into two heaps, so as to know where the "key" card lays. If the confederate shifted the cards from the wrong packet the trick would fail, and the sharper would lose his money. But this is precisely what never happens.

THE CARD IN THE POCKET.

A rattling good card trick depending absolutely upon sleight of hand and skillful address. It has an advantage over many card tricks in that it may be presented anywhere, at any time, and with any cards.

EFFECT—A spectator shuffles the pack and mentally selects any card, remembering its number from the top. When the pack is returned the performer holds it behind his back and removes a card, which is placed in the coat pocket on the right side —or in the trousers pocket if preferred. This is done quite slowly, in order that the audience may note every move. The spectator is now requested to name the number at which his card stood. Let us assume that the number is thirteen. The conjurer throws thirteen cards, one at a time, face downward, on the table, after which he asks the spectator to show the last card (that is to say, the thirteenth card, assumably the one he drew) to the audience. The spectator declares that it is not his card. "What is your card?" asks the conjurer. "The ten of diamonds," answers the spectator, although, of course, any other card might have been selected. "Believe me," replies the conjurer, "I knew your card the instant you made the selection, and

The Art of Magic

it is now in my pocket." The spectator is invited to remove the card himself.

TIME OCCUPIED—Three minutes.

REQUISITES AND PREPARATION—An ordinary pack of cards; no preparation.

PRESENTATION OF TRICK—The secret is as simple as it is ingenious. After a card has been decided upon in the manner described, the performer holds the pack behind his back. He now takes any card from the vicinity of the bottom of the pack, and, bringing this card forward (keeping its back to the spectators), places it in the coat or trousers pocket. The right hand is immediately withdrawn and the pack taken in that hand. In reality, however, the card is not left in the pocket, but is palmed in right hand and placed top of the pack in the simple act of transferring the pack from the left to the right hand. "Ladies and gentlemen," says the conjurer, "I call upon you all to witness the apparent fairness of the experiment. So far I have asked no questions, and you must admit that it would be impossible for me to know what card you mentally selected. However, in order to be on the safe side I will deal your card face downward on the table. What was your number, sir? Thirteen? That's unlucky for me"—or any other remark to suit the occasion. The performer throws thirteen cards face down on the table, requesting the spectator to satisfy himself that the last card dealt is the one he selected. The spectator immediately denies knowledge of the card in question. The conjurer feigns embarrassment. "What was your card?" he mildly asks. "The ten of diamonds," is the answer. "Believe me," replies the conjurer, "I knew your card the instant you made the selection, and placed it in my pocket." While the attention of the audience was focused on the thirteenth card, the conjurer palmed the next card, the fourteenth, which, thanks to the fact that the card which the performer pretended to put into his pocket was in reality placed on top of the pack, is the selected card. The palmed card must now be loaded into the pocket. This can be done while the spectators are looking at the cards on the table; but the

The Art of Magic

better plan is to wait until the performer addresses the audience in the words quoted above. As he says "and placed it in my pocket," the performer drops the palmed card into the pocket, immediately throwing the plam outward so that it faces the audience, the thumb holding the pocket open at the end nearest the front. If the body is turned slightly toward the left at the instant the card is dropped into the pocket, and the hand is immediately turned palm outward, the effect is that the thumb only is inserted, in order to facilitate the introduction of the spectator's hand. A little practice before a mirror will convince the student of the practicability of this move. For this reason the coat pocket is preferred to the trousers pocket.

The following is a more ingenious and interesting method of performing this trick: A spectator shuffles the pack and divides it into two nearly equal packets. He is then requested to note a card in either of the two packets, and to remember its number from the top. While the spectator is obeying instructions the performer turns his back or even leaves the room. When the card has been selected the performer asks the spectator to indicate which packet it is in. "Thank you," says the performer, "I shall perform the trick with the other packet." He picks up this packet, carefully selects a card, and, without showing it to the audience, places it in his coat pocket. He really palms the card, however, as described in the first method, and picking up the packet which contains the selected card, he places the palmed card on top. The trick is then concluded in the manner described in the first method.

HOUDINI'S TORN CARD TRICK.

This simple trick is the invention of Harry Houdini, the celebrated "King of Handcuffs." We use the word "simple" advisedly. The method by which the effect is attained is assuredly simple; but to present the trick effectively requires an absolute mastery of the two-hand pass, nothing more nor less. At this point we may say that Mr. Houdini performs the conventional two hand shift noiselessly and invisibly. It is impossible

The Art of Magic

for the sharpest eye to detect the slightest movement of the packets as they are transposed, even though the performer accomplishes the movement directly under a spectator's nose. The ease and celerity with which Mr. Houdini makes the shift is remarkable, and goes to prove that there is no limit to the dexterity that may be attained—and Houdini's mastery of this sleight is the result of fifteen years of assiduous practice.

EFFECT—A card is selected from the pack, and the conjurer tears off a corner in order that the card may be identified. The card is now placed on top of the pack, which is held in the performer's left hand, and, without any visible movement on the part of the performer's hands, or apparent manipulation of the pack, the top card mysteriously changes into a different card, which also has a corner missing.

TIME OCCUPIED—Two minutes.

REQUISITES AND PREPARATION—An ordinary pack of cards, one card of which, say the eight of diamonds, is prepared by tearing off the upper right hand corner.

PRESENTATION OF THE TRICK—At the beginning of the trick the prepared card (the eight of diamonds) is at the bottom of the pack. Allow a card to be drawn—it is not necessary to force a card for this experiment. While the spectator is noting the card, make the pass, bringing the eight of diamonds to the center, and insert little finger above it, so that when the pass is made again the eight will be brought to the top. The pack is held in the left hand in readiness for the pass. Place the drawn card on top of the pack, and tear a small piece out of the upper right hand corner, taking care that it is about the size of the piece torn from the eight of diamonds. Draw attention to the fact that the chosen card is on top of the pack, and as the right hand closes on the deck, with the apparent intention of squaring the cards, the pass is made, by which move the eight of diamonds is brought to the top. As its corner is missing, the spectator will have no suspicion that the conjurer has manipulated the cards. The performer addresses the spectator as follows: "As you see, sir, I place your card on top of the deck, where it is in plain view.

The Art of Magic

Watch me carefully so that I shall not deceive you." (By this time the spectator is keeping the top card under a steady espionage). "Before proceeding with the experiment, however, it will be necessary for me to know the name of the card you drew. The ten of clubs? Thank you, sir. But are you sure it is the ten of clubs. You are? Then, of course, there's nothing more to be said. Ah, one moment, please. Are you troubled with astigmatism or myopia? Really, I do not doubt your word, sir, not in the least; but it is absolutely necessary to know the precise card you drew, or my experiment, which is of a very delicate nature, will be a failure. You say that your card is the ten of clubs." The performer slowly turns up the top card, and, if the trick has been adroitly performed, the spectator's eyes will boogle out when he discovers that his card has changed under his very eyes. There is no more to the trick, the whole effect depending upon the execution of the two-hand pass. There is one element in the performer's favor. The change is accomplished before the spectator realizes that the trick has actually begun.

BARRINGTON'S TORN CARD TRICK.

The author takes keen pleasure in presenting this splendid card effect to his readers. It is by long odds the subtlest and most mysterious of the many torn card tricks, and is the invention of Mr. Frederick Barrington, by whose permission it is now explained for the first time in print. The drawing room conjurer will find this incomprehensible effect a valuable addition to his programme.

EFFECT—From the beginning of the performance an envelope is suspended in full view of the audience. A card is selected and torn into four pieces which are handed to a second spectator, who selects one of the pieces (not forced). The remaining three pieces are burned, the ashes loaded into a pistol and fired at the suspended envelope. The envelope is opened and inside a second envelope is found; when this is opened a third envelope is found; and so on until four or five envelopes have been opened, the last one of which is addressed to the person who selected the card.

The Art of Magic

This person opens the envelope and finds his card restored, with the exception of one corner. The piece retained by the second spectator exactly fits the missing corner.

TIME OCCUPIED—Five minutes.

REQUISITES AND PREPARATION—A pack of cards; a card box; five envelopes, one fitting inside the other, four of them containing a card similar to the one to be forced, except that one-fourth of the card is missing. The four envelopes are secretly numbered 1, 2, 3, 4. These envelopes are nested so as to have one card in each envelope to match the one to be drawn. The four corners or pieces that have been torn from the cards are numbered to correspond with the cards in envelope. In other words, the envelope marked "1" will contain the card whose missing corner is also marked "1." These four numbered pieces are placed in a card box, or any other piece of exchange apparatus, or they may be exchanged by sleight of hand, as the conjurer elects. Each of the four envelopes containing a torn card is addressed to the person on whom you intend to force a card. The four are then nested and sealed and placed inside a large envelope. This is hung in the room where you are going to perform.

PRESENTATION OF TRICK—Let us assume that the envelopes are loaded with duplicate sixes of diamonds. Force a six of diamonds on the lady or gentleman whose name is on the nested envelopes. He or she is requested to tear the card in half. The two halves are put together and torn in half once more, making four. Collect these four pieces in the card box, and, in turning to request a second person to select a corner, make change in box, and, of course, this person will select one of the corners that belong to the duplicate cards in the nested envelopes. You must notice the number on the selected piece, as the whole trick depends upon it. Now burn the other pieces, load the ashes into a pistol, and fire at suspended envelope. Open and take out first envelope, which is marked No. 1, and inside of which is No. 1 card. If the spectator selected the corner marked No. 1, then this envelope contains the card to match corner. In other words, you continue to open the envelopes until you come to the one that has

The Art of Magic

the torn card to match the selected piece. You hand the envelope to first person to identify the address, and then take out card and hand to second spectator to match the corner. Remember, all the nested envelopes are addressed to the person who selects the card.

CARD DISCOVERED BY SENSE OF TOUCH.

A quick, startling little trick, suitable for any occasion, and one of the most effective impromptu effects in the category of card magic.

EFFECT—The conjurer fans the pack and requests a spectator simply to touch a card. The pack is immediately closed and may be shuffled either by the conjurer or the audience. The performer takes pack in his left hand, riffles the edges with his thumb, and instantly the card touched by the spectator appears, face upward, on top of the pack.

TIME OCCUPIED—A minute or two.

REQUISITES AND PREPARATION—A pack of cards; no preparation.

PRESENTATION—After shuffling the performer fans a pack of cards with both hands so that the audience may see the faces. He requests a spectator merely to touch the top of one of the cards. The cards are spread in such a manner that the performer can see the back of the card touched, and at the same moment that the spectator indicates his selection the performer bends slightly the lower left hand corner of the card. He hands the pack to be shuffled, or performs the operation himself. But no matter how well the cards are mixed the bent corner makes a break by which the chosen card can be instantly located. Direct attention to the fact that neither the top nor the bottom card is the one selected. Holding the pack to the left ear riffle the thumb over the edges of the cards at the left side. This will allow you to insert the tip of the thumb under the break made by the bent corner. To facilitate this movement the pack is held between the first finger of the left hand at the upper end and the little finger at the lower end, while the second and third

The Art of Magic

fingers assist in steadying the pack at the side opposite the thumb. When the thumb is inserted under the bent corner at the lower left end is slid to the center of the pack. The thumb raises the upper packet about an inch and a half, imitating exactly the movement of making the one-hand Charlier pass. When the upper packet has been raised the requisite distance the thumb continues its upward movement, the lower card of the upper packet (the card with the bent corner) is drawn out in the direction of the wrist, and, making a half revolution, falls, face upward, on top of the deck. Of course, in actual practice this sleight is instantaneous, and if, at the same moment, the left arm makes a sort of flourish and at the conclusion the thumb riffles the cards, the eye cannot detect the maneuver. The sudden appearance of the card on top of the pack is startling, particularly if the pack is riffled at the instant the card is disclosed. The reader may deem the trick too simple to add to his repertory, but we assure him that after a trial he will be convinced that it is quite as effective as many more elaborate card experiments.

CAUTION—The student is advised to make the fan of cards as wide as possible, so that when a card is touched there need be no extra movement of the cards to enable him to bend slightly the lower left hand corner.

CONCLUDING OBSERVATIONS AND SUGGESTIONS—The bent corner idea of locating a card is susceptible to elaboration, and the ingenious performer will at times find it a very useful expedient.

THE FLYING CARD (First Method).

This is one of the standard card tricks, ranking in age and respectability with the "Four Ace" trick, the "Rising Cards," the "Cards Up the Sleeve," and the "Ladies' Looking Glass." It is not always entitled the "Flying Cards," but is variously known as the "Multiplication of Cards," the "Precipitation of Cards," or "From Pocket to Pocket." In some form or other it has been described and explained in every pretentious work on card conjuring since the time of Robert-Houdin. We shall first describe the familiar method of passing several cards from one person's pocket to that of another, for the reason that it is one of the most perfect tricks in the whole range of card conjuring; but in the course of explanation we shall introduce several improvements, which, in our opinion, justify the inclusion of the trick. The second method, however, is the invention of Mr. Downs, and, if anything, is more brilliant in effect than the old trick. In either form, however, the trick is one of the best ever invented and should form a part of the programme of every magician. It has the advantage of being one of the few card tricks suitable for the stage.

EFFECT—The performer requests two members of the audience to assist in the experiment. One of the volunteer assistants counts off thirty-two cards from a shuffled pack, and the other assistant verifies the count. The pack of thirty-two cards is divided into two packets, and each assistant puts a packet in his breast pocket and buttons up his coat. The performer now transfers any number of cards the audience may determine from the pocket of one assistant to the pocket of the other. The assistants remove the packets themselves and count the cards in order to prove that the performer's commands have been obeyed.

TIME OCCUPIED—In order to get the maximum amount of effect, and to invest the trick with the requisite amount of patter, at least ten minutes should be devoted to this charming experiment.

REQUISITES AND PREPARATION—A pack of cards; no preparation.

PRESENTATION OF TRICK — For this experiment you must have the assistance of two volunteers from the audience. Request one of the gentlemen to stand on the left of your table and the other on the right, squarely facing the audience. Hand pack to the assistant on your left to shuffle, after which invite him to count off thirty-two cards, one by one, on the table. After he has done so request the assistant on your right to verify the

The Art of Magic

count. The performer counts out loud, "One, two, three," up to thirty-two, as each card is laid on the table. This double count serves two purposes: it corrects any error that the assistant on the left may have made in counting, and it drives the fact of thirty-two cards being used into the minds of the spectators. This last point is very important; for the effect of the experiment is lost if, at its conclusion, some spectator naively remarks that he didn't know how many cards were used. It is insistence on such little details that makes for effect in a card trick.

After the second count the performer picks up the thirty-two cards, squares them, and while doing so asks the assistant on the left if he has an inside breast pocket, and if it is empty. If not empty, he requests the assistant to remove its contents for a few moments. He makes the same request of the second assistant, and, for additional effect, might request the gentlemen to pull out the lining of the pockets in order to satisfy the audience that they are really empty. While this is being done the performer palms four cards and places the remaining twenty-eight on the table. Right here we may remark, more or less parenthetically, that most writers on magic, in describing this particular trick, direct the student to palm five cards. In this important detail, as will be hereafter explained, our version of the trick differs from all others we have seen. With this exception we shall follow more or less closely the admirably clear and logical arrangement of the experiment written by Mr. Lang Neil in his excellent treatise on conjuring. Mr. Neil's advice to palm five cards is sound enough for the stage performer, or for the magician who is accustomed to work before large audiences; but it is advice that will often put the drawing-room performer in a predicament.

After the assistants have removed the contents from their pockets and proved to the satisfaction of the audience that they are empty, request the assistant on the left to cut the cards into two heaps, as nearly equal as possible, and then choose one of the heaps. Whichever heap he chooses, request him to pick it up, place it in his empty pocket and button up his coat. Now

The Art of Magic

request the assistant on the right to count the cards in the remaining heap, one by one, on the table. Let us assume that there are fourteen cards in this heap. The performer, looking directly at the audience, says: "How many cards has this gentleman?" (pointing to the assistant on the left, who has the other packet in his pocket). "You tell me, sir (turning to assistant on the left). There are fourteen cards on the table and fourteen from thirty-two leaves how many?" "Eighteen," answers the assistant. "Correct," replies the conjurer. "There are eighteen cards in your pocket and fourteen on the table." During the first part of the dialogue, when the conjurer says, "You tell me, sir * * * There are fourteen cards on the table" he brings the hands containing the four palmed cards down on those on the table, picks up the cards, squares them, and requests the assistant on the right to place the packet in his pocket and button up his coat.

Turn to the audience and continue: "Please impress three facts upon your minds: first, that the gentleman on the left has eighteen cards in his pocket; second, that the gentleman on my right has fourteen cards in his pocket; and third, that during this experiment I have not touched the cards. You will remember that both gentlemen counted the cards; the gentleman on my left cut the cards, selected one heap, and immediately placed it in his pocket, while the gentleman on my right did the same with the other heap. Therefore, it is manifestly impossible to accuse me of any deception." This harangue, of course, is all hocus-pocus, but the magician must be as skillful in drawing the long bow as he is dexterous in handling the cards. This perversion of the truth is really the strongest part of the trick; for the fact that the packet of cards in possession of the assistant on the left is never handled by the performer readily influences the spectators to believe that the performer never touched a card during the entire experiement. It is unusual, indeed, if, after the performance of this trick, the spectators do not comment upon this fact among themselves. It is a good thing for the modern magician, that the

The Art of Magic

mind of the average spectator is not logical in its workings and not given to analyzing from effect back to cause.

The performer continues: "My trick is this. I purpose to take a few cards from the pocket of one of the gentlemen and pass them into the pocket of the other gentleman. The spirits of magic, as you may know, always work with three numbers — three, four, or five. Now, how many cards shall I transfer, three, or *four*—or five?" The emphasis is on the "four," and there is a slight pause before the voice, with a falling cadence, utters "or five." The chances are that the audience will say "four," in which event your trick has succeeded without any more deception on your part. Should some say "three" and some say "five," you ignore these and turn in the direction where you heard "four" called, and proceed with the trick. This diversity of choice will happen, of course, where there is a large audience, — in which case, as we said in the beginning, it does not matter if the performer does palm five cards. In a small drawing-room performance, however, the conjurer cannot afford to burn his bridges behind him, for the reason that where there are only a half dozen spectators or so, there is likely to be only one response to the performer's request for the selection of a number; and if the reply be "three" the performer is not in an enviable position, for the expedient commonly resorted to in this case does not add to the effectiveness of the trick. We shall proceed with the description of the trick, assuming that "four" is the number chosen, and, at the end, shall explain an expedient of our own for getting out of the difficulty if another number is chosen.

If "four" is the number chosen, address the audience as follows: "Ladies and gentlemen, you have determined that I shall pass four cards invisibly from the pocket of the gentleman on my left into the pocket of the gentleman on my right. Remember, you chose your own number — four! Observe the simplicity of the operation." Make a grab in the air near the pocket of the assistant on the left and pretend to have caught a card between the fingers and thumb. "Ah, yes, here is one card,

The Art of Magic

or rather the astral body of a card. Can you see it, sir?" Hold fingers toward assistant. "You cannot? Well, that does not surprise me, for it is only after long and arduous training that one becomes able to detect an astral card. But here it is—the ten of diamonds." This is all make believe, of course, but the naming of the card adds to the verisimilitude of the trick. "I shall now pass this astral card into the pocket of the gentleman on my right, where it will at once regain its material and normal shape." Make a tossing movement toward the assistant on the right. "Did you see it go? No? Well, it traveled at a rate of nine thousand million miles a minute. I could hardly see it go myself. One card, the ten of diamonds, has passed. I shall take the second card on the tip of my wand." While speaking the performer touches the outside of the pocket with the tip of his wand. Call attention to the fact that the second card, say the ace of clubs, is on the tip of the wand, and then pass it into the pocket of the assistant on your right. "Two cards have passed from one pocket to the other. Now for the third." Again grab near the pocket of the assistant on the left; name the card apparently held by the fingers and thumb, and pretend to toss it toward the audience, and with the right hand point after it as though following its flight with your eye, saying: "There it goes, look! Right down into that corner. No! it has flown up again and hit the ceiling. Ah, here it comes along the edge of the wall. There! It has disappeared into your pocket, sir, as a homing pigeon darts into its nest. You now have three extra cards. The pocket is a little heavier, is it not? Yes, I thought so. Now for the fourth. This card you will not see pass, as it will travel at the speed of a wireless message. One, two, three, pass!" Make a rapid sweep with the right hand, which holds the wand, from the left to the right. "I have passed four cards from the pocket of the gentleman on my left into the pocket of the gentleman on the right. At the beginning of the experiment the gentleman on my left had eighteen cards. He should now have fourteen cards. The gentleman on my right had fourteen cards. He should now have eighteen cards. Remember, my hands have not touched the cards during this experiment. Now, sir (to the assistant on the left), take the cards out of your pocket and count them one by one on the table, so that every one may see and hear. You had eighteen cards, and you now have fourteen." As he throws the cards down one by one, you count with him, and when you come to the last, or fourteenth card, you add, "You see, you have lost four cards; so you, sir (turning to the other), must have the four extra cards in your pocket. Will you, please, take out your cards and count them." He counts, "One, two, three," up to fourteen (the number he had originally) when you join in counting with him, "fifteen, sixteen, seventeen, eighteen."

Now let us consider the possibility of the audience not being complaisant enough to choose the number "four." Let us suppose that of the three magic numbers they choose "five." The performer need not be disconcerted. "Very well," he rejoins, "the audience elect that I shall transfer five cards from the pocket of the gentleman on my left into the pocket of the gentleman on my right. So be it. Shall I pass the cards visibly or invisibly?" The answer is always "visibly," for an audience can never resist an opportunity to see how it is done. "Visibly? Very well. Nothing easier, I assure you. Will you, sir, (turning to the gentleman on the left) place your hand in the pocket containing the cards? Now take out one card. Thank you. Now you, sir, (turning to the gentleman on your right) will you be so kind as to place this card into your pocket? Thank you. One card, ladies and gentlemen, has passed. I shall not proceed to pass a second card *visibly* from one pocket to the other." But by this time the audience is laughing, and one or two spectators are protesting that it is no trick at all, that any one could pass cards that way. Whether they say so or not, you imagine they are making some such comment. "Ah," you say, in a rather grieved tone, "I heard some one whisper that I was perpetrating a practical joke. I assure you that such is not the case. Believe me, I would not hoax my audience in such a way. I am merely carrying out your own directions, to pass five cards *visibly* from

The Art of Magic

the pocket of this gentleman into the pocket of this gentleman on my right. One card has passed *visibly*, and if you will have patience I shall make the other four cards pass in the same manner. Ah, you smile. That is no trick, you say. I agree with you perfectly. But your conditions left no alternative. In order to pass a card *visibly* it must be done by material means. Now, if you had said *invisibly*, that would have been another story. In that case I would have recourse to the marvelous principles of the magic art. Perhaps you would like to have me pass the other cards *invisibly*. Very well. It will be more difficult, of course; but I shall take pleasure in proving to your satisfaction that my experiments are not practical jokes."

The reader will understand that by this stratagem he has succeeded in getting the extra card into the pocket of the assistant on the right, and this, too, in the most natural manner, without arousing the slightest suspicion. Indeed, if the performer is a good actor, and has a ready tongue, he will be able to get a good deal of comedy out of the incident, and the trick will really have more effect than if the audience had chosen "four" in the first place. Far from believing that the conjurer is in a difficulty, they will believe that it is a part and parcel of the trick. And having seen one card pass by material means they will marvel all the more when the performer passes the other four cards invisibly from one pocket to the other. In fact, the mixing of the material and the magical is so effective that the conjurer may consider himself fortunate if the audience choses "five" instead of "four."

If "three" is chosen, the modus operandi is varied in one detail. The "visible or invisible" expedient is worked in the manner described, but the *visible* card is passed from the gentleman on the right into the pocket of the gentleman on the left (for which reason nothing is said about passing the cards from left to right until after the number has been chosen. Now in passing the three cards *invisibly* they are passed from the pocket of the gentleman on the left, into the pocket of the gentleman on the right, as in the two former instances. The performer should call attention to the increased difficulty of the experiment, inasmuch as he will cause the card that has just been *visibly* transferred from right to left, to travel back *invisibly* from left to right, followed by two other cards. The reader, however, will seldom have to take advantage of this expedient, for the number chosen will almost invariably be four or five, and usually four.

CAUTION—There is no reason why this trick should fail in the hands of even an indifferent performer, for exceptional skill is not demanded. The only sleight employed is the palm. A good deal of practice is necessary, however, to develop the dramatic features, or the plot, so to speak. Presented with clever patter, there is no trick in the whole range of card magic that has more effect.

CONCLUDING OBSERVATIONS AND SUGGESTIONS—Some performers present this trick with forty cards, or even with a complete pack. This is a mistake; for the time consumed in counting the extra cards detracts materially from the effect. Indeed, thirty cards are sufficient.

THE FLYING CARDS (Second Method).

This method is the invention of T. Nelson Downs, and in clever hands is a remarkably fine piece of card deception. It demands a greater degree of dexterity than the first method, more address on the part of the performer, and—shall we call it sangfroid or boldness? The effect, however, is so startling that the trick is well worth the time spent in mastering it.

EFFECT—Two spectators are invited to assist the performer. They stand on either side of the table, as in the first method. One of the assistants counts thirty-two cards on the table. The performer then takes this packet and requests the assistant on his left to hold out his right hand. The performer counts, slowly and distinctly, sixteen cards, placing each card unmistakably on the palm of the assistant's hand. The remaining sixteen cards are then given into the keeping of the assistant on the right. The two assistants hold their respective packets tightly in their

The Art of Magic

hands. Now a third spectator is invited to assist in the experiment. He is requested to select a number of cards from the packet held by one assistant and to add the cards to the packet held by the other assistant. The performer then causes the cards that have been *visibly* transferred from one packet to the other to return *invisibly,* so that both assistants, at the conclusion of the experiment, have sixteen cards, as at the beginning.

TIME OCCUPIED — About eight minutes.

REQUISITES — An ordinary pack of cards; no preparation.

PRESENTATION OF THE TRICK — Invite two members of the audience to assist you, and station them on either side of the table. Request the assistant on your right to count thirty-two cards on the table. When this has been done, the performer picks up the packet and requests the assistant on the left to hold out his right hand. He then deals sixteen cards, one at a time, on the palm of the hand. So far there is no deception; but, as the acute reader has already guessed, more than sixteen cards are really put into the assistant's hand. This is how it is accomplished: When you have placed the sixteenth card in the assistant's palm, your own hand naturally returns to the packet, and as it does so three cards are quickly palmed. "How many cards have you, sir," the performer asks of the assistant on the left. "Sixteen," answers the assistant. "That is correct," replies the performer. "Now, sir, will you place this packet of sixteen cards between your hands like this?" The performer slaps his right hand over the packet in the assistant's hand, which, of course, adds the three palmed cards to the sixteen. The assistant now has nineteen cards, but if the performer has managed his part of the experiment in an easy manner neither the assistant nor any one in the audience will have any suspicion that any cards have been added to the packet. Of course, this part of the trick must be adroitly performed, and at the outset the student will find it rather difficult to palm three cards quickly and smoothly. A very good way is to palm the three pasteboards before counting the cards on the assistant's hand. After the assistant on the right has counted thirty-two cards on the table,

The Art of Magic

the performer, in picking up and squaring the packet, palms three cards in the right hand. He holds the pack in the left hand and with this hand deals sixteen cards on the assistant's hand, the right hand, with the palmed cards, hanging naturally at his side. Everybody, of course, watches the left hand. Dealing with one hand is not difficult. The thumb simply pushes each card off the pack. When the sixteen cards are dealt on the assistant's hand the performer drops the remainder of the pack on the table. After the one-hand deal the cards naturally lie rather awry in the assistant's hand, and nothing is more natural than that the performer should square them with his right hand, at the same time requesting the assistant to cover the packet with the left hand and hold the packet tightly. Of course, in the act of squaring the cards the three extra pasteboards are added. Now lead the assistant forward three or four steps, and request the other assistant to take the remaining sixteen cards from the table and hold them tightly between his hands. Invite a third spectator to take part in the experiment, and as he comes forward ask him to draw a few cards from the hands of either assistant. "Just take a few cards," says the performer, carelessly, "but be sure to take an odd number, for the spirits of magic, like Rory O'More, prefer odd numbers. Should you select an even number the experiment might fail." You apparently give him the option of selecting cards from either assistant, but in reality he is not allowed to exercise any choice. It will be remembered that the assistant who holds the packet of nineteen cards stand well in front of the table, while the assistant who holds the packet of thirteen cards stands at the rear of the table. As the third spectator comes forward the performer stands a little to the right and just back of the forward assistant, so that the spectator, if he elected to choose cards from the assistant at the rear of the table would have to walk around the forward assistant as well as around the performer and the table in order to reach the second assistant. This he will not do. He will follow the line of least resistance, and take the cards from the forward assistant. It is essential that the spectator should

The Art of Magic

take exactly three cards. If the assistant holds the cards tightly between his hands, as requested, it will be difficult for the spectator to take many cards, and, as you have impressed upon him the necessity of selecting an odd number, there really is not one chance in a thousand that he will take more than three. A single trial will convince the reader that there is nothing to be afraid of at this stage of the trick, provided the assistants are properly arranged, and the forward assistant holds the cards tightly between his hands. When the spectator has selected the cards the performer asks how many cards he has selected. The spectator replies "three." "Very well," adds the performer, "I wish to impress upon your minds, ladies and gentlemen, what has been done. This gentleman" pointing to the spectator, "has taken three cards from the sixteen held by the gentleman on my left. He had his own choice of packets and selected his own number of cards. Will you be so kind, sir, as to place the three cards on the packet held by the gentleman on my right? Thank you. The gentleman now has how many cards in his hands? Nineteen! Correct. And this gentleman (pointing to assistant on the left) how many cards has he left? Thirteen? That is correct. Now, my trick is this: I propose to make the three cards pass back, *invisibly,* into the hands of the gentleman from whom they were taken originally. Observe the simplicity of the operation." It is not necessary, however, to explain the conclusion of the trick, as the performer can make use of the patter presented in the first method.

CHAPTER V

Sleight of hand with cards (continued).

THE CARDS UP THE SLEEVES (First Method).

This is one of the stock feats of the magician, and one of the best; and as aged, probably, as the Rising Cards and the Four Ace trick, though not susceptible of so many variations. It was a major card experiment in the days of Robert-Houdin, and today is found in the repertory of every performer who handles the cards with any pretension to skill. Unfortunately, however, the trick is not always performed so dextrously as it deserves; and even professional magicians sometimes come a cropper, so to speak, when essaying this feat. The trick is performed in a score of ways; every performer worth his salt having his own method of performing it and his own peculiar wrinkles. Some conjurers pass the whole pack up the sleeve, while others execute the trick with twelve cards. Many magicians pluck the cards from the waistcoat, as was the custom in Robert-Houdin's day; some produce the pasteboards from the coat pocket; and still others—and they are in the majority—pass the cards into the trousers pocket. Some writers on magic affect to regard it as bad form for an entertainer to put the hand in the trousers pocket: but in our opinion there is nothing obnoxious in the practice; and we hold it ridiculous to imagine for an instant that even the most fastidious audience will take offense at the trick performed in this manner. We shall describe several methods of performing this interesting feat of sleight of hand, leaving the reader to select the one that appeals to his artistic conscience; but we strongly recommend the student to master each method; for versatility will stand him in good stead if he is called upon to perform the trick more than once before the same audience.

The Art of Magic

EFFECT—The performer holds twelve cards in the left hand at arm's length, and causes them to pass, one at a time, along the sleeve into either the waistcoat or trousers pocket.

TIME OCCUPIED—About five minutes.

REQUISITES AND PREPARATION—A pack of cards; no preparation.

PRESENTATION OF TRICK — FIRST METHOD — This is the method employed by Mr. Downs. The performer should wear trousers with pockets that open along the seam on the side, or else have a double pocket on the right side, so that a number of cards may be concealed, although the pocket is pulled out in order to convince the spectators that there is no hocus-pocus. If the single pocket is used, the cards are pushed to the extreme top corner remote from the opening. With the cards in this position the pocket may be turned inside out without the slightest danger of exposing them. This method is more artistic than the double pocket.

Before presenting the trick conceal three cards in the pocket. The performer offers the pack to be shuffled, and while this operation is being performed he pulls out the trousers pocket and draws attention to the fact that it is empty. He leaves the pocket hanging out for the time being. When the pack is returned he counts off twelve cards, laying the pack on the table two or three inches to the left of the packet containing the twelve cards. In squaring up the twelve cards, three cards are palmed off in the right hand. The packet of nine cards is taken in the left hand, and at the same time the right hand picks up the deck, of course replacing the palmed cards, and with the same movement the pack is handed to a spectator to hold during the experiment. The performer draws particular attention to the fact that he has only twelve cards in his left hand, and also to the empty pocket; and carelessly showing that the right hand is empty he pushes the pocket back into place. Now, holding the cards at arm's length in the left hand, the performer announces that he will cause them to pass up his sleeve, one at a time, and travel into the trousers pocket, which his just been shown empty.

The Art of Magic

He riffles the cards, (which is done by running the third or little finger sharply across the edges of the corner of the pack, making a clicking sound), and carelessly showing his right hand empty, although not verbally calling the attention of the spectators to this fact, he thrusts it into the pocket and slowly produces one of the three cards. If the other two cards are still in the upper corner of the pocket, as in the beginning of the trick, the performer can show the pocket is empty after each production. If the pocket is shown empty at the begining and the conclusion of the experiment, however the natural inference is that it was empty throughout the trick, and that the cards in some mysterious manner really found their way invisibly into the cloth receptacle. After the production of the first card, the performer really has nine cards in his left hand, but not minding this fact he says: "One card has passed. Remember, we had twelve cards in the beginning, and therefore, we should have eleven cards left. Let us see if this is correct." The conjurer miscounts the nine cards as eleven, slowly and distinctly, in the manner described in "The Twenty Card Trick." The second card is now snapped into the pocket, and the nine cards in the left hand are miscounted as ten. A third card is then caused to pass along the sleeve and thence into the pocket, and the cards in the left hand are counted as nine. There is no miscount this time. While counting the cards the performer inserts his little finger underneath the seven top cards, and in the act of squaring up the packet the seven cards are palmed in the right hand and pocketed in the act of showing that the pocket is still empty. The cards are produced from the pocket one or two at a time until the last two are reached. Let us assume that these two cards are the king of clubs and the three of hearts. Hold one in the left hand and the other in the right, both cards facing the audience. "Which card shall I make go up the sleeve first?" Asks the conjurer. "The king of clubs? As you will. King of clubs pass! Did you see it go? No? Well, it went up the sleeve like a bolt of lightning, and here it is in the pocket." This last effect is simple. When the spectators choose the card that is to pass up first (in this instance the king of clubs) you return the card to the left hand, in the rear of the other card. In this case the king of clubs is back of the three of hearts, and the two are held horizontally, facing the audience. The king of clubs, the rear card, extends below the three of hearts about three quarters of an inch. The two cards are held between the thumb and the second finger of the left hand. In order to make the king of clubs vanish, the right hand covers the greater part of the three of hearts, and also the portion of the king of clubs that extends below the front card. By a rapid downward sweep of the right hand the rear card is carried away in the right palm. The card may be held in the palm or between the fingers and thumb, and the student need not be at all alarmed if a goodly portion of the pasteboard is visible. The eyes of the spectators will not follow the movement of the right hand. Their eyes are ont the two cards in the left hand, and, therefore, the performer must also keep his eyes focused on the card in that hand. As the right hand moves away it presses rather heavily on the front card, which causes a loud click the instant the two cards are separated, and this noise materially assists in deceiving the audience. The effect on the spectators is that the card leaves the left hand at the instant the click is heard; but curiously enough no suspicion is attached to the right hand, which immediately plunges into the pocket and slowly produces the card. This is a singularly effective sleight, as a single trial will convince the reader. One card remains. This is held for a moment in the right hand; it is then apparently placed in the left, but is really palmed in the right. The back of the left hand is turned toward the audience, as if containing the card. After a slight crumpling movement of the fingers the left hand is turned over and shown empty, and an instant later the right hand produces the card from the pocket.

CARDS UP THE SLEEVE (Second Method).

The effect of this method is more elaborate than the one just described, as not only twelve cards are passed along the sleeve

The Art of Magic

into the right trousers pocket, but afterwards the remainder of the pack passes up the right and left sleeves alternately. This is a brilliant and bewildering card experiment, but demands exceptional ability to palm, both with the right and left hands, and also considerable address on the part of the performer. In order to get the maximum of effect the conjurer should not attempt to accomplish the trick under at least eight minutes, for a certain amount of patter is necessary to a complete illusion.

A pack of cards is offered to a gentleman in the audience to shuffle, and upon the cards being returned to the performer he divides the pack into four heaps on the table. One of these packets is freely chosen by the audience, the performer shuffles it and deals twelve cards on the table, remarking that as the audience selected the packet there can be no possibility of the performer possessing duplicates of the twelve cards. The remainder of the cards and the packets are stacked together and laid to one side, preferably at the upper hand of the table — that is to say, the performer's left hand. The performer, standing on the right of his table, picks up the packet of twelve cards and passes them rapidly from right to left, requesting the audience to remember the cards. The cards are passed so rapidly, however, that the audience cannot remember more than one or two, and he offers to show them again, this time more deliberately, counting each card as it is passed from the left hand into the right. When he comes to the seventh card it is placed a little below the others, so that its lower end projects about half an inch below the packet of six, forming what gamblers call a "jog." The remaining five cards are placed in the same position, the "jog" marking the division between the two packets of six cards, so that in the act of squaring up the cards the performer will have no difficulty in palming the top six cards of the packet. The squaring up and the palming of the cards should be practically one movement, and the instant the cards are palmed the other six are taken between the thumb and first finger of the right hand. The left hand is extended and carelessly shown to be empty. Any exhibition of haste or nervousness at this point should be avoided; for this is the crucial stage of the trick, and if the right hand is held easily and naturally the spectators will never dream that the performer has palmed any cards. Begin as follows:

"My object in this experiment is to illustrate the possibilities of the sleeve in conjuring. I am aware that most prestidigitators are averse to acquainting their audiences with the secrets of their profession; but I believe that it adds zest to an entertainment to reveal, occasionally, a secret or two of this fascinating art. It is my purpose, therefore, to show you how magicians make use of the sleeve. Magicians, as a rule, pooh-pooh the idea that the sleeve is employed for the purpose of secreting articles; but you know as well as I do that their denials must be taken with a grain of salt. As a matter of fact, the coat sleeve is to the conjurer what a trunk is to a woman going on a summer vacation. It is the receptable of his paraphernalia. It is the hiding place of the rabbits and elephants and kangaroos and other wild animals that he so deftly produces from a derby hat. Where does he get his endless supply of roses, of eggs, of bonbons or feathers? From his sleeve! Where do the cannon balls and bird cages and even his ladylike assistants disappear? Up his sleeve, of course! I shall prove the truth of the sleeve theory by a demonstration. Now, watch me carefully. I shall place these twelve cards in my left hand." Of course, you only place six cards, but in magic the maxim is that the truth is not to be told at all times. "You will observe that every time I make a click like this (riffling the cards with the third or little finger) one card will leave the packet, travel up the sleeve (here the conjurer gives a dainty little pull with the right hand at the left elbow) and pass invisibly into my pocket, which, as you see, is quite empty." Suit your actions to your words and thrust the right hand into the trousers pocket, hiding the six palmed cards in the upper corner and pulling out the pocket as explained in the first method. "Now, ladies and gentlemen, please watch me very closely and perhaps you will see the cards pass. Observe that

The Art of Magic

the pocket is absolutely empty." Here you slowly replace the pocket, and once more take the cards in the right hand, in exactly the same position as before. "Once more I place the twelve cards in the left hand. I shall now make the first card pass." The click is made, and the right hand plucks at the left elbow. "One card has passed. Did you see it go? No? Well, sometimes the cards pass so rapidly that it is almost impossible to see them. But I felt the jar when it flew into my pocket. By the way, does any one remember what the first card was? The queen of diamonds. (It will be recalled that when the performer passed the cards slowly from the left hand to the right, at the beginning of the trick, he urged the spectators to remember the cards.) Then the queen of diamonds must be in my pocket." Carelessly showing the right palm, the hand is thrust into the pocket and the card slowly produced. Throwing the card on the table, remark, "Now I have eleven in my hand. I shall make another pass into my pocket." Execute the riffle again, pluck at the left elbow, and take the second card out of the pocket. "Another," and a third card is removed. "Another," and the hand plunges into the pocket, but is withdrawn without a card. "That's strange," remarks the performer, with a slight emotion of embarrassment. "I seldom fail in this experiment, especially when explaining it." While speaking he pats his clothes on the right side with his right hand, then across the breast, and down the left arm, until he comes to the left elbow. "Ah," he remarks, "it jammed at the elbow. It often does that unless I am careful." Lightly jerk at the coat sleeve. "There it goes. I felt it arrive," and quickly pull out the card. Another riffle, a little pluck at the left elbow, and the fifth card is removed.

"Five cards have passed up the sleeve and into my pocket. How many should I have now in the left hand?" "You, sir (to any gentleman in the audience). Five from twelve?" "Seven," is the answer. "Thanks. Let us see if the gentleman is a good mathematician." Count the cards. As the performer has but six cards he executes the false count, making it appear that he has seven cards. With the cards in the left hand, and once more showing the pocket empty, the conjurer walks among the audience and requests two spectators to hold his wrists. "Seven cards in my left hand and the pocket empty. I shall command another card to pass. Hold my wrists as tightly as possible." Again the riffle and the performer makes a slight lunge forward, announcing that the cards has arrived in the pocket. The spectators will look as if they doubted this, but the assistant holding the right wrist is requested to put his hand into the performer's pocket. He does so, and to his amazement discovers that the performer has told the truth. The card is produced, and the performer, while in the midst of the audience, counts the six cards remaining in the left hand.

In squaring up the six cards the performer apparently places them in the left hand, the back of which is immediately turned toward the audience; but he really palms them (face to the palm) in the right hand. The left hand is now turned around and exhibited empty, and the cards are produced from the mouth, see Fig. 5. Again the performer squares up the six cards, during which maneuver the top three are palmed. Remarking that "the cards can go all in a bunch or one at a time," he introduces the three cards into the pocket and takes out one. "One more card. That makes seven. Another! That makes eight. I should have four cards in my hand." The performer rapidly counts the three cards as four. "I shall make another card pass. Watch me closely." Click! The card is taken out of the pocket. "Three remain. Shall they go singly or together? Very well." The performer does not wait for the spectators to express their preference, but immediately takes the three cards in the right hand, back palms them, quickly recovering them fanwise from behind the right knee. He places them in the left hand, face down, in about the position that cards are held for dealing, the thumb near the top of the cards. The instant the cards touch the left palm, the hand is turned over so that the back is toward the audience, and during the movement the left thumb pushes upward, which causes the card

The Art of Magic

to rise up above the hand. In order to explain the move clearly we have mentioned the left hand only. But in reality the right hand plays just as an important part in the manipulation as the left. As the cards are placed in the left hand the four fingers of the right are placed at the upper edge of the cards, and as the left hand is slowly reversed the right fingers press down on the cards until the upper end is flush with the extended first finger of the left. In this position, when the hand is reversed, the left thumb is naturally across what is now the lower edge of the cards. The four fingers of the right hand make a slight rubbing movement across the lower part of the left hand, and this movement conceals the left thumb, which pushes the cards up behind the left hand. The effect to the eye is that the rubbing movement of the right finger tips causes the cards to rise behind the left hand. The illusion is perfect and very effective. It is essential that the two hands should work in harmony, and there must not be a break in the movement. In actual practice the various details of the sleight become one movement. The right hand places the cards fanwise (as taken from the right knee) into the left hand, and while the left fingers are squaring the cards (between the fingers and the crotch of the thumb) the tips of the four fingers of the right hand cover the top edge of the cards, the left hand begins to reverse, and simultaneously the right fingers push downward on the cards. The moment the hand is reversed the left thumb continues the work of the right fingers, pushing the cards up instead of down, and while the right fingers are lightly brushing the back of the left hand, the cards rise slowly behind the hand. There is no cessation of movement. As the cards rise the performer remarks: "That is the way the cards really go up the sleeve. I shall do it again more slowly so that you can actually follow the cards as they pass into the sleeve."

While talking turn over the left hand and take the cards once more in the right. Immediately replace them in the left hand as before. The right fingers are immediately placed on the top edge of the cards, only this time the upper corners are gripped

The Art of Magic

between the first and second fingers and the third and little fingers. In other words, the cards are held exactly as in the familiar manipulation of the continuous palm with cards. The right fingers, which have the same appearance as before (the corners of the cards not showing between the fingers) push down on the cards, as in the first instance, and the left hand is reversed as before. But this time, at the beginning of the reverse, the left thumb is withdrawn from the back of the cards, the right hand, which holds the cards, completely covering the movement. The right fingers stroke the back of the left hand, as before, and then move slowly toward the left elbow, the effect on the audience being that this movement has something to do with the passage of the cards up the sleeve. The moment the right fingers reach the elbow the left hand is turned palm to the audience, the fingers outstretched, and at the same instant the right hand goes back of the left elbow, and under cover of the sleeve the cards are back palmed and the right hand brought down again, palm to the audience, the finger tips touching the tip of the left elbow. Both hands are thus shown empty. Hold this position long enough for the spectators to realize that the cards have actually disappeared.

The left arm is now lowered slightly until the coat sleeve covers the palm of the right hand, when the cards are reversed into the palm. The two hands fall down in front of the performer and swing into their natural positions on the left and right sides. The right hand is then thrust into the pocket and the three cards removed one at a time. We have described this vanish and reproduction of the last three cards at great length, but we wish to make every detail clear, for it is by far the most effective method of performing the concluding movement of the cards up the sleeve.

With the majority of performers the trick ends at this point, and the reader may make his bow if so disposed. It is highly effective, however, to continue the trick until all the cards of the pack have passed up the sleeve and been produced.

The Art of Magic

This requires exceptional dexterity in palming, and a goodly store of audacity.

Leaving the twelve cards on the table the performer takes up the pack, as if the trick were concluded. Squaring up the pack he palms ten or twelve cards, and remarks: "Now that you know how the trick is done, you can do it yourself after a few years of practice. After ten years you should attain the requisite rapidity and accuracy. I have been doing this trick for so many years that I can often make my hands move faster than the cards. For instance," (the performer holds pack in left hand and riffles the cards three times), "I shall send three cards up the sleeve and intercept them at the shoulder. Here they are," producing three cards. As he says the words "intercept them at the shoulder," he thrusts the right hand into shoulder of coat and leaves the palmed cards on the right shoulder, where they are held securely by the pressure of the coat. He takes out three cards and tosses them on the table. "Let us try it again." Three more riffles of cards, and the right had, palm unmistakably empty, sweeps quickly to the right shoulder and removes three cards. By this time the audience will be on the alert and determined to catch the performer; and undoubtedly were he to continue to palm cards from the top of the pack he would meet his Waterloo. The spectators are watching the right hand like lynxes, and it is at this critical moment in the trick that the performer baffles the enemy completely by a strategic movement that makes the trick more mysterious than ever. He palms a dozen cards in the left hand from the bottom of the pack, and goes on producing them from the left shoulder. As the method of palming more than one card in the left hand is not very well known we shall describe this movement at length.

After the reproduction of the last three cards from the right shoulder, the right hand grasps the pack, which is in the left hand, the left arm being outstretched. The spectators, shrewdly guessing that the performer is up to something, is watching the two hands very closely. The right hand must seize

The Art of Magic

the deck in a particular manner, which must be thoroughly understood in order to accomplish the sleight easily and without detection. Seize the deck with the right hand on top, between the first joints of the second and third fingers at the upper end, and the thumb at the lower end, the fingers close together, and the third finger and the thumb close to the right corners, so as to expose as much of the deck as possible. The left hand changes its position and seizes the deck at the lower end (the right thumb end), between the first and second finger tips and the crotch of the thumb, the thumb lying straight across the top close to the lower end. If this position is accurately attained the tips of the left thumb and second finger touch the right thumb, as all three are at the same corner of the deck, and almost all of the deck is exposed. At the beginning the deck is held perpendicularly, the right edge pointing toward the audience. The performer, whose right side has been toward the audience, now makes a half turn, so that his left side is toward the audience. During this turn the two hands, all the time together, make the swing from left to right. The cards are palmed in the left hand during the swing. To palm, grip the bottom cards (say a dozen, or as near that number as can be determined by the sense of touch) at the lower right corner with the tip of the left second finger, pressing the packet in against the root of the thumb, and pull down over the tip of the right thumb about a quarter of an inch. This will cause the outer-end corner of the under cards to project a little at the side, under the right third finger. Catch the projecting corner with the right little finger-tip, pressing the cards firmly against the palm under the left thumb, and draw them in toward the right thumb, at the same time straightening out the left fingers, until the under cards lie fairly along the left palm. Slightly close the left hand with the palmed cards. This palm can be made undetectably if the hands are at rest, for movement, when once the knack is attained, is simple and rapid; but in order to perform it neatly the exact position of the cards must be understood. With the swing of the two hands from left

The Art of Magic

to right, during the half turn of the body, the palm is greatly facilitated.

After the half turn of the body the right arm is outstretched, and the cards are held in the right hand exactly as in the left. A riffle is made with the right fingers, and the left hand is thrust into right shoulder, withdrawing three of the palmed cards, leaving the remainder in the shoulder of the coat. "They travel equally well through either sleeve," remarks the performer. Riffle the pack three or four times and produce some more cards from the left shoulder. Transfer the pack to the left hand, and, with a careless wave of the right hand to show the palm empty, click the cards, and after each click remove a card from the left shoulder; and then transferring the pack to the right hand repeat the same movements with the left hand, taking out cards from the right shoulder after each riffle, until the stock of cards under the coat is exhausted. This part of the trick should be done rapidly, with no pause between the productions, and the movements of the hands should be such that the right and left palms are always shown empty.

There will be now from sixteen to twenty cards remaining in the deck, which is in the right hand at the conclusion of the movements just described. Do not pause, but place deck in left hand, really placing only five or six cards in the left hand, the remainder being palmed in the right. The left arm makes several vigorous up and down movements, the fingers riffling the cards. "Pass!" exclaims the performer. The right hand reproduces the palmed cards in a fan from beneath the vest and throws them on a table, remarking, "Quite a bunch went that time. Let us see how many we have left," counting, "One-two-three-four-five-six. Please note what they are. The king, jack, tray, ten, seven and ace (or whatever they happen to be). Shall I pass them all at once? Very well. Go!" Bring the left hand, which holds the cards, face upwards, between the thumb at the inner edge and the tips of the second and third fingers at the outer edge, the first and little finger tips below the cards. Lower the left hand below right, then, in repassing right with a quick upward and outward movement, propel cards into right palm with left first finger, making a snapping noise. Point right index finger at empty left hand for an instant, then thrust the right hand into either the left shoulder or under the waistcoat and slowly reproduce the cards.

THE DISSOLVED CARD.

Tricks in which articles dissolve in water have always been favorites with magicians. One of the earliest experiments of this kind was the dissolving coin, which is even now a popular parlor trick, in spite of the fact that it has been explained in a thousand and one treatises on conjuring and in every juvenile paper or magazine. Time was when the amateur or professional magician never thought of going abroad without his glass disc, in order that he might be prepared to perform this trick at a moment's notice. When billiard ball tricks rolled into favor a few years ago, an enterprising manufacturer of magical apparatus devised the dissolving ball, the apparatus consisting of a half shell of glass, which was exchanged for the solid ball and dropped into a tumbler of water. The idea was eventually extended to eggs, and now an ingenious magician has applied the principle to cards.

EFFECT — A card is drawn from a shuffled pack, covered with a handkerchief, and held by a spectator over a glass of water. At the performer's command the card is pushed into the water, after which handkerchief is removed. Lo! the card has vanished.

TIME OCCUPIED — Three minutes.

REQUISITES AND PREPARATION — An ordinary pack of cards; a handkerchief; and a piece of transparent celluloid cut to the shape and size of a playing card. The celluloid should approximate the thickness of a playing card, so that it will neither curl nor wrinkle. The celluloid can be bought at any dealer in art materials.

The Art of Magic

PRESENTATION OF TRICK — In the right coat pocket are planted a fairly large cotton handkerchief and the celluloid feke. The feke is in such a position that it can be readily palmed in the act of removing the handkerchief. Offer the pack for shuffling; request a spectator to select a card; and while he is marking the card, remove the handkerchief from the pocket, palming the celluloid feke. Hand the handkerchief to a spectator for examination. Take the chosen card in the left hand, immediately transferring it to the right, which movement covers the card with the feke. The card may safely be held in view of the audience; for the celluloid being transparent the sharpest eye cannot detect the presence of the feke. When the handkerchief is returned the performer throws it over the card and hands both to a spectator to hold. At least this is what he apparently does. In reality he palms the card, and it is the celluloid feke that the spectator holds beneath the handkerchief. This substitution and palm are easily made while the performer's hand is under the handkerchief. Take up the pack, adding palmed card to it; shuffle, and hand the cards to another spectator for safekeeping. Now fill a small tumbler with water, nearly to the brim, and hand it to the spectator who is holding the covered card, the performer relieving him of the latter burden. Throwing the handkerchief over the glass so that the lower edge of the supposed card is directly above the mouth of the glass the conjurer requests the spectator to hold it in that position in his disengaged hand. Remarking that at the word "three" the spectator is to thrust the card into the water, the performer counts, "One, two, three!" The spectator does as requested, and the performer whips off the handkerchief, at the same time taking the glass in his right hand and holding it aloft so that all may be convinced that the card has disappeared. The celluloid feke is absolutely invisible even at a distance of three or four feet. The card is then discovered in the pack, or in any manner that the magician may elect.

CAUTION — If possible the performer should use a glass at least an inch taller than a playing card, and if filled only within a half inch of the brim the glass may be left in the spectator's hand without any danger of the feke being detected. If the glass is so small, however, that the feke extends above the level of the water, the glass must be held higher than the plane of vision, or placed on a table a tolerable distance from the spectators. A cotton handkerchief is used in preference to silk, as the extra thickness precludes the possibility of the spectator discovering the substitution of the celluloid for the card.

THE MYSTERIOUS CARD.

A new and mysterious experiment with cards, and which requires skill and mental adroitness to perform with success. It is one of Mr. Down's specialties.

EFFECT — A pack of cards is shuffled and cut into five packets. One packet is chosen (not forced). The performer spreads this packet face up on the table and a spectator is requested to think of one of the cards. The performer then produces the card.

TIME — Three minutes.

REQUISITES AND PREPARATION — An ordinary pack of cards; no preparation.

PRESENTATION OF THE TRICK — The performer watches the direction of the spectator's eyes as he mentally chooses a card. The wider the spread the easier it is to determine which group of cards the chosen card is among: that is to say, the right, the center, or the left. As a rule the most prominent card of the group will be selected. In picking up the cards palm this prominent card, after placing the other two likely cards of the group at the top and the bottom of the pack. A little practice will enable you to get the chosen card every time, as there are three chances in your favor. Ask the spectator to name his card. If he names the palmed card, pick up pack in left hand, riffle the cards, as in the cards up the sleeve, and produce the chosen card from under the coat at the left shoulder. If he mentions the card at the bottom of the pack, simply strike the pack a blow with the fist, turn the pack over and reveal the card. If the top card is named, command the chosen card to appear at that position, allowing the spectator to turn it over himself.

The Art of Magic

THE CARD AND HAT.

An excellent impromptu trick for the office, the club, or restaurant. Neatly performed it will prove very mysterious. The invention is claimed by Mr. Henry Hardin, the originator of the "Princess Card" trick.

EFFECT — A pack of cards is handed to a spectator with the request that he shuffle it, place it on the table face downward, and then to peep at the top card, leaving it on the deck. Cover the pack with a soft felt hat (which must be worn for this particular trick), and command the top card to change. Upon removing the hat, the spectator discovers that the performer's command has been obeyed.

TIME — Two minutes.

REQUISITES AND PREPARATION — An unprepared pack of cards; a soft felt hat, preferably of the Fedora style; and in the left sleeve a stick shaped like a lead pencil and about four inches long — although the exact length will vary with the size of the hat. On one end of the stick is a pellet of conjurer's wax.

PRESENTATION OF THE TRICK — While the spectator is looking at the top card the performer casually removes his hat and introduces the stick into it. Cover the pack with the hat, the waxed end of stick hanging down; the other end being held by the pressure of the fingers on the crown of the hat. The stick is pressed onto the top card, and, after muttering some mystic gibberish, the hat is removed and replaced on the head. The card and stick of course, are concealed inside the hat.

THE STABBED CARD.

A new method of performing an old and well-known trick. A card is drawn from the pack, replaced, and the pack is shuffled by a volunteer assistant. The beauty of this method is that the performer does not need to keep track of the chosen card, as it is really shuffled into the deck. Nevertheless, when the cards are spread on the table, the performer experiences no difficulty in stabbing the selected card with a borrowed penknife. As the old methods of working of the trick are so widely known

The Art of Magic

we shall confine our description to the bare details of the new method of locating the chosen card.

The only preparation necessary is a minute pellet of conjurers's wax affixed to the top card of the deck. After a spectator has selected a card, and while he is holding it up for the benefit of the spectators, the performer makes the pass, bringing the waxed card to the center. The selected card is replaced on this card, and the pack squared up. A little pressure of the fingers and the selected card will adhere to the waxed card, so that the pack may be shuffled for twenty-four hours without the two cards being separated. The method of bringing the trick to a conclusion should now be clear. In spreading the cards on the table, the double card is instantly distinguished by the sense of touch. A slight pressure of the fingers will instantly separate the cards, during which operation, of course, the hands never cease the mixing operation. The chosen card is kept in sight, and the trick brought to the usual conclusion. In another chapter *we* shall give a new, original and absolutely undetectable method of performing this interesting and always effective trick.

THE GREAT POKER TRICK.

This is a startling trick for the club or drawing-room and will enhance the performer's reputation as a skillful manipulator of cards. Incidentally, it will wean any person from the ambition to play poker with a magician or card expert. It is a particular favorite of Mr. Adrian Plate, a very skillful and ingenious conjurer, by whose permission it is included in this volume.

EFFECT — A new pack of cards is taken out of the wrappers. The performer riffles the cards and the pack is cut by the spectators as many times as they desire. Seven poker hands are then dealt, and the six players each have a full house, while the performer throws down a straight flush.

TIME OCCUPIED — Three to five minutes, according to the amount of fancy shuffling and false cuts indulged in by the performer.

The Art of Magic

REQUISITES AND PREPARATION — A pack of cards direct from the manufacturer. A pack that has not been tampered with will run as follows, from the bottom upwards: Ace, king, queen, jack, ten, nine, eight, seven, six, five, four, three, two, for each suit; or Ace, two, three, four, five, six, seven, eight, nine, ten, jack, queen, king for each suit. For the purpose of this trick it makes no difference which order is used. There are a few brands of playing cards, however, among them the "Steamboats," which are not packed according to either of the above arrangements.

PRESENTATION OF THE TRICK — The performer removes the pack from the wrapper, calling attention to the fact that the cards are fresh from the manufacturer. He throws away the joker and gives the pack a false shuffle, using whatever method he is most adept at. If versed in fancy blind cuts he may indulge in a series of manipulations of this kind; but for the purpose of the trick it is sufficient to give the cards a false shuffle. Then allow the spectators to cut the cards. They may cut as many times as they wish without destroying the order of the cards, as the halves simply revolve around each other. This is, in fact, the strongest feature of the trick; for most persons believe that the conventional cut completely disarranges any prearranged order of the pack.

Now deal the cards out to six persons, giving the top card to No. 1; the second card to No. 2; the third card to No. 3; the fourth card to No. 4; the fifth card to No. 5; and the sixth card to No. 6. Begin the round again, dealing the seventh card to No. 1, and so on to No. 6. As soon as the twelfth card is dealt, shift the next card (the thirteenth) to the bottom of the deck, and continue dealing two more rounds. As soon as the twenty-fourth card is dealt, shift the twenty-fifth card to the bottom of the pack, and then deal around once more, handing one card to each player. Now deal five cards from the top of the pack for your own hand. Ask the spectators to turn over their hands, and each one will be astonished to find that he holds a full house. The performer then turns over his own hand, exhibiting a straight flush.

The Art of Magic

CAUTION — If the order of the pack is Ace, two, three, four, etc., up to the king, the performer must take note of the bottom card of the deck after the cut; for should the bottom card be a jack, the trick will not come out as described. Another cut will obviate this difficulty.

CONCLUDING OBSERVATIONS AND SUGGESTIONS — The weakest point in this trick is the necessity of shifting the thirteenth and twenty-fifth cards to the bottom of the pack; for the conventional two-hand pass is rather awkward to make while dealing, especially if the performer is seated at a table with six spectators around him. For this reason we advise the performer to stand up and not use a table; but to deal the cards on the spectator's hands. In moving from one person to another the performer will have an excellent opportunity to shift or slip the two cards from the top to the bottom.

ANOTHER POKER TRICK.

Properly speaking, this is not a conjuring trick, but a gambler's artifice; for a certain number of cards are stocked, and, in dealing four hands at poker, the desired cards fall to the dealer. The conventional riffle shuffle is used, supplemented with fancy cuts and a peculiar and rather effective movement known as the "haymow" shuffle, which used to be employed in rural districts before the riffle shuffle was generally rnown. This method of "putting up" cards is the simplest and most effective known; and the conjurer can use it to good effect in explaining why he does not play cards.

We shall assume that three cards are to be stocked or "put up," so that in dealing four hands at poker these three cards shall fall to the dealer, although four or five cards may be stocked as easily as three. For the purpose of explanation let us see three aces. Place the three aces in center of pack, keeping the little finger above them. Now make the "haymow" shuffle. This is accomplished by drawing out the under half of the pack, that is to say, the packet *below* the little finger, and slapping it rather forcibly on the top packet. Now undercut [1] about three-quarters

The Art of Magic

of the pack, and allow the cards to drop in small packets on the packet remaining in the left hand. As the three top cards of this packet are the aces, the little finger must be kept on top of the packet. The final movement is to draw out this undermost packet and drop it on top. If the movements are performed slowly and naturally the effect is exactly as if the cards were thoroughly mixed and the three aces hopelessly lost.

The three aces, however, are on top of the pack. Riffle the cards in the ordinary manner, taking care not to disturb the three aces, but allowing one card to fall on the top ace. Repeat this shuffle three times, allowing one card to fall on top of the pack after each riffle. When the four shuffles are concluded there will be four indifferent cards above the three aces. "It must be apparent," you explain to the spectators, "that the cards are thoroughly shuffled, and that the three aces are mixed in the pack. They are not on the bottom (here you turn over the cards and show three or four of the bottom cards); nor on the top (you turn up the three top cards, and if the spectators desire to see the next card, you can turn that up also, as it is an indifferent card). You see, I do not know where the aces are. To convince you that there is no deception about this experiment I will even give the pack another thorough shuffle."

Riffle the cards as before, keeping the top stock of seven cards intact. After the shuffle make the following cut: Seize the deck with left hand at side, near end, between the second finger and thumb, the first finger tip resting on top. Seize the upper portion of deck with the right hand, at sides, near end, between the second finger and thumb. Raise the deck slightly from the table with both hands and pull out the upper portion with the right hand but retain the top card in the left hand by pressing on it with the left first finger tip. Immediately drop the left-hand packet on table and bring the right hand packet down on top with a slight swing, and square up. This cut displaces the top card, sending it to the middle. Therefore, if you riffle the cards four times, making this cut after each riffle, the four top cards will be transferred to the center of the pack, and at the

The Art of Magic

conclusion of the shuffles the three aces will be on top, although the spectators would be willing to wager that these particular cards were hopelessly mixed in the pack. The trick proper now begins. All the movements and manipulations just described are mere flourishes, introduced for the purpose of convincing the spectators that the aces are hopelessly lost in the pack. Address the audience substantially as follows: "Perhaps you think I do not really shuffle the cards; but I assure you that the shuffle is neither an optical illusion nor any sort of hocus-pocus. To convince you that the cards are really shuffled I shall repeat the operation, only this time I shall riffle the cards so slowly that there can not be even the suggestion of trickery. (Cut the cards and place the two packets in position for the riffle shuffle). Now, watch my hands very closely. See; every card is riffled into the pack. No deception of any kind." The action is suited to the words. The packets are slowly riffled into each other. The first part of the shuffle is performed rather carelessly, but when you come to the last four or five cards, you must slow up and see to it that an *indifferent card is riffled between each ace*. The second shuffle completes the stocking of the aces. It is performed exactly as the first riffle, only in this instance the last six cards of each packet are alternately riffled into each other. If this manipulation has been correctly performed the twelve top cards will be arranged in the following order, counting from the top of the pack: Three indifferent cards — ace — three indifferent cards — ace — three indifferent cards — ace. It will be readily seen, from this order, that if the cards are dealt out in four hands, as at poker, the three aces will fall to the dealer. In case you should not calculate correctly, and one of the riffles should leave two or three extra cards over the top ace, the contremps need not disturb your mind. All you have to do is to cut as many times as you have superfluous cards, as described in the first part of the trick. This extremely useful sleight will shift the useless cards to the center of the pack. On the other hand, should the cards in the right hand run out first, and there is no indifferent card to place on top, all that is necessary is to give

The Art of Magic

the pack an extra riffle, leaving the top stack undisturbed, and conclude by dropping an indifferent card on top of the pack.

By using five cards this system of stocking may be employed in a very effective card trick. Allow five cards to be selected, marked, and returned to pack, which is now shuffled by the performer, who, sitting at the table, invites four spectators to surround him. After the series of shuffles described, supplemented by some fancy cuts, four poker hands are dealt, and the five selected cards will fall in the performer's hand. The effect of this trick will be enhanced if, after shuffling, the performer "bridges" the cards and allows a spectator to cut the cards. The "bridging" should be done at the end instead of the side, and is performed in the act of cutting. For complete instruction in fancy cuts and shuffles, as well as in other artifices employed by those who woo the goddess of fortune at the gaming table, the reader may be referred to S. W. Erdnase's excellent treatise, "The Expert at the Card Table."

THE DISAPPEARING QUEEN.

A remarkably fine card experiment, brilliant and bewildering, the invention of that exceedingly ingenious conjurer Mr. Adrian Plate, and now explained for the first time.

EFFECT — A pack of cards is shuffled, and, when returned, the performer removes all the picture cards. These face cards are exhibited to a spectator, who is requested to remember the bottom card, to remove it from the packet and place it on his left hand, covering it with the right. This is repeated until all the picture cards have been similarly disposed of. The performer draws attention to the remainder of the pack, showing that it is composed wholly of spot cards, and places this packet on an inverted tumbler, covering all with a handkerchief. "Ladies and gentlemen," says the performer, "be so kind as to name the cards that you have in your hands, the cards that you selected. Name them at the same time, when I count three. Now, then, One! two! three!" "Queen of heart!" respond the spectators in chorus. "What!" exclaims the performer. "The

Queen of hearts? Everybody? That is impossible, for there is only one queen of hearts in every honest pack, and at this moment her majesty is reclining at ease underneath the handkerchief." The performer removes the handkerchief, and turning up the top card of the packet shows that it is the queen of hearts. The spectators are now requested to look at their cards, and much to their surprise they will find a different picture card in their hands.

TIME OCCUPIED — Five to eight minutes.

REQUISITES AND PREPARATION — A pack of cards; no preparation; a tumbler and a handkerchief. A half card (the queen of hearts) is also used. Take a duplicate queen of hearts and cut it in half. Use only one of these halves, and conceal it under the vest, or in any convenient pocket, so that it will be instantly accessible.

PRESENTATION OF TRICK — Give a complete pack of cards to be shuffled, and upon its being returned remove all the face cards except the queen of hearts, which you leave on top of the packet of spot cards. Run the spot cards before the eyes of the spectators, exercising care to draw the queen of hearts behind the pack. Place this packet on an inverted tumbler and cover with a handkerchief. The queen of hearts, unknown to the audience, is the top card of this packet.

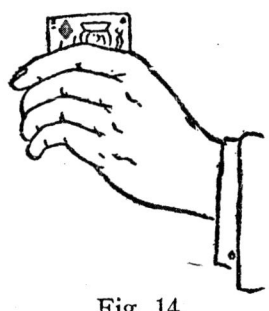

Fig. 14.

The performer now takes up the packet of picture cards and, getting possession of the half card, places it at the bottom. Hold the pack in the left hand in such a way that the fingers

The Art of Magic

cover the lower half of the pack, the first finger concealing the half queen of hearts, as shown in Fig. 14. Advance to a spectator and show him the bottom card. All he sees is the queen of hearts. Request him to take away this card, place it in his left hand, and cover it with his right.

At this juncture the performer lowers the pack face downwards and the right hand grasps the pack, the thumb at the end towards the body and the middle finger at the front. While keeping the left hand in its place and retaining the half card, the right hand shoves the pack a little forward. The result of this maneuver will be that the half card will be at the place where the right thumb is, instead of near the tips of the fingers of the same hand. The right hand is now removed and the spectator takes the bottom card. He thinks, of course, that he is taking the queen of hearts, whereas he is really taking the bottom card of the packet.

Now place the right hand again on the pack and shove the half card to the front. Advance to another spectator and exhibit the bottom card (the half queen of hearts), requesting him to remove it. Go through the same maneuver as with the first spectator, and repeat until all the cards are taken. When only one card remains in the hand press the half card well against it, palming the half card neatly when the last card is given to a spectator to hold. Every one imagines that he or she holds the queen of hearts; and when the performer requests the spectators to name their cards at the word "three," the chorus will be "Queen of hearts." They will be very much surprised to discover they are holding entirely different cards.

All that remains is to show that the queen of hearts is really on top of the packet on the inverted tumbler.

CAUTION — The trick as described can only be worked among a tolerably large audience; for the spectators who draw cards should be separated from each other, so that they cannot compare notes. In a small audience the performer can work the trick with, say four or five picture cards; but, of course, in this event, much of the dramatic effect is lost.

The Art of Magic

THE CARD THROUGH THE HANDKERCHIEF.

The trick of shaking a card through a handkerchief is one of the most popular of latter-day card effects, and is no doubt included in the repertory of the majority of amateur magicians. So far as we have been able to trace its history, it was the invention of a well-known German conjurer, St. Roman, although it is claimed by at least a half hundred modern wizards. Although one of the best card tricks ever invented, it has been "done to death." It is so widely known, in fact, that there is more or less danger in presenting it before a clever, up-to-date audience; for it invariably happens that there is some one among the spectators that is acquainted with the secret. The following trick may be described as a variation of the card through the handkerchief, although the effect is quite different. It is equally mysterious, however; and in the hands of a clever performer may be made a very fine card experiment. It is a splendid impromptu trick, and as this is the first time its secret has been explained, we advise the reader to add it to his programme. It is one of the specialties of the ingenious Mr. Leipsig.

EFFECT — A card is chosen from a shuffled pack, returned, and the pack shuffled by a spectator. Performer calls attention to the fact that the drawn card is neither on the top nor the bottom of the pack. The deck is laid face down on the table and covered with a handkerchief, which is folded over the cards. The performer seizes two corners of the handkerchief and pulls them apart, when the card rises visibly through the handkerchief.

TIME OCCUPIED — Three minutes.

REQUISITES AND PREPARATION — An ordinary pack of cards, no preparation; a fairly large cotton handkerchief, preferably of a dark color; a small pellet of adhesive wax.

PRESENTATION OF TRICK — A card is selected and returned to the pack. It is shifted to the top and palmed and the pack offered for shuffling. In taking back the pack the palmed card is returned to the top, and the pack placed on table. Exhibit a moderately large handkerchief of a dark color (cotton is preferable to silk as it is more opaque). Allow the spectators to examine the handkerchief, and while they are thus engaged get possession of the minute pellet of adhesive wax (a good place to keep the wax until wanted is on one of the vest buttons). In taking up the cards press the wax on the center of the top (the

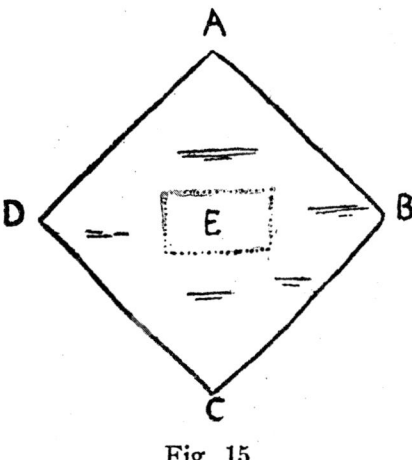

Fig. 15.

selected) card. Call attention to the bottom card and ask if it is the selected card. The reply, of course, is in the negative. Remove the two top cards, holding them as one, and ask if it is the selected card. The reply is also a negative. Replace the pack on the table, face downward, and cover with the handker-

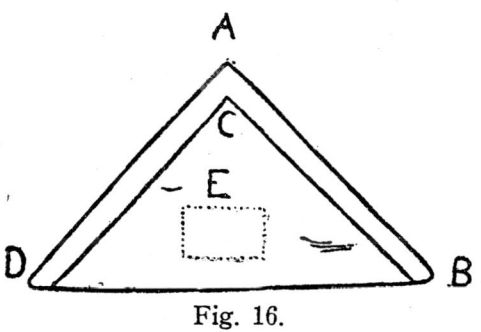

Fig. 16.

chief, as in Fig. 15. In the drawing, A, B, C, D represent the four corners of the handkerchief which is spread over the pack, E. The pack is drawn with dotted lines, so as to represent it as being under the handkerchief. In spreading the handkerchief over the pack the center is pressed on the top card, so that it will adhere to the pellet of wax. Now for the method of folding the handkerchief, upon which the success of the experiment depends. The reader will find it easier to following the directions with the materials actually at hand. Fold C over towards A, until the point C is about two inches from the point A, see Fig. 16. Now fold C about half way back, as in Fig. 17. When the fold is in the position of Fig. 17 the pack is under three thicknesses of the handkerchief. Now grasp the handkerchief on either side of the pack, at about the positions marked F and G in Figure 17. The fingers should be underneath and the thumbs on top of the handkerchief. With both hands lift the handkerchief about

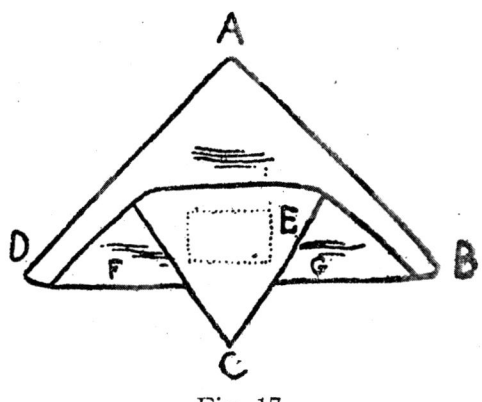

Fig. 17.

ten inches above the pack. The top card, of course, adheres to the underside of the handkerchief. Lift handkerchief high enough so that the front half, the part marked A, is free from the table. Now swing A in toward the body (above the pack, of course), and let it fall over the cards and onto the table, only this time it occupies the original position of C. The chosen card is now securely hidden between the folds. Grasp the corner C in the right hand and the corner A in the left hand. Pull C to the right and A to the left. By means of this maneuver the handkerchief is opened and the chosen card is presented face upward on top of the handkerchief. The sudden appearance of the card

The Art of Magic

is nothing short of startling, and the effect is precisely as if the card actually passed upward through the meshes of the handkerchief. The directions for folding the handkerchief may seem rather confusing at first. It is a very simple operation, however, and in actual practice consumes not more than two or three seconds. If the reader will follow each move with a handkerchief on the table he will experience no difficulty in "catching the hang" of the operation, so to speak.

The performer who does not mind going to a little extra trouble in order to increase the effect of his experiments can refine this trick by working it in connection with the "kinetoscope" or "Flying Card" trick, explained in Chapter III. In order to present the trick in this manner, arrange the pack, as described for that trick, so that in ruffling the cards a king of spades will appear as the king of clubs. The real king of clubs is on the top of the pack. It is forced on a spectator, due care being taken not to disarrange the order of cards. The king is replaced and brought to the top (still keeping care not to disarrange the order of the pack). The performer gives the pack a false shuffle, places it on the table and covers it with the handkerchief, which is folded in the manner already described. After the handkerchief is folded the performer remarks, rather apologetically, that he forgot the most important part of the trick. "I forgot to show you that your card was not at the bottom or at the top of the pack (removing the handkerchief and exhibiting the top and bottom cards). Oh, yes, sir, the card is in the pack. I have not juggled it away. Will you see if your card is still in the pack, sir?" This to the spectator who drew the card. Ruffle the pack before his eyes, and he sees what is apparently the king of clubs. It is really the king of spades, the card he drew being wrapped in the handkerchief. Request the spectator to shuffle the pack, and then lay it on the table and cover it with the folded handkerchief. Take hold of the ends A and C and pull them in opposite directions, when the king of clubs will apparently rise through the handkerchief. Permit the audience to examine the pack so as to convince themselves that a duplicate card was not employed. As the spectator shuffled the pack, the cards are so mixed that they afford no clue to the mystery. If the cards were left in their original order a keen-witted spectator might reason out the modus operandi.

THE CARD IN THE WATCH (First Method).

This mystifying trick used to be one of the specialties of the Italian conjurer Yank Hoe, who created something of a sensation among magicians in this country about fifteen years ago. It is not a trick that every conjurer will accomplish; but those who once acquire the knack of opening the case of a watch will make a decided hit with this mystifying feat.

EFFECT — A watch is borrowed, wrapped in a handkerchief, and the bundle given to a spectator to hold. A card is drawn and returned to pack. The card disappears and a miniature of it is found inside the case of the borrowed watch.

TIME OCCUPIED — From three to five minutes.

REQUISITES AND PREPARATIONS — An ordinary pack of cards; a miniature card, say the ace of clubs, the back of which is prepared with a sticky substance, like the dried glue on labels, so that it is necessary only to moisten with the tongue in order that the card will adhere inside the watch case.

PRESENTATION OF TRICK — Yank Hoe came forward with the miniature card palmed, the back moistened. He borrowed a watch, and on the way back to the stage deftly opened the case and inserted the miniature card. He was so expert that he could open the most stubborn case with one hand. Such facility, however, is acquired only after a diligent practice, and only then when one possesses stout finger nails. The card once inserted and the watch wrapped, in a handkerchief the trick, so far as the performer is concerned, is over. All that remains is to force an ace of clubs, and cause it to vanish according to the fancy of the magician. An excellent method is to perform the diminishing card trick with the ace of clubs, causing the smallest sized card to vanish, to be discovered eventually in the watch.

The Art of Magic

THE CARD IN THE WATCH (Second Method).

In this variation of the trick the performer has a miniature card pasted in the back of his own watch. Let us assume that this card is the ace of clubs. The performer forces an ace of clubs on a spectator. The card is returned to the pack and the deck shuffled. The performer asks the spectator to hold the deck to his own forehead, and to think intently of the selected card. He takes out his watch and opens the case and holds it so that the spectator cannot see the card in the cover. Now if the timepiece is held at the proper angle the card will be reflected in that part of the case that covers the works. In gold watches this surface is highly polished and the card is reflected with startling distinctness. With the proper patter this trick can be made very effective. An excellent method of performing the trick is to have the person who drew the card hold to his forehead one end of a long piece of thin wire, or string. The performer holds the other end over the watch, and invites another spectator to see what he can see. He sees the reflection of the very card that the other spectator is thinking of. Produced with the proper dramatic effect this method is startling.

CHAPTER VI

CARD TRICKS BASED ON A NEW AND ORIGINAL SYSTEM OF LOCATING A CHOSEN CARD.

In this chapter we shall describe a series of sleights by which a chosen card may be located in the pack, without the use of the shift, or without resorting to any of the multifarious and conventional devices employed by magicians to obtain knowledge of a card that has been sighted or selected by a spectator. This new and original system of subterfuge is the invention of T. Nelson Downs, who has built upon the basic idea a superstructure of subtle and bewildering illusions with cards that will appeal particularly to the devotee of sleight of hand. These tricks are susceptible to development and variation, and in the hands of an adroit performer and clever talker will furnish adequate material for a thirty-minute act. The experiments form an ideal card combination for club work, or for an impromptu performance in the home, hotel or newspaper office, in that no preparation is required and any cards may be used. The performer, however, will soon discover that the best results are obtained by the use of a new, or comparatively new, pack of cards. Equipped with such a pack, and with a small table or stand of any kind, the student, assuming that he possesses the requisite skill, will be able not only to mystify the uninitiated, but also to baffle those who may have a knowledge of sleight of hand. So much for the intrinsic merits of this new system of deception. It is more to the purpose to present a brief description of the effects obtained by the various subterfuges.

The performer removes a pack of new cards from its case and wrapper, and offers the same to a spectator for shuffling. This preliminary duty performed, the conjurer, holding the pack downward in the left hand, requests some member of the audience to look at a card — not to draw a card, or in any way disturb its position in the pack; but simply to lift slightly the upper right-hand corner of the pack and sight a card. During this operation the performer partly turns his back to the spectator, extending the left arm backward, in order that he may not catch a glimpse of the card. After the card has been sighted, and the pack restored to its normal condition, the performer draws attention to the fact that the cards are squared up, and even allows the spectator to take the pack in his own hand and examine it. Nevertheless, the performer can instantly produce the chosen card in any manner he may choose, or, as performed by Mr. Downs, can make the card appear at any number from the top of the pack that may be desired by the audience. This is the general effect of the experiment, the groundwork of the ingenious system, so to speak; but in repetition — and this is one of the very few card tricks that can be safely performed more than once before the same audience — in repetition a number of different methods are employed to obtain secret knowledge of the card sighted, and the method of reproducing the card is varied. We shall describe each method in turn, but the reader must remember that the bewildering effect of the experiment consist in combining the different methods into one general trick. In other words, the effect is cumulative, developing to a climax.

FIRST METHOD — The pack is held face downward in the left hand, in the usual manner of holding the cards for dealing, except that the four fingers on the outside press the pack rather firmly into the crotch of the thumb. The first joint of the first, second, third and fourth fingers are pressed against the outer edge of the pack. The thumb extends slantingly across the top of the pack, pointing toward the first finger. In this manner the cards are presented to the spectator, who is requested to lift the upper right hand corner of the pack and remember one of the cards. The performer impresses rather strongly upon the spectator the importance of looking at one card only. While the spectator is engaged in this duty, the performer partially turns his body and head, so that he cannot possibly see the card sighted by the spectator, who, after making a mental note of the card, allows the upper portion of the pack to fall back into its original position. If, however, the pack is held as directed, and a rather firm pressure maintained by the first and second fingers against the outer edge of the deck, it will be found that a small part of the fleshy tip of the first finger will be wedged between the two portions of the pack, forming a break, the bottom card of the upper portion being the spectator's card. If, at the same time, the left thumb is pressed rather heavily on the top of the pack, this break will not be visible. As you turn around and bring the hands together, the tip of the left first finger is inserted further into the break and then pushed upward and outward, which movement forces the chosen card (that is, the card at the botom of the lower packet) outward until it extends about

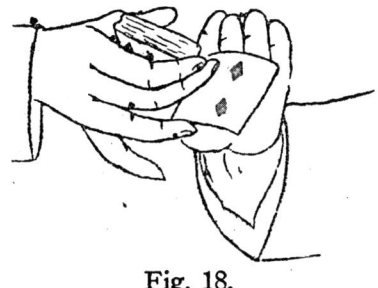

Fig. 18.

half an inch from the right side of the pack. The right hand, which covers the pack during this operation, grips the extended card between the first joint of the thumb (at the lower corner) and the second joint of the third finger (at the upper corner), see Fig. 18, and slips the cards to the top of the pack. Deftly performed, with the back of the right hand toward the audience, the movement cannot be detected by the sharpest eye. When the card is safely on top the performer impresses the audience with the idea that it is an utter impossibility for him to know what card was sighted, or to know the location of the card in the pack; and he draws attention to the fact that the cards are squared up, even allowing spectator to take the pack in his own hands. In order to make the trick appear more difficult, however, he shuffles

The Art of Magic

the pack, taking care, of course not to disturb the top card. He now requests a spectator to name a number. Let us suppose that the number ten is named. The performer stands apparently wrapped in deep thought, and pays no attention to what the spectator says. Then, suddenly he becomes all animation. "What number did you say, sir?" he inquires politely. "Ten? An excellent number for the experiment. I really knew beforehand that you would select ten, and consequently have already commanded the chosen card to fly to that number. You look incredulous, sir. Fortunately, however, I can prove my assertion. Will you, sir, oblige me by holding the pack in your own hands and counting off the desired number of cards. Pray observe that there can be no deception. One, two, three, four, five, six, seven, eight, nine — stop! You have counted off nine cards; and,

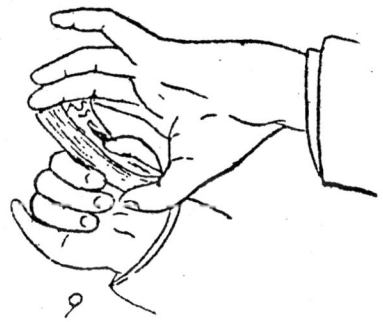

Fig. 19.

therefore, if the experiment has been successful the next card should be the card selected by this gentleman. Will you kindly name the card before it is turned up? The five of clubs? Then the tenth card should be the five of clubs. Turn it up yourself, sir. Thank you. The experiment has been a complete success."

The method by which the desired card is brought to the required number from the top of the pack is at once simple and ingenious. The pack is held in the left hand, face downward. The lower portion of the pack is bent slightly upwards, and the bottom cards are released, one at a time, by the thumb of the right hand, see Fig. 19. The pressure of the thumb enables the performer to count exactly the number desired (in this case nine); the little finger is slipped between them and the rest of the pack and the pass made, which operation brings the chosen card to the desired number in the pack.

A the outset the student may object that this method of counting is rather slow; but after a modicum of practice the thumb becomes accustomed to the work and the desired number of cards will be counted off noiselessly, rapidly and without the slightest hesitation. Indeed, there is no limit to the skill that may be acquired in this really valuable sleight, and it will be found in time that the desired number of cards will be secured more by the intuitive sense of touch than by the conscious act of counting. In the actual performance of the trick it will expedite matters if the performer begins counting before asking a spectator to think of a number. Let him thumb off, say, ten cards, which he separates from the rest of the pack by inserting the little finger of the left hand. Now, if a greater or smaller number than ten is chosen, it will be a simple matter to add to, or take away from, the ten cards. Experience teaches that the number chosen, ninety-five times out of a hundred, will be between seven and fifteen, and with ten cards already counted it will require only a second to shift the requisite number to the top of the pack. In case the performer is not certain that he has transferred the exact number of cards to the top of the pack, it will be wise to vary slightly the method of concluding the trick. Hand the pack to a spectator, as already described, but instead of allowing him to count down to the desired number, the performer himself takes off the cards, one by one, from the top, counting audibly as each card is removed, and glancing swiftly at each card as he places it in his left hand. Let us suppose that the card is to be found at number ten from the top, and that the performer, in taking off the cards, discovers that the chosen card is at number nine. He does not hesitate an instant but places this ninth card on top of the packet in his left hand, and then takes up the tenth card. He does not show the face of this card, however, but places it on top of the packet in the left hand, and

The Art of Magic

addresses the audience somewhat as follows: "The conditions of the trick require that the card chosen by the gentleman shall be found at the tenth number in the pack. I have already counted off ten cards from the pack, and if my trick has been a success this card (here the performer touches the top card with the right forefinger) should be the one selected. (This is a fabrication, of course, for the chosen card is second from the top; but there would be no such thing as magic if mendacity were a penal offense). Before turning over the card I shall prove that I have known its identity all along. (The performer, of course, after shifting the card to the top of the pack, in the manner described, took occasion to sight it. Let us assume that it is the four of hearts). Will the gentleman kindly think of the card intently. Do not allow your thoughts to wander from the cards. Is your card a red one, sir? The gentleman says that his card is red. Strange, isn't it, how I can look in a person's eye and tell what—he has eaten for supper? Your card is a diamond, is it not? The gentleman says that his card is a diamond. I could see in your left eye that it was a diamond. Strange, isn't it? Really, I do not see how I can do it for the money. But to proceed. It is a spot card, is it not? I was sure of it. I am rarely mistaken on spot cards, and particularly when the card in question is the four of diamonds. Am I correct, sir? The gentleman says that the four of diamonds is his card, which should be on the top of the packet in my hand, as it is the tenth card I took from the pack." During the latter part of this patter the performer has ruffled the ten cards in his left hand with the right thumb and has slipped the left little finger underneath the two top cards. By this maneuver he is enabled to take off the two top cards and exhibit them as one. As the four of diamonds is the bottom card, the audience is satisfied that the experiment is a complete success. "The chosen card," continues the performer, "has appeared, as requested, at number ten in the pack. Of course, had any other number been chosen it would have made no difference in the result. (Here the performer takes with his left hand the pack from spectator.) "Will any one else kindly

The Art of Magic

name a number at which they would like this four of diamonds to appear, counting from the top of the pack. (At the words "top of the pack" the performer carelessly places the double card, which the spectators think is the four of diamonds only, on the top of the pack). But in order to make the experiment still more difficult I shall place the four of diamonds on the table. (Suiting the action to the word the conjurer deals the top card on the table. The spectators believe, of course, that the four of diamonds is on the table; but in reality the four is on the top of the pack). Will some one mention a number. Fifteen? Very good, sir. I was certain that you would select fifteen, and I assure you that the card has already traveled to that position in the pack. Watch me carefully. (The performer counts the cards and turns up the four of diamonds at the fifteenth. This surprising result is accomplished by dealing seconds). I shall now place the four of diamonds in the center of the pack (suiting the action to the word) and it immediately flies to the bottom of the pack. (This is accomplished either by the shift, or by the "Voisin twist," or "dovetail pass," described on Page 16 of "More Magic," by Prof. Hoffman. Had you commanded the four of diamonds to appear on the top of the pack, it would immediately have obeyed. (Shift again and show four of diamonds at the top of pack). Will you, sir, kindly touch one of the cards in the pack. Turn it over, please, and name the card. The four of diamonds? Ah, ladies and gentlemen, you must admit by this time that the four of diamonds is really ubiquitous, and agree with me that no matter what number you may select the four of diamonds will instantly appear at that number."

This last effect is accomplished by forcing. As the performer says, "Will you, sir, kindly touch one of the cards," he advances toward one of the spectators, at the same time making the shift, which brings the four of diamonds to the center. It is now a comparatively easy matter to force a spectator to touch this card. If, inadvertently, or with malice prepense, he touches some other card, you need not be disconcerted. Take out the card designated, and, without showing it, place it on the table.

The Art of Magic

Request another person to touch a card, and force the four on this spectator. If he touches the right card, place it face downward on the table. Request another spectator to touch a card (it does not matter which card is touched) and also place this one on the table. These three cards should be arranged so that the four of diamonds is in the middle. Request a spectator to select one of the three cards, and the chances are ninety-nine to one that the center card, the four of diamonds, will be chosen. If the middle card is not selected, the performer may still force the four of diamonds by taking up the card designated and then forcing the four by means of the familiar "right or left" equivoque. This method of terminating the trick allows the performer three chances to force the four of diamonds, and if he fails in three trials there is very little hope of his ever being a magician.

Having explained at length the modus operandi of terminating the trick when the performer does not shift enough cards from the bottom to the top of the pack, it will not be out of place to give a hint as to how to bring the trick to a successful conclusion in case the performer transposes more than the requisite number. Let us assume that the conjurer has shifted ten cards from the bottom to the top, instead of nine. This would bring the chosen card number eleven from the top, instead of number ten. As the performer takes the cards, one at a time, from the pack, held by the spectator, he glances at them quickly. When the tenth card has been removed he turns up the corners of the eleventh and twelfth cards and remembers what they are. Then he addresses the audience as follows: "Ladies and gentlemen, I have removed ten cards, the number selected by yourselves, from the top of the pack. Therefore, the next card should be the selected one. Will you kindly name the card, sir. The four of diamonds? Thank you, sir. Will you kindly turn up the top card. It is the four of diamonds and my trick has been successful." This is the procedure in case the chosen card is number eleven. Should the four of diamonds be the twelfth card, the performer takes off ten cards, throws them on the table, and, taking the pack from the spectator turns up the two top cards, exhibiting them as one card, and concludes the trick in the manner described. It is seldom, however, that the conjurer will make a mistake of more than one card in his secret count; but it is the part of wisdom to have a plan of campaign in case the unexpected happens. The magician cannot afford to burn all his bridges behind him.

SECOND METHOD — A spectator sights a card as described in the first method, but the performer in this case does not insert the little finger, after the break is made, and slip the card to the top of the pack. Instead, he bends the right hand corner of the pack slightly upward, so as to form a permanent break, and lays the pack on the table, calling attention to the fact that it is impossible for him to know the location of the spectator's card. Of course, the pack must be laid down so that the break will not be visible to the audience. In picking up the pack, the performer can instantly bring the chosen card to the top by means of the slide or slip as described in the first method, or he can shift the card to the bottom by inserting little finger in the break and making the pass. This method is preferable, as it varies the method of operation. The card may then be found at any number in the pack, as already described.

THIRD METHOD—In this method the spectator holds the pack in his own hand while sighting a card, and he squares up the pack before handing it to the performer. Nevertheless, the conjurer causes the desired card to appear at the desired number in the pack, or, in order to vary the method of reproduction, may snap the card up the sleeve and produce it from the breast pocket or armpit. When the conjurer introduces this variation the effect will be rather electrical on those who know, or think they know, some of the good things of magic. As a matter of fact, or rather, as a matter of magic, what could be more bewildering than allowing a spectator to hold a pack of cards in his own hands and simply look at one of the cards, neither removing it nor handling it in any manner, after which the performer, who may turn his back to the spectator during the preliminary part of the trick,

The Art of Magic

instantly reproduces the card! This is real magic. In spite of the brilliancy of the effect, the method by which it is attained is simple. Before handing the pack to a spectator the performer should spring the cards from one hand to the other, a fancy sleight, or flourish, that is familiar to all conjurers. The student who is not familiar with this flourish will find it described in most of the older books on magic, and we give as the most convenient reference, Page 37 of "Modern Magic." The execution of this flourish will correct any bend that may be in the cards after performing the trick by the first two methods. In order to insure success the pack must, when squared up, be without a break. Hence the importance of using new cards.

After performing the fancy flourish, square up the cards, and hand the pack to a spectator. The springing will leave the pack slightly rounded or convexed. This is absolutely essential to the success of the trick. Request the spectator to lift up the pack as before and to remember the card he sees. This bends a portion of the pack in the opposite direction and forms a break at the chosen card. By cutting, or making the shift at this break, the chosen card is brought to the bottom. Glance at the card and shuffle the card to the top. Palm it in the right hand and ask the spectator to name his card. If he names the right all you have to do is to snap the pack in the left hand and produce the palmed card from under the coat, either at the armpit or from the breast pocket, calling attention at the same time to the ease with which you can make a card leave the pack and travel up the sleeve. If, as it may occasionally happen, you have not secured the right card, you will have to vary the procedure. Every conjurer worth his salt will have his own method of getting out of a difficultly; for, as Robert-Houdin said, the true test of a magician is not how he does a trick, but how he can turn failure into success. In case of a contremps at this stage the performer need not be at all disconcerted. Hand the pack to the spectator and request him to note the number of his card in the pack counting from the top, when he has done so take back the pack and replace the palmed card on top (the one you had palmed in the expectation that it was the spectator's card). Now ask the person to name the number his card is in the pack. For the purpose of explanation we shall assume that it is number nineteen. That is to say, it *was* number 19; but since adding the palmed card to the deck the chosen card is *now* number 20. Deal nineteen cards on the table, and as you thrown down the nineteenth card request the spectator to turn it over. This will draw all eyes to the table, affording the performer an opportunity to palm the twentieth card (the spectator's card) and introduce it into the pocket. The spectator, of course, remarks that the nineteenth card is not the one he chose. The performer appears embarrassed, and, after a little byplay, asks the spectator to name his card. The spectator complies. "Ah! you must have been mistaken," answers the conjurer, "for the seven of diamonds (assuming that is the card) has been in my pocket all the evening." Suiting the action to the word he removes the chosen card. This method of getting out of a difficulty is not original, but is based upon the "Card in the Pocket" trick described in another chapter. This subterfuge will be found useful in many instances where the performer, through some error, loses sight of a chosen card. If the performer is not successful in finding the card sighted by this method — that is, if the spectator does not bridge the cards enough, he can remedy the difficulty by snapping a small rubber band across the middle of the pack. This method, while adding to the effect of the trick, makes it impossible for a person to lift up one end of the deck for the purpose of sighting a card without bridging the pack. A spectacular variation is to invite a spectator to insert a paper knife into the pack thus treated with a rubber band. The performer slightly raises the handle of the knife, in order that the spectator may not note the card; and this movement bridges the pack so that the spectator's card may instantly be located. The performer's ingenuity will suggest different methods of utilizing this clever ruse.

FOURTH METHOD — The spectator holds the pack in his own hand, as in the third method; but in this case it is not necessary

The Art of Magic

to bridge the cards. He may cut the pack, or lift the cards up, or note a card in any manner he desires. Nevertheless, the performer instantly produces the card. Cleverly performed this has a stunning effect upon an audience, the more imaginative of whom will almost be persuaded that the performer has a Machiavellian mastery over the cards.

The means by which this surprising result is brought about are in reality very simple, although the bungling and unobserving performer will meet his Waterloo in this experiment. The keen-eyed, ready-tongued and adroit performer, however, will experience no difficulty whatever in this method, the secret of which lies in locating the selected card by *observing where the spectator breaks the pack.* For convenience arrange the pack as follows: First, seven or eight clubs; then the same number of hearts, followed by about the same number of spades and diamonds. These suits are not arranged in any order. With a little practice you will be able to locate within five cards where the pack is broken by the spectator in selecting a card. In rapidly running over the cards (which can be done as you return to the table) remove these five cards, placing one on top of the pack, another at the bottom (remembering, of course, which is which), and palm the remaining three cards, remembering their order. To facilitate the memorizing of five cards the pack is arranged in suits, as described; for it is easier to remember five cards of one suit than five of different suits. After a little practice, however, the performer should be able to perform the trick without any pre-arrangement of suits. When these preliminaries have been accomplished, request the spectator to name his card. You then know whether the card is on the top or at the bottom of the pack, or in your hand; and you act accordingly, exhibiting either the bottom or the top card, or producing the selected card from the pocket, leaving the other two behind. With a little practice the performer will find that, nine times out of ten, he will be able to come within three of the chosen card, and seven times out of ten he should be able to locate the exact card. For the sake of safety, however, it is advisable to palm three cards and place

The Art of Magic

the other two as directed. In case the performer does not locate the card in his five chances, he can bring the trick to a successful conclusion in the manner described in the Third Method. At first blush the reader may think that this variation is not practical; but we hasten to assure him that it is practical in every sense of the word, and that adroitly performed it has an astonishing effect. That it is one of Mr. Downs's favorite tricks is an adequate recommendation of its value.

FIFTH METHOD — This is one of the most mystifying and artistic methods of the series. Count down from the bottom of the pack (in the manner described in the First Method), a dozen or fifteen cards — the exact number makes no material difference. Insert the little finger between the cards and the pack and make the pass, bringing the packet to the top. Keep the packet separated from the pack by means of the little finger. Now fan out the cards, at the same time requesting a spectator to draw one. As the cards are fanned the packet of fifteen is spread into the right hand, where they are held so that the spectator cannot select one from them. Count the cards as you fan them, sliding them one at a time with the left thumb upon the fifteen in the right hand, mentally counting sixteen, seventeen, eighteen, nineteen, twenty, twenty-one, twenty-two, etc., until the spectator selects a card. Let us assume that he draws the twenty-third card, in which case you will have twenty-two cards in the right hand. Keep on sliding the cards, one at a time, from left hand to the right, secretly counting as you do so, twenty-three, twenty-four, twenty-five, requesting the spectator to replace his card. Let us assume he replaces his card in the fan just as you have counted twenty-five. His card, therefore, will be the twenty-sixth, counting from the top. Immediately square up the deck and request the spectator to name the number at which he would like his card to appear. If he says sixteen, you simply count off ten cards from the top and shift them to the bottom. The counting is done in a manner similar to the bottom count already described. Lift up a bunch of cards from the top of the pack, inserting the little finger of left hand between them and the rest of the pack, and then count the cards in packet by allowing the ends to escape from the right thumb. When the right number is secured shift them to the bottom. With a little practice the right thumb should pick up the required number without hesitation. Some performers have brought this feat to such a degree of skill that they can cut any number called for, without missing once in a dozen times. By way of variation, the performer may cause the card to appear at any number from the bottom of the pack. If the performer is working with a full pack, and the chosen card is number twenty-six from the top it is number twenty-seven from the bottom. If the spectator names sixteen, the performer must shift eleven cards from the bottom to the top of the pack.

Sixth Method — The manner in which the chosen card is located in this method is decidely ingenious, and the resourceful conjurer will find the little feke an invaluable assistant in a hundred and one ways in experiments with cards. The author complaisantly believes that if this book contained no other novelty than this its existence would be justified. And like all the good things in magic this feke is absurdly simple and may be prepared by anyone in five minutes. It is simply an improvement on the old and well-known long card; but the device is so clever that its employment will baffle the astutest eye and mystify even old hands at the business. The feked card is illustrated in Fig. 20. A glance at the illustration will convey the idea better than a page of description. To prepare the card, split it at one end and insert a small square piece cut from another card. Glue the card together and your feke, when dry is ready for use. If you use a glazed card, the easiest way of splitting is to insert the end in warm water. The wetting will not injure the card, and as soon as it is dry the split portion may be glued together. For this purpose liquid glue is preferable to mucilage or paste. The feke should not be large. Its greatest width, at the point where it leaves the card proper, should be three-sixteenths of an inch, and it should not extend more than one-eighth of an inch. The projection should be slightly rounded, as shown in the illustration. Instead of a duplicate piece of card the feke may be made of very thin metal, aluminum preferred. A card thus prepared will last indefinitely.

The use of this prepared card will be apparent at once to the reader, and also, we believe, instantly appreciated. The simplest mode of using it is to offer the pack to some one to select a card. "Replace it, please," says the performer, at the same time cutting at the prepared card so that the drawn card may be replaced beneath it. The performer may now shuffle

Fig. 20.

the pack with a very small risk of the two cards being parted, and he has only to cut at the prepared card in order to bring the chosen card to the top.

The following is the way the card is used in the series of tricks described in this chapter. Up to this time the prepared card has been in the pocket. The performer adds it to the top of the pack, and requests a spectator to select a card. While the card is being noted the performer brings the prepared card to the center by means of the shift. Placing the pack on the flattened palm of the left hand the performer requests the spectator to replace his card, at the same time cutting at the prepared card. Replace packet on top of drawn card and square up the pack, holding it between the first and second fingers at the top end and the thumb at the lower end. As the thumb completely hides the small projection, the performer allows the spectator to scrutinize all sides of the pack, at the same time calling attention to the impossibility of his being able to locate the chosen card. The performer may now bring the chosen card to the top by the simple expedient of cutting at the prepared card, when the spectator's card may be found at any number in the pack that the audience may name. This is only one method of using this ingenious card; but the reader will find it an invaluable adjunct to many card tricks. The card can be added to the pack at any moment, and, when it has served its purpose, can be instantly palmed and replaced in the pocket.

THE UBIQUITOUS CARDS—(First Method).

This brilliant and effective trick is based upon the sleights and stratagems just described. It is one of the leading items in the repertory of Mr. Nate Leipzig. This is the first time that the trick has been made public, and we are satisfied that our readers, after they have mastered the manipulations, will never willingly relinquish it from their programme of card problems. As an experiment for the parlor, the club, or any impromptu occasion, this card feat, in the opinion of the author, eclipses the majority of card tricks.

EFFECT — The pack is thoroughly shuffled by the audience, and three spectators sight a card each, after the manner already explained. The pack is again shuffled and laid face downward on the table. The performer removes several cards from the top of the pack, one at a time, and requests a spectator to tell him when to stop. At the word "Stop" the performer exhibits the last card taken from the pack, and it proves to be one of the cards sighted by the audience. The second card is produced in the same manner. The performer then hands the pack to a spectator, who deals the cards, one at a time, into the conjurer's hand until the signal "Stop" is given. Turning up the last card

The Art of Magic

dealt from the pack it also proves to be one of the sighted cards.

TIME OCCUPIED — In order to get the maximum effect out of this experiment it should be performed deliberately; and invested with the proper amount of patter it should take up at least six minutes.

REQUISITES AND PREPARATION — An ordinary pack of cards, dexterity and audacity.

PRESENTATION OF TRICK — The pack is handed to a member of the audience with the request that it be thoroughly shuffled and cut, or, if he choose, the performer may do the shuffling himself. Holding the pack in the left hand he requests a spectator to lift up the end and peep at a card — "just one card," the conjurer urges, "for if more than one card is sighted I may be unable to perform the trick." This little explanation forestalls any desire on the part of the spectator to ruffle the pack in order to make a selection from several cards. When the spectator has sighted a card, the break is made with the first finger, as already described. The performer does not immediately bring the card to the top, but holding the pack at his side in such a manner that the break is not visible, he says: "I wish to impress upon your minds that a card has not been drawn from the pack, but merely sighted by this gentleman. Consequently it is impossible for me to know either the name of the card or its location in this pack of fifty-two cards. Will another gentleman oblige me by looking at a card?" The conjurer makes a half turn toward some other member of the audience, and at the same time slips the first card sighted to the top of the pack, in the manner that is now familiar to the reader. The pack is immediately extended so as to enable the second spectator to sight a card. This maneuver is repeated for the selection of the third card, after which the performer gives the deck a false shuffle. Laying the pack on the table the performer proceeds to remove a few cards, one at a time, and requests the spectator who selected the *last* card to tell him when to stop. He removes the cards with the right hand, immediately trans-

The Art of Magic

ferring them to the left, where the cards are held face down as in the ordinary position for dealing. The three selected cards, of course, are on the bottom of the packet in the left hand, the card last selected being the undermost. When the signal to stop is given, the right hand immediately grips the packet, the fingers at the top and the thumb at the bottom, as if squaring up the cards. During this maneuver the third finger tip of the left hand pushes the bottom card out at the side of the packet, and it is grasped by the fingers and thumb of the right hand and slipped to the top, as explained in the First Method of this chapter. With a little practice this movement is undetectable, as it is performed with the back of the right hand toward the audience. The performer is further protected by a clever and very natural "stall." When the spectator says "Stop," the performer asks in a peremptory tone: "Did I influence you in any way, sir, to stop at this particular card?" This brings all eyes away from the conjurer's hands for an instant, and in that instant the movement is executed. At the words, "this particular card," the performer strikes the top of the packet rather smartly with the tip of the first finger of the right hand, and at the same instant the left thumb pushes the top card of the packet slightly forward. The spectator, naturally enough, answers "no" to the performer's question. "Very well, sir," responds the conjurer. "If my trick has been successful, then this card (tapping the top card with right forefinger) should be yours. Will you be so kind as to name your card? The queen of diamonds? Thank you, sir. Then this top card should be the queen of diamonds." The performer turns over the top card, which proves to be the queen of diamonds, or whatever the card may be.

The remaining two cards, it will be remembered, are on the bottom of the packet in the left hand; and in order to proceed with the trick it is necessary to bring them to the top of the deck. This may be accomplished by means of the shift, but the easiest and most natural method is to give the packet an ordinary overhead shuffle, throwing the last two, or bottom

The Art of Magic

cards on top of the packet. This packet is then placed on the pack, which is shuffled, the top cards being left undisturbed. Replacing the pack on the table, the same effect is repeated with the second card, but the production of the third card is varied by placing the pack in the hand of one of the spectators, preferably the one who sighted the last card. The working of the trick, however, is the same.

This is the trick as performed by Mr. Leipzig, but it may not be out of order to describe, briefly, a method by which the repetition of the movement of slipping the card from the bottom to the top of the packet is obviated. Three cards are sighted as described, and after they are brought to the top and the pack subjected to a false shuffle, the performer thumbs six cards from the bottom, and this packet is divided from the pack by the little finger. The conjurer requests some one to think of a number between one and ten, throwing a slight emphasis on the word "ten." Nine times out of ten the number seven will be chosen, in which case he has only to make the pass, bringing the six cards to the top, and hand the pack to the spectator who sighted the last card. This card will now be number seven from the top, and the performer requests the spectator to count off six cards from the top and look at the seventh. The spectator does so, and is astonished to discover his card at the chosen number. Of course, it would make no difference what number was chosen, for it is a simple matter to thumb the required number of cards; but as it is almost certain that seven will be chosen, the performer can gain time by having the six cards already counted down and separated from the rest of the pack by the little finger.

The card turned up, and also the six cards counted off, are now placed at the bottom of the pack, which leaves the other two chosen cards on top of the deck. The pack is now false-shuffled and laid on the table. The second chosen card is produced in the manner explained, the performer taking the cards off the top of the pack, one at a time, and slipping the card from the bottom at the signal to stop. The packet in the left hand

The Art of Magic

is now shuffled, so that the bottom card is brought to the top. The packet is then replaced on the pack, which is once more false-shuffled. Now the pack is handed to the spectator whose card is to be discovered. He is asked to think of any number between one and fifty-two, and not to tell the performer what the number is. He is requested, in order to provide against any mistake, to whisper the number to one of the audience. When this is done, the performer directs the spectator to deal the cards off the top of the pack until he arrives at the number chosen. The spectator does as requested, but the card at the chosen number does not prove to be the one he sighted. The cards are replaced on the deck, which is handed to the person to whom the spectator communicated the number, and he is requested to try his luck. He does so, and, much to the surprise of the audience, turns up the right card. This last effect is achieved by an absurdly simple ruse, but presented deliberately and with the proper patter has an astounding effect. The fact that the performer does not know the number selected by the spectator is what makes the trick so inexplicable to the audience. When the performer hands the pack to the spectator to count down to his number, the spectator's card is really on top of the pack. The cards are counted face downward on the table. Let us assume that the spectator chooses the number twenty. He deals off twenty cards. The twentieth card does not prove to be his card, and the performer pretends to be embarrassed. He cannot imagine how the trick has failed. It never failed before. During his talk he replaces the twenty cards on top of the pack, by which maneuver the chosen card is now number twenty, for the spectator in counting the cards on the table naturally reversed their order. The performer hands the pack to the person to whom the spectator confided the chosen number, and upon his counting down to number twenty the right card is turned up. As a matter of fact, the failure of the first spectator to find his card at the chosen number adds to rather than subtracts from the effect of the experiment. The success of the

The Art of Magic

second spectator is entirely unexpected, as the audience really believes that the performer has failed.

THE UBIQUITOUS CARD—(Second Method.)

This is T. Nelson Downs's method. Its general effect is the same as described in the preceding method, except that two cards are drawn instead of three. In describing this trick we take pleasure in acquainting the reader with a new and valuable artifice in card conjuring—a method of dealing seconds with one hand. This sleight is one of the numerous specialties of Mr. Downs.

Two cards are sighted and shifted to the top in the manner that is now familiar to the reader. The performer false-shuffles the pack, and concludes by palming the top card in the right hand and laying the pack on the table. "Now, ladies and gentlemen," he says, "I haven't the slightest idea as to the identity of the two cards noted, neither do I know their position in the pack. Even if I did possess this knowledge it would have nothing to do with the trick I am about to perform. However, I will attempt to read the mind of the gentleman who looked at the last card. Ah, by gazing into his left eye I get the mental impression that his card is red (or black as the case may be) while the right eye informs me that the card is a king (or whatever it is) — a king of hearts. Is that correct, sir? Thank you. However, this knowledge really has nothing to do with the experiment; for the reason that I propose to cause this gentleman's card, namely the king of hearts, to appear at any position in the pack the gentleman commands. I shall take off the cards one at a time. (He suits the action to the words, lifting off the cards one at a time with the left hand, the deck lying on the table). I shall stop at any card you desire. Whenever you say stop, sir." When the command is given the performer picks up the packet of cards with the left hand and places the palmed card on top. Holding the packet in the left hand, the performer, pointing to the top card, says: "I would like to ask you, sir, did I influence you to stop at this particular card? No, sir, I did not? Very well." The card is now turned over and proves to be the spectator's card.

The second sighted card is now at the bottom of the packet. Secretly count three cards from the bottom, insert little finger, and make shift, bringing the desired card the third from the top. At this point the performer pretends to overhear some comment on the part of the spectators. "Ah, I heard a lady in the back part of the room remark that there is some trick about it," says the conjurer. "I assure you, ladies and gentlemen, that I would not resort to any chicanery or deception. To prove to you beyond the shadow of a doubt that no deception is practiced I shall deal the cards with one hand only, making it physically impossible for me to indulge in any of the reprehensible arts of hocus-pocus." Holding the pack in the left hand the performer deals the cards, one at a time, from the top of the pack, and at the word of command the other spectator's card is exhibited. The first two cards are actually thrown face upward on the table. The third card, which is the spectator's card, is retained on top until the signal to stop is given.

This is accomplished by means of a one-hand second deal. Hold the pack firmly in the left hand in about the usual position for ordinary dealing, save that the pack is gripped between the tips of the four fingers and the crotch of the thumb. The fingers should be pressed firmly so as to arch, or "bridge" the pack slightly, the convex shape of the pack being necessary to the proper execution of the sleight. The left thumb extends across the upper part of the pack so that it just touches the tip of the first finger, the convex shape of the pack making this long reach possible. To deal the second card proceed as follows: Draw back slightly the left thumb, which movement arches the top card so that the tip of the thumb touches the outside border of the second card. Push this second card outward with the thumb, at the same time turning the hand over with a sweeping movement of the arm. The instant the palm of the hand is toward the table the pressure of the thumb is relaxed, which allows the second card to fall face upward on the table.

The Art of Magic

This is the mechanism of the sleight, so to speak, and at the outset the movement may be somewhat difficult to achieve. A little practice, however, will soon overcome all difficulties; and when the sleight is mastered the student will have at his command an indetectable method of dealing seconds. The sweeping motion of the arm and the turning of the hand completely baffle the sharpest eye, so that it is impossible for even those acquainted with second dealing to say whether the top or the second card is dealt. When the performer attains to a perfect mastery of the movement he will be able to deal the second card without turning the hand over. The method described, however, is more effective in the trick of the "Ubiquitous Cards."

CHAPTER VII

CLAIRVOYANCE WITH CARDS

One of the oldest of card tricks, as well as the most generally known, is that in which all the cards in a shuffled pack are named "without seeing them," although the words in quotation marks must be taken in a Pickwickian sense. There are a hundred methods, more or less, of achieving this interesting effect, from the primitive pre-arranged deck and memoria technica to the small concave mirror held in the palm of the artist, but most of them are either suggestive or uncertain. In this chapter we shall acquaint the reader with a number of new methods of reading cards, methods that have not been explained in treatises on the magic art. A knowledge of the ordinary methods of performing the trick—such as the glass mirror, the reflecting ring, etc.—is pre-supposed. We shall begin the series with a very simple method of naming a single card and conclude with what is really one of the finest effects and most perfect tricks in this particular department of card conjuring.

First Method—The pack is spread fanwise, the face of the cards toward the audience. A spectator is invited to touch the top of one of the cards. The instant he does so the performer names the card. The explanation is absurdly simple. As the spectator touches the top of a card the performer with the left thumb slightly raises the lower left hand corner of the same card; and as the fanned pack is held quite away from the performer, and also rather high a glimpse of the index is afforded. Although this effect may be repeated, the wise conjurer will be satisfied with the single exhibition of his clairvoyant power.

Second Method—In this form of the trick any number of cards are named in succession without the performer (apparently) seeing them. This is a new, original and very suitable method of reading cards, and undoubtedly will be appreciated by the reader who is attracted by artistic card work. The secret lies in the use of a little feke that reflects the index of the cards. This feke is nothing more or less than an ordinary German silver, or nickel-plated, thumb tack, such as artists and architects use to pin sheets of paper to a drawing-board. The kind with the slightly convexed head is the best for this purpose. With a pair of pliers, or other sharp instrument, cut off the tack part close to the head. With a pellet of conjurer's wax attach the head to the back of the upper right hand corner of a playing card. Palm this prepared card and offer the pack to be shuffled, or the card may be in the pocket while the audience has possession of the pack. Whichever subterfuge may be adopted, the card is eventually placed on the bottom of the pack. Holding the pack in the left hand, with the bottom card squarely facing the audience, the performer slides all the cards but the bottom one downward, so that the head of the drawing pin is visible. As the back of the left hand is toward the audience the palm masks the cards, so that there is no reason to suspect that the pack is not squared. With the thumb of the right hand slowly push up the card on the back of the pack. As it rises the index is reflected in the polished surface of the thumb tack, and the performer is thus enabled to announce its name. This may be repeated until nearly all the cards have been named, but the conjurer will find that reading ten or a dozen cards is just as effective as calling off the entire pack. If any one suspects a preparation of the pack, it is a simple matter to remove the feke, when the pack may be passed out for examination.

THIRD METHOD—This, in the opinion of the author, is the most perfect method of reading cards ever invented. It is really a brilliant and bewildering trick.

The effect is as follows: A pack of cards is offered to the audience for shuffling, and while in possession of the audience a number of cards are drawn—six, eight, ten—any number, in fact, although six will be found the most effective number for the trick. These cards are replaced and the pack is held to the performer's forehead, whereupon he divines the name of each selected card. The cards are not forced, nor does the performer employ the pass or palm or any other sleight. Furthermore, the method is abolutely undetectable. The trick, we believe, is the invention of Theodore L. DeLand, Jr.

In order to accomplish this effect two packs of cards are necessary. One pack is quite unprepared, but the other is not so innocent as it appears. Two of the cards are unprepared, but each of the remaining fifty has one of its indexes cut out, as in Fig. 21. Consequently, if an unprepared cards is replaced in a pack so prepared the index is plainly visible. The working

Fig. 21.

of the trick will now be clear to the reader. The six cards, of course, are selected from the unprepared pack. While the cards are being marked the performer changes the unprepared pack for the prepared one, which can be done on the table or in the pocket. The faked pack has an unprepared card on top and one on the bottom, so that it does not differ in appearance from the ordinary deck. Holding the pack with the prepared end in the crotch of the left thumb, the performer riffles the other end and invites the spectators to return their cards, calling attention to the fact that the cards are replaced in different parts of the pack, and that everything is square and aboveboard. Now slip the unprepared card from the bottom to the top of the deck, and, if the pack is placed to the performer's forehead (the back of the cards, of course, toward the audience) it is a simple matter to read the index of the first card, or, more properly, the card nearest the front of the pack. The card should not be named immediately. The performer should press the pack to the forehead and endeavor to create the impression that the result is achieved by clairvoyance. After naming the first card the performer fans the pack, removes the card, and, handing it to spectator, requests him to identify the mark. The reader will understand that it is necessary to remove each card after it has been named, in order that the index of the card next nearest to the front may be seen. Whenever the face of the pack is exhibited cover the missing index with the flat of the thumb.

We have explained merely the bare bones of this effective trick, leaving it to the individuality of the performer to present it in as dramatic a manner as possible, and with suitable patter. As the index of each card must be neatly cut out with mathematical precision, it is impossible to prepare a pack without machinery made especially for the purpose. The publishers of this book have had special machinery made for the manufacture of this pack and they feel assured that the conjuring fraternity will be glad to know that they can supply the prepared pack in any style of card at a reasonable cost.

CHAPTER VIII

A SERIES OF CARD TRICKS BASED ON A NEW AND ORIGINAL SYSTEM.

In this chapter the author presents a series of absolutely new and original experiments with cards. The effects, which are unknown to the profession, are among the most mysterious and baffling in the whole category of card magic. The different tricks described are based on one principle, which is, of course, susceptible to an infinite variety of combinations and arrangements. With these effects at his command the performer will not have the slightest difficulty in deceiving even those who are thoroughly conversant with the mysteries of card magic. To the uninitiated the feats will savor of the preternatural, and there will be a disposition to regard the conjurer as in league with the evil one. There is absolutely no clue by which those unacquainted with the secret can offer even the shadow of a solution. For club, parlor or close work these experiments are perfect, inasmuch as the spectators may surround the operator in a circle and yet be no wiser for their proximity. Before describing the different tricks in detail let us acquaint the reader with the principle on which the effects are based.

In the first place, it must be explained that the tricks described in this chapter can be performed only with cards that have a scroll design back, and of the many varieties that come under this category the "Angel Backs" are to be preferred. The tricks are based on the fact that in all scroll designs there are more or less irregularities. These irregularities, of course, are imperceptible to the eye unacquainted with the secret; but when one knows where to look the slight differences in the design are as plain as a moon in a cloudless sky. A glance at Fig. 22 will make this matter plain. In the upper left hand corner of the figure one of the small leaves is marked with a circle, at A. The leaf marked B, in the lower right hand corner, diagonally opposite, so to speak, is larger and of different shape. The difference in size and shape is very perceptible when attention is called to the irregularity; but a person might examine the card for months, if he did not know where to look, without observing the difference in design. On this slight irregularity depends all the tricks described in this chapter.

Fig. 22.

The pack should be previously arranged so that all the cards are in the position shown in Fig. 22, that is, with the small leaf in the upper left hand corner. A little practice will enable the performer to keep the pack always arranged in this manner. It is obvious that if a card is drawn and replaced in a reversed position, the card can be instantly located, no matter how much the pack is shuffled. The card thus reversed has the large leaf, B, at the upper left hand corner, and is readily located by ruffling this corner with the left thumb. With a little practice the card can be located in the fraction of a second,

The Art of Magic

when it is a simple matter to insert the little finger and bring the card to the top. When the card is drawn the performer must watch closely to see if the spectator reverses the card while it is in his hands. If the card is not reversed the performer must reverse the pack. It will be found, in actual practice, that not once in a hundred times will a spectator reverse a card in his hands. It is not advisable to reverse the pack openly, for this might lead to the suspicion that the performer is using strippers. Simply give the pack a shuffle while the spectator is noting his card, and during this operation the pack is reversed in the most natural manner. A very effective method is to hold the pack behind the back when the card is drawn. In wheeling around the pack will be in the proper position for the return of the card. The most effective method, however, is to spread the cards on the table. A card is selected, and if the spectator reverses it while in his hand request him to replace it; then gather up the cards and shuffle the pack. If he does not reverse the card, gather up the cards yourself, shuffle and reverse the pack, request the spectator to replace his card, immediately offering the pack for shuffling. So much for the system itself. We shall now describe a series of incomprehensible effects based upon this method of detecting a card. The first we shall call

MIND READING WITH CARDS.

EFFECT—A small packet of cards is handed to one of the company with the request that he or she will think of a small number and then transfer that many cards from the top to the bottom of the packet. The performer turns his back during this operation so as not to see how many cards are transferred; but when he receives the packet he spreads the cards on the table, and, taking the spectator's hand, directs it to a card which, when turned over, has the same number of spots as there were cards transferred. Thus, if five cards were transferred, the performer turns up a five spot.

TIME OCCUPIED—About two minutes.

The Art of Magic

REQUISITES AND PREPARATION — A packet of "Angel Backs"—ten cards, arranged in sequence from ace to ten spot, the top card being the ace. The cards should be of different suits.

PRESENTATION OF TRICK—Exhibit the ten cards fanwise in the right hand, and in closing up the fan insert the little finger between the eighth and ninth cards (counting from the top), and make the pass, thus bringing the last two cards, the nine and ten spot, to the top.

Hand the packet to a spectator and request him to think of a number between one and ten, and to transfer that number of cards from the top to the bottom of the packet. The performer turns his back while this is being done. Now take the packet and spread the cards on the table, remembering that the second card from the top will indicate the number of cards transferred. Take the hand of the person who made the transfer and pretend to read his or her mind. After much maneuvering finally turn up the second card, which will reveal the number of cards transferred.

This is the orthodox method of performing the trick, and is known to every conjurer. It does not require a very acute mind to figure out that the secret of the trick lies in the fact that the cards are arranged in a certain order, although this intelligence will not enable one to perform the trick. Having performed the trick in this manner some one in the audience may remark that the cards are arranged. At any rate, the performer picks up the packet and remarks that the audience is skeptical as regards the experiment being based on mind reading. To convince the audience that such is the case the performer allows a spectator to shuffle the ten cards. Taking back the packet the conjurer shows the bottom and top cards of the packet, and declares that he will not change the position of the cards in any way. He now requests some one to transfer a number of cards from the top to the bottom, as before. The cards are thrown on the table, and the spectator is asked to think intently of the number of cards transferred; and placing the latter's hand to his forehead, the performer, simulating mind reading, reveals the number as dramatically as possible.

This bewildering effect is achieved by simple means. The ten cards are really shuffled. Taking back the packet the performer directs attention to the bottom card, after which the top card is turned over and exhibited. In the act of turning the top card back to its original position it is reversed, so that nine cards are arranged as A in Fig. 22, while the top, or tenth card, is arranged as B in the same figure. One of the company now transfers any number of cards from the top to the bottom. Let us suppose that five cards are transferred. The performer spreads the cards on the table and sights the reversed card. In this case it will be the fifth card from the end, counting from the bottom. The performer holds the spectator's hand to his forehead, and, after the proper amount of hesitation, reveals the number of cards that were transferred. Worked in connection with the first method, this little trick will prove as effective and mysterious as the most fastidious performer could desire. The next experiment performed by means of this subtle system is entitled

DIVINITION EXTRAORDINARY.

This is a mysterious card experiment and is particularly effective for close work.

EFFECT — A pack is shuffled by the audience; the cards are spread on the table; a spectator is requested to take out a card, write its name on a piece of paper, and to lay the card face downward to one side of the table. This is repeated until ten cards have been taken and their names written on the paper, which the assistant folds and places in his pocket, the performer standing away from the table during these operations. The ten cards are now replaced, one at a time, in different parts of the pack, which is shuffled by the audience. The performer deals the cards into four packets. One of these packets is selected and is found to consist of the ten chosen cards.

TIME OCCUPIED—About three minutes.

The Art of Magic

REQUISITES AND PREPARATION — A pack of "Angel Back" cards arranged according to the system; a pencil and a sheet of paper.

PRESENTATION OF TRICK — The working of the trick should be apparent to the reader who thoroughly understands the system. The ten drawn cards, of course, must be reversed when replaced in the pack. In distributing the cards into four packets the reversed cards are dealt into one packet. A good plan is to use forty cards for this trick, so that each packet will consist of just ten cards. The packet containing the ten chosen cards is, of course, forced. The performer should stand near the table while the assistant is drawing cards and writing their names down, so as to see if any of the cards are reversed during this process. This is not likely to be the case, for the assistant is instructed to leave the chosen cards on the table. The performer, in gathering them together, can discover at a glance if they are in the proper position. After the cards are selected and their names written down, the assistant folds the paper and puts it in his pocket, during which operation the performer reverses the pack so that the chosen cards may be returned, one by one, after which the pack is offered for shuffling. The performer deals the cards into four packets, and the trick is brought to the conclusion described.

THE TRANSFIXED CARD.

In a previous chapter* two methods of performing this splendid trick were explained, but the method which follows is superior to any other known to magic. The performer who presents the trick according to the directions that follow will never need to use any other method, for the secret will never be discovered no matter how many times he repeats the trick before the same audience. Of how many other tricks can this be said?

EFFECT — A card is drawn from the pack returned, the pack shuffled and the cards spread on the table. The performer —

---

*See Chapter 3, page 52.

The Art of Magic

blindfolded if he prefers — now transfixes the chosen card on the point of a knife.

TIME OCCUPIED — About five minutes.

REQUISITES AND PREPARATION—A pack of "Angel Backs" arranged according to the system; a pen knife.

PRESENTATION OF TRICK—Allow the pack to be shuffled and then spread the cards in a row on the table. Request one of the company to draw a card, impressing upon his mind that as the cards are on the table it is impossible to influence his choice. Turn your back while he exhibits the card to the audience. Request him to place the card face downward on the table and cover it with his hand. When the card is on the table you glance at it to see if it has been reversed. If so you leave the pack spread on the table. If the card has not been reversed, which is likely, pick up the cards, and in squaring them up reverse the pack. You explain that the object in having the spectator press his palm on the card is in order to impregnate it with magnetism. After the pasteboard has been sufficiently "magnetized" it is replaced and the pack shuffled. As the drawn card is reversed the spectators may shuffle the pack until the cows come home, as the saying is, without disturbing the performer's equanimity.

Request the spectator to divide the pack into five or six packets. It is possible that the drawn card may be on top of one of these packets. But it makes no difference whether it is or not. The performer, beginning with the first packet on the left, flips the cards about on the table, watching them carefully so as to catch a glimpse of the reversed card. He treats each packet in turn in this way, and when he comes to the reversed card it is flipped to one side, and, using both hands, he thoroughly mixes the cards, taking good care, of course, not to lose sight of the reversed, or chosen, card. After the mixing process the conjurer takes a penknife in his right hand, and explains that he will endeavor to discover the chosen card by means of the implement. "It is simply an experiment in magnetism," says the performer. "By placing his hand over the card the gentleman impregnated it with a magnetic fluid. Now, it is well known that steel is attracted by magnetism, and taking advantage of this natural law I shall endeavor to find the gentleman's card by means of this steel blade. The card will act as the magnet and the knife-blade as the pole." The performer circles the knife over the cards with a slight trembling movement of the hand, and suddenly plunges the knife into a card. Requesting the spectator to name his card, the performer lifts up the knife and exhibits the chosen card. As he has kept the reversed card in sight all the time this part of the trick is not difficult. The whole feat, in fact, is the acme of simplicity, and there is no possible way, with ordinary precaution, by which it can fail. The author believes, however, that few card tricks are as astounding as this, and it can be used a lifetime without any one discovering the modus operandi.

THE MAGICIAN'S WILL POWER.

This is the title of a rather old, but very good, card trick. We shall first explain the method used by Mr. David Devant, as explained in his valuable little book entitled "Magic Made Easy," and will then describe our own improvement, which makes the simple experiment a veritable marvel of mystery.

EFFECT—A pack of cards is spread face downward on the table, and the performer undertakes to make any member of the audience draw such cards from the pack as he "wills" him to draw.

TIME—Three to five minutes.

REQUISITE AND PREPARATION—Any pack of cards; no preparation.

PRESENTATION OF THE TRICK—In this trick, to quote Mr. Devant, you undertake to make any member of the audience draw such cards as you may "will" him to draw. You are positive you can exercise your will power, and so you ask him to take out a certain card from the pack spread face downward on the table. You name a card and ask the person to pick it out of the pack. He will naturally say that he does not know where it is,

The Art of Magic

but you assure him that with your mystic will power you will direct him to the card you have named, which, let us say, is the six of spades. The spectator picks up a card and hands it to you. Thank him and assure him that he is quite right; that it is the six of spades. You then ask for another card—say the ten of diamonds. The spectator picks up another card and hands it to you. "Quite right," you remark. "It is the ten of diamonds." But add that you can do it quicker yourself. Explain that you often have curious presentiments, and that on this particular occasion you have a presentiment that a certain card you will touch will be the ace of clubs. You pick up a card and announce that your presentiment has been fulfilled. Turning to the person who has assisted in the experiment you say: "Let me see, I asked you for the six of spades and the ten of diamonds, and I said that I would take out the ace of clubs. There are the three cards."

The trick is accomplished by sighting the bottom card of the pack. When you throw the pack down carelessly, and separate the cards on the table, you really keep the bottom card in sight all the time, and remember what it is. In this case we will suppose it is the six of spades. You ask your volunteer assistant to hand you the six of spades. The chances are fifty-one to one that he will pick out some other card, which (for sake of explanation), let us say is the ten of diamonds. You then ask for the ten of diamonds, and, let us say, get the ace of clubs. When you announce that you will select a card yourself, you pretend to pick up the ace of clubs, but in reality pick up the card which you know to be the six of spades. In this way the interested spectator has apparently handed you the two cards which you told him to pick out, and you have taken out the card which you announced that you would find. This trick requires no practice, but it goes the better if the conjurer will invent a little suitable patter and will take care that the cards are strewn carelessly over the table. The performer's eyes must not be fixed on the card which he knows. Let him sight it when he throws the cards down, and then remember its whereabouts on the table.

The Art of Magic

The improvement on the trick is as follows: Use a pack of "Angel Backs," and instead of sighting the bottom card have one card reversed—say the six of spades. Allow the pack to be thoroughly shuffled, after which it is divided into five or six packets, as explained in the "The Transfixed Card." Now by spreading the cards carelessly on the table you locate the reversed card, and the trick is concluded in the manner already described. It frequently happens, if you leave the reversed card in a prominent position, that the spectator will pick up this card, which, of course, brings the trick to a still more effective conclusion, inasmuch as you do not have to draw a card yourself. If this is the case, the performer, naturally, makes as much capital out of it as possible in his patter.

PROPHECY DOWN-TO-DATE.

One of the favorite tricks of the card wizard is to foretell a card or cards that will be thought of, or selected. There are a hundred and one methods of achieving this effect, which makes an extraordinary impression upon an audience. In some methods special apparatus is employed, and in other various sleights are used; but none of them compares in simplicity and effect with the method which we shall now explain. Few card tricks have such a bewildering effect upon an audience, this effect being due, in great measure, to the fact that during the entire experiment the cards are under the control of the spectators. As a matter of fact, the pack literally is not once in the hands of the performer.

EFFECT—The performer begins by handing a sealed envelope to a spectator. He then introduces a pack of cards still in the wrappers, with the government stamp affixed. A spectator is requested to remove the pack and shuffle it thoroughly. The performer calls particular attention to the fact that throughout the experiment he will not touch the cards. The spectator who has shuffled the pack is directed to deal the cards face downward in five packets on the table, ten cards in each packet, with the exception of the last packet, which, of course, will contain twelve

The Art of Magic

cards. This done the audience is requested to select one of the packets. This packet is shuffled by a spectator, who is told to deal the cards face downward on the table in two rows of five cards each, or, if the packet containing twelve cards is chosen, in two rows of six cards each. One of these rows is chosen. Five (or six) cards remain on the table. The audience is requested to select one of these cards. When they have made their choice, this card is turned over, and the spectator is requested to open the envelope. He finds therein a slip of paper on which is written the name of the identical card which has just been turned over on the table. As the performer has never touched the cards for an instant, and as the envelope was given to the spectator before the cards were taken from the case, the spectators are quite at a loss to account for the fact that the conjurer correctly foretold the card that would be chosen. But one pack of cards is used, and there is no exchange of envelopes.

Time Occupied—Five to seven minutes.

Requisites and Preparation—A sealed envelope containing a card, or a slip of paper, on which is written the name of a card, which, for the purpose of explanation, let us say, is the ace of spades, although any other card may be used; a pack of "Angel Backs" arranged in the manner that is now familiar—that is to say, all the cards with the exception of one arranged as A in Fig. 13. The one exception is the ace of spades, which is reversed. The pack thus arranged is replaced in the wrappers and case, and the government stamp gummed on so as to afford ocular proof that the contents of the case have not been tampered with.

Presentation of the Trick — The performer begins by handing the sealed envelope (containing the name of the ace of spades) to a spectator to hold, or place in his pocket. Another spectator, at the same time, removes the cards from their case and shuffles them. The performer requests the spectator to come to the table, and to deal one card face downward, another at its side, and so on until five cards have been dealt on the table, side by side. The volunteer assistant is now directed to deal the sixth card on top of the first; the seventh card on top of the second; the eighth card on top of the third; and so on until the entire fifty-two cards have been dealt into five packets. The reason the cards are dealt in this manner is to make it easier for the performer to follow them and to note in what packet the reversed card (the ace of spades) falls. If one packet were made at a time the cards would be dealt so fast that the performer's eye might not detect the reversed card. Dealt in the manner described, however, the performer cannot fail to locate the card. This knowledge gained it is a simple matter to force the right packet on the company. The performer leaves this packet on the table, taking away the other four. One of the company is requested to shuffle the cards in the chosen packet, and deal them face downward in two rows of five cards each. A glance at the cards acquaints the performer with the position of the reversed card, and he forces that row on the spectators, taking away the other row. The card must now be forced on the audience; but this will be a simple matter to the reader versed in the conjurer's subtle equivoques. For instance, let us suppose that the reversed card is No. 4, counting from left to right. Ask a spectator to select one of the five cards. If he chooses No. 4 the trick is finished without any more trouble on your part. Let us suppose, however, No. 3 is chosen. In this case, the performer immediately takes away No. 3 and returns it to the pack, which is on one corner of the table. "There are now four cards left, two inside and two outside," says the performer. "Which will you select, the inside or the outside?" The probabilities are that the inside cards will be selected, in which case the performer takes away the outside cards. If, however, the company selects the outside cards. The performer says, briskly: "Thank you," and takes away the outside cards. Only two cards remain now, Nos. 2 and 4, and No. 4 is forced by means of the familiar right or left dodge. The card is turned up by a spectator, the envelope is opened and the name of the card announced to the audience. Perhaps it is more effective to have the envelope opened and the name of the card read before the card on the table is turned up.

The Art of Magic

CAUTION—Little can be said under this head. With ordinary care there is no possibility of the trick failing. At the outset give the cards for shuffling to some one who is accustomed to handling cards. If, inadvertently, he should drop a few cards, step forward quickly and pick them up yourself. Glance at them to see if the reversed card is among them. If it is not, toss the cards aside carelessly, offering no explanation.

CONCLUDING OBSERVATIONS AND SUGGESTIONS—It may sometimes happen that the performer will be obliged to perform this trick with cards other than "Angel Backs." He may not have his own cards with him, or at the time his own pack may not be arranged according to the system. In such a case he may vary the procedure, as follows: Offer the pack to be shuffled, and, in taking it back (in this method the performer is obliged to handle the pack for a moment), and while walking to his table, he glances at the third card from the bottom, which, let us say, is the six of spades. He drops the pack on the table and calls attention to the fact that in the experiment he will not touch the pack at all. He then writes the name of a card (the six of spades) on a piece of paper, of course not showing what he has written to the audience, places this slip in an envelope, seals the envelope, and hands it to some one for safekeeping. He now requests a spectator to cut the pack into four packets, as nearly equal as possible. He forces the packet containing the six of spades (the third card from the bottom), and asks the assistant to count the cards of this packet face downward on the table. The number of cards in the packet is not essential to the success of the experiment; but by this means the order of the cards is reversed, and the six of spades is third from the top. In order to make the trick more difficult, the performer explains, the spectator is requested to place the top card in the middle of the packet, and this maneuver leaves the six of spades second from the top. The performer direct the spectator to deal three cards face downward on the table, side by side. This leaves the six of spades in the middle. The audience is requested to choose one of the three cards, and ninety-nine times out of a hundred they will select the middle card. This card is then turned over and compared with the name in the envelope. This method, of course, is neither so artistic nor effective as the first method, but it is a valuable subterfuge to have at one's command. The skillful conjurer, like the skillful carpenter, or any other good workman, never complains of his tools. He does the best he can under all circumstances, adapting his tricks and his methods to the means at hand.

CHAPTER IX

THE RISING CARDS.

One of the most effective of all card tricks and certainly one of the oldest. Investigation, we believe, has disclosed the fact that the modus operandi of "the trick that mystified Herrmann" was known and practiced in the middle of the seventeenth century. There is an old Dutch book on magic in which there is an illustration of the thread stretched between two doors, which recalls the proverbial saying that there is nothing new under the sun. In spite of this, however, the author hopes to include some genuine novelties in this chapter and to promote an increased respect for this venerable trick.

Although there are many variations of the rising cards, the mechanical means of accomplishing the effect are limited. The favorite method of causing cards to rise is by the use of "the conjurer's faithful friend," the black silk thread. The thread is operated in divers ways. Sometimes it is drawn by the performer himself, standing behind or beside his table; sometimes it is manipulated by a concealed assistant; or it is operated by mechanical means. One of the oldest methods was to have the thread attached to a small cylindrical weight within a pillar filled with sand. By moving a trigger at the foot of the pillar the sand was allowed to trickle slowly into a cavity in the base, and the weight, being deprived of its support, gradually sunk down and pulled the thread. This form of self operating mechanism was commonly used in conjunction with a piece of apparatus known as the card lyre, a rather awkward contraption, which would excite the risibilities of the modern audience. Another method of drawing the thread is by a clockwork arrangement in a table. The most practical method, however, and the one commonly adopted, is to have the thread pulled by an assistant behind the scenes, or, in the case of a drawing-room performance, in the rear of a convenient screen. The most serious drawback to the mechanical methods of drawing the string is that the unintelligent force will not always obey orders and is likely to go back on the performer in the midst of the trick, which, to say the least, is not a recommendation. If the thread is pulled by an assistant, the performer may take his own time, and introduce many minor effects to the enhancement of the illusion. The first trick in this chapter we shall call

THE TATTLINGS OF TOTO.

This is a combination of old materials presented in such a novel form that the trick will be practically new to many readers. The author is indebted to the French publication, "The Illusioniste," for the idea of the amusing illusion, although he has added several effects of his own and arranged the patter so that it is suitable for American or English audiences.

EFFECT—Six cards are drawn and returned to the pack, which is placed in a glass tumbler. A penny is borrowed and dropped into another glass tumbler. The penny indicates the drawn cards by jumping in the glass, after which the selected card rises out of the pack. One of the cards rises with its back toward the audience, and after it has been pushed back into the pack it rises properly and bows politely to the spectators.

REQUISITES AND PREPARATION—A duplicate penny attached to a thread; two glasses; a pack of cards with several cards arranged with a thread. The thread attached to the coin is passed behind the scenes — or a screen — into the hands of an assistant. As three of the six selected cards are forced, duplicates of these the jack of spades, the ten of clubs, and the queen of hearts are previously threaded. In reality two jacks of spades are used, so that one of them may rise with its back toward the audience. One of the jacks is weighted at the bottom by a strip of very thin metal glued between the front and back. This is the first card to thread. In the center of the card, just one inch from the lower edge, make a small hole with a needle. The

The Art of Magic

thread is put through this hole and a knot made on the front of the card so that the thread will not pull through. Lay this card face downward on the table, allowing the thread to pass along the center of the back of the card, toward the top, and on it lay, face downward, an indifferent card. The thread is returned along the center of this card, and on it place the second jack of spades, face upwards, so that in the actual performance of the trick this particular card will rise with its back to the audience. Thread up again along the center of the face of this card, and place an indifferent card on it. Again thread down the back, and on it place the ten of clubs, face downward. Thread up again and on it place an indifferent card. Thread along back and place the first card that is to rise, the queen of hearts, on this, and place two or three cards on the queen. Lay this part of the pack just behind the handkerchief on the table, face upward, the end from which the thread emerges pointing toward the center of the table. Leave a couple of feet of slack thread on the table. The thread extends over the back edge of table, in a line with the glass and plate on the center of the table. At the spot where the thread goes over the edge put into the cloth or covering one of the black pins, making it pass out of the cloth, over the thread, and into the cloth again. Let the thread fall to the floor, and similarly insert a pin into the carpet, over thread, and into carpet again. The thread then passes along the floor to where the assistant is concealed behind a screen, or into another room. The thread attached to the penny should be arranged in a similar manner with the other two pins. The glass and plate for the cards stand in the center of the table, while the other glass is a little to the left of the plate. The penny, attached to the thread, is just behind this glass. The pack of cards is in front of the plate. On top are three cards of the same suit and denomination as those that are to rise from the pack.

PRESENTATION OF TRICK—Picking up the pack and shuffling it, taking care not to disturb the three cards on top, which are to be forced, the performer advances toward audience and re-

The Art of Magic

quests a number of ladies and gentlemen to select a card each. Some six or eight cards are drawn, during which operation no difficulty should be experienced in forcing the three required cards (the queen of hearts, the ten of clubs and the jack of spades). The forced cards are returned first, so that the spectators may shuffle the pack. The performer makes the most of the opportunity saying, "Take the pack into your own hands, place your card in and shuffle." When the other cards are replaced, however, the performer makes the pass, bringing each card to the top, and sighting it as he moves toward the next chooser. If possible, arrange a code with the concealed assistant, so that a few simple and natural phrases, such as "Thank you," or "Much obliged," or "Watch me carefully," etc., he may become acquainted with the cards. The reason for this will be patent later on. This arrangement, however, is not absolutely necessary, but it adds much to the effect of the experiment.

Returning to the table the performer places the pack, face upward, on the threaded packet that lies behind the handkerchief, at the same time picking up the handkerchief with which he proceeds to wipe the glass. Then he drops the pack into the glass, the face of the cards towards audience, the end from which the thread emerges being uppermost, taking care that the thread between the cards does not slip out of position. He calls attention to the fact that the glass is quite isolated, raising the plate and glass a few inches from the table, and then directs attention to the other glass. "Now that you are quite convinced that everything is fair and aboveboard," says the conjurer, "I would like to borrow a penny. (Loud noise off stage). Do not be alarmed; they are merely closing the doors. I assure you that when I borrow a penny I *always* return it. If it were a $20 gold piece I might be tempted to become a captain of industry and organize a syndicate. You are quite sure that this is a genuine penny? Thank you. One cannot be too careful, even in small matters. I am going to put this penny in this glass (dropping it into the smaller glass). Oh, yes, the glass is quite unprepared." He lifts the glass and drops the penny on the table.

The Art of Magic

After exhibiting the glass and tapping it with his wand, he replaces it on the table, the bottom covering the borrowed penny, and at the same time he picks up the penny attached to the thread and drops it into the glass. This penny has been lying on the table back of the glass, and when the performer replaced the handkerchief on the table he dropped it in such a position as to conceal the penny against the glass being removed.

"And now," continues the performer, "I am going to christen the penny. As I intend to hold a conversation with it that might be a little long, I think it would be more agreeable to call the piece by some more striking name than penny. Ah, some of you smile incredulously. You do not believe it possible to hold a conversation with a coin. Perfectly reasonable, I assure you—money talks. How do you like the name of Toto? All right. From this moment we shall call this copper Toto."

"Now I shall magnetize Toto." The performer makes several passes with his hand or wand, at the same time looking expectantly into the glass.

"Toto, are you asleep?" (No answer).

"He does not answer because he is asleep. But I will make him understand me and answer my questions. I will make him talk in his sleep." (He blows on glass).

"And now, Toto, do you hear me?" (The coin jumps in the glass).

"What do you do when you say 'yes'?" (The penny jumps).

"And to say 'no'?" (The piece does not move).

"All right, Toto. (He turns to audience). You understand. Toto jumps to say 'yes,' and does not move to say 'no.' Well, this is enough. We shall understand each other."

Let us assume for the sake of illustration that six cards were drawn—three of which were forced. The performer, of course, has sighted and remembered the other three cards, and if he has not communicated this information to his assistant he pretends to read the minds of the spectators who drew the cards. "Whenever I look at any one through my wand," says the performer, squinting along the magic stick, "I can tell all they are thinking

The Art of Magic

about. But, pray do not be alarmed, I shall not divulge any secrets. I shall content myself with naming the card you selected. You are thinking of it now. It was (naming card); and yours was (naming the next person's card); and yours was (naming the third person's card)." But the more artistic way is to communicate the requisite information to your assistant, so that the penny—or rather Toto—can reveal the cards. We shall assume that this is the method employed.

"Toto, my friend, do you know the card that this lady drew?"—referring to the first of the freely drawn cards, say the five of hearts.

The assistant pulls the thread and the jumping coin answers "yes."

"He knows it. He knows more than I do. Is the card red?"

"Yes." (Coin jumps).

"Among the red cards are hearts and diamonds. Is it a heart?"

"Yes." (Coin jumps).

"Is it a picture card?"

"No." (Coin doesn't move).

"Then it is a spot card. Will you please jump as many times as the card has spots?" (The piece jumps five times).

"The five of hearts. Is that correct?" (Performer appeals to the one who drew the card, and she is obliged to admit that Toto has correctly told her card).

The performer then goes on to reveal the second of the freely drawn cards, say the six of clubs.

"Toto, do you also know this gentleman's card?"

"Yes." (The coin jumps).

"Is it red like the first one?"

"No." (The coin doesn't move).

"Then it is a black one?"

"Yes." (Coin jumps).

"Of course, if it is not red it must be black." (Coin jumps madly in glass).

"Among the black cards are spades and clubs. Is it a spade?"

"No." (Coin doesn't move).

"Then it must be a club?"

"Yes." (Coin jumps).

"Is it a picture card?"

"No." (Coin doesn't move).

"Then it is a spot card?"

"Yes." (Coin jumps).

"How many spots? (The penny jumps six times). The six of clubs. Is that correct, sir?"

The same operation is gone through with the third freely drawn card, and also with the first of the forced cards, which is the queen of hearts. When Toto has revealed the queen of hearts the performer asks the spectator if she would like to see her card. She naturally answers in the affirmative.

"Madame, you have only to command the card to appear and it will rise out of the glass." The lady says "Rise," but the card does not appear. The performer affects to be disconcerted. "Try again," he says to the lady. She does so, with no better result. The performer suddenly brightens up. "Ah, I know what the matter is," he says. "I forgot that your card is the queen of hearts. One cannot expect a lady—much less a queen—to be commanded in so peremptory a manner. Let me try. May it please your Majesty (with a profound bow) to favor us with your gracious presence. Please rise." The assistant pulls the thread and the queen "obligingly" rises from the pack. The second forced card, the ten of clubs, is likewise named and produced from the pack. The last card is the jack of spades.

"I believe the last card was taken by this gentleman," says the performer, pointing to the spectator. "Do you know that card, too, Toto?"

The coin raps out "Yes."

"Is it a black one?"

"Yes."

"Is it a spade?"

The Art of Magic

"Yes."
"A picture card?"
"Yes."
"Is it a king?"
"No."
"A queen?"
"No."
"Then it must be a jack?"
"Yes."

"Is that correct, sir? Thank you. Toto seldom makes a mistake. Would you also like to see your card? Very well. Jack of spades, appear! (The card appears with its back toward the audience). Well, well, what's that! (He removes the card). It is the jack of spades, but he has a peculiar way of presenting himself to society. I have a good notion to give him a lesson in politeness. What do you think of it, Toto? (The piece jumps up and down several times)." The performer returns the jack of spades to the pack, taking care to replace the card in front of the arranged part.

"Now appear!"

This time the jack of spades rises with his knavish countenance toward the audience.

"Ah, here you are, you impudent fellow! Aren't you ashamed of yourself! How dare you appear before such a charming audience showing your back! I should think you would feel like hiding yourself!" The jack suddenly disappears, an effect accomplished by the assistant suddenly slacking the thread, the weighted end of the card carrying it down.

"Ah, he is really sensitive. We can afford to be lenient. Appear. The ladies forgive you." (Jack appears).

"Bow to the ladies."

The jack bows three times—that is to say, the assistant manipulates the string so that the card slowly falls and rises three times.

"And to the gentlemen."

This time the jack bows three times very lively.

The Art of Magic

"Good." (The performer takes jack and lays him on the table). "Now, ladies and gentlemen, here is the jack of spades, here is the glass and here the deck of cards. (He removes cards from glass and springs them from hand to hand to demonstrate that they are unprepared). But I am not quite through with Toto. He knows people just as well as he knows cards, and to prove this assertion I will ask him to indicate the biggest story teller in the room. Toto, my friend, do you know who is the biggest story teller in this room?"

"Yes." (Coin jumps).

"Are you disposed to name the person to us this evening?"

"Yes."

"Is it a man?"

"Yes."

"Is he on the right?"

"No."

"Then he must be on the left."

"No."

"What! He is neither to the right nor to the left. That is odd. Of course, you do not refer to me?"

"Yes, yes, yes." (Coin jumps madly).

"Stop, Toto! You are a prattler." The conjurer quickly throws the glass over, picks up the borrowed penny and returns it to its owner. "Look out for this penny. It talks too much."

DE KOLTA'S RISING CARDS.

One of the finest performers of the rising cards was the late Buatier De Kolta, who worked this trick in such a deceptive manner that even the most expert magicians were puzzled. We refer to his old method of performing the trick, and not to the one in which all the cards rise from the glass, an effect that will be explained in due course. We doubt if the secret of Buatier's original rising card trick is known to the profession at large. We have seen many explanations of the trick in print, not one of which was more than fifty per cent. accurate. Here is Professor Hoffmann's explanation, from "More Magic," Page 94: "Some

The Art of Magic

performers, notably the celebrated Buatier De Kolta, work with a prearranged pack, and force a corresponding series of cards, but dispense with the aid of any assistant. The free end of the silk is, in Buatier's case, attached to one of the hinder cards, which he rolls up into a little tube through which to blow at the cards in the houlette, such blowing being the ostensible motive power to cause their ascent. The gradual withdrawal of the body, naturally bent in the act of blowing, draws the silk taut and produces the desired effect."

We give this explanation of the usually well-informed Professor Hoffmann for two reasons: first, because it describes the effect of the trick; and second, because it is the nearest correct of the many explanations we have seen. The following is the correct method of performing the original rising card trick of Buatier De Kolta:

The three cards destined to rise are threaded on the same general principle of all rising card tricks but with a slight difference—a difference, so to speak, that made all the difference in the world between Buatier's rising card trick and the tricks of his contemporaries. Instead of the thread being drawn *over* the top of each indifferent card used as a fulcrum, it is drawn through a tiny hole near the top of each indifferent card. The hole should be drilled in the exact center of the card and about an eighth of an inch from the upper edge. Arranged in this manner the glass or houlette, while containing the pack, may be handed to the audience for examination without any one being the wiser. But what of the free end of the thread? asks the acute reader. A very natural question. "The free end of the silk," says Professor Hoffmann, "is attached to one of the hinder cards, which he rolls up into a little tube through which to blow at the cards in the houlette, such blowing being the ostensible motive power to cause their ascent." This explanation is correct so far as it goes, but it does not go far enough. The "hinder card" is in reality a double card. That is to say, the edges of two cards are glued together around three sides, leaving the lower end open, thus forming a sort of envelope or pocket. Into this space the

The Art of Magic

free end of the silk—two or three feet, as the case may be—is concealed. The end of the silk, of couse, is permanently attached inside the double card. The thread should not be crowded into the double card in a helter-skelter manner, but should be neatly laid zigzagwise. The working of the trick will now be plain to the reader. The cards are threaded as described, the residuum of the silk being neatly laid in the double card. The arranged cards, face upward, are on the table, behind a handkerchief or some other object. The performer forces three duplicates. When these are replaced the pack is shuffled by the audience. Returning to the table the performer drops the pack face upward on the arranged packet, at the same time taking up the glass and handkerchief. He wipes the glass in order to prove that it is without preparation. The cards are now dropped into the glass and the "apparatus" is carried into the audience and freely exhibited. Owing to the fact that the thread does not pass *over the top* of the prepared cards, and that the free end is concealed inside the double card, there is absolutely no danger in handing the glass to a spectator for cursory examination. When, a moment later, the glass is placed on a table or chair, near the front of the stage, or, if a drawing room performance, in front of the spectators, and the selected cards rise at the command of the conjurer, there is something really "spooky" in the effect. The method of making cards rise is simple. The conjurer simply removes the hinder card, that is to say, the double card containing the thread. As he removes the card the thread is pulled out of the envelope. The performer rolls the card into a little tube, through which he blows toward the glass. The gradual withdrawal of the body, naturally bent in the act of blowing, draws the silk taut and produces the desired effect, as Professor Hoffmann says. The Editor of this book (Mr. Hilliard) uses a human hair instead of a thread, and allows a member of the audience to hold the glass while the cards ascend. In an artificial light and against a reasonably dark suit of clothes the hair is absolutely invisible. Care must be exercised in selecting the hair for this experiment. Some hairs are more brittle than others, and some have a betraying sheen or glint. If a stout hair of a dull dark color be used, there is absolutely no danger of its being detected, even though the trick be performed directly under a strong light and in the midst of an audience.

DE KOLTA'S NEW RISING CARDS.

This is one of the triumphs of the inventor of the "Flying Bird Cage," "Flowers from the Cone," the "Vanishing Lady," "Handkerchiefs and Soup Plate," the "Growing Die" and many other famous tricks and illusions. It is certain that if this master among modern conjurers had invented no other trick or illusion, his "Rising Card" trick, in which all the cards fly from the glass, would be sufficient to carry his name to posterity.

EFFECT—Three cards are drawn from a pack, returned and the pack shuffled. The pack is dropped into a glass, which is placed either on a table or a chair. At the conjurer's word of command the three chosen cards rise, one at a time, from the glass, after which all the cards leave the tumbler, one at a time.

TIME—Five to seven minutes.

REQUISITES AND PREPARATION—A pack of playing cards; a glass tumbler, preferably of the kind with a foot; and a reel of black silk thread.

The method of threading the pack in this trick differs radically from all other methods known to magic. Here is the method: Take a card in the left hand and the thread in the right. In beginning the threading process, leave a loose end of the thread, about twice the length of a card, hanging below what will be the bottom of the pack when all is ready for the trick. Pass the thread *up* the back of this card, which we will designate as No. 1, *over* the *top* and thence down the face of the card. Now place the second card on the face of the first (the thread, of course, being between), and bring the thread up in front of the second card, passing it *over* the *top* of the *two cards* and thence *down behind the rear card*. Place a third card at the rear (on top of thread) and pass the thread *up this card*, over the top of the three cards, and down the front again. Place a fourth card

The Art of Magic

in front, and pass the thread up and over the top of the four cards and thence down the rear card. Place a fifth card on the rear and continue passing thread alternately back and front, over the top each time, until the whole pack, save one card, is threaded. This last card, which should be a king of clubs or spades, has a slit in its lower edge. This slit should be large enough so that the thread may easily be drawn away and not pull the card with it. Pass the loose end of the thread, hanging below card No. 1 (in the center of the pack) towards the front of the pack, under this extra card which is placed on the front of the pack, thence up over its face and down behind the extra card, and just through the slit, where it is knotted so that the thread cannot be drawn through the slit. The last three cards threaded not counting the extra card at the front should be duplicates of the three that you are going to force. The pack thus arranged is lying in readiness on the table behind a handkerchief or some convenient object. The free end of the thread passes to the concealed assistant. In order to make the cards rise the thread must be pulled perpendicularly; that is to say from the "flies," or if in a drawing-room, the thread may pass over a gas fixture and thence to the hand of the concealed assistant. The simplest and best method of performing the trick in the drawing-room, however, is to stand the glass on the seat of a chair. The thread, passing over the top of the chair, gives the necessary perpendicular pull. It is also possible to accomplish the effect without the perpendicular pull. In this case the thread is pulled sideways; that is to say, at right angles with the glass. If this method is adopted a small notch should be cut in the bottom of each card to hold the thread, so that in pulling from the side there is no danger of the thread slipping from the card. Some performers do not take the trouble to fix the last card in the manner described, but we advise the reader that the extra trouble will not be wasted. As the cards rise alternately from the back and the front of the pack, the spectators would soon arrive at the conclusion that the cards are fixed in some manner, although of course, they would never dream of the real solution. The extra card, however, masks the cards that rise from the front of the pack, as it is the last to leave the glass. Furthermore, without this extra card, one of the chosen (forced) cards would of necessity be on the front of the pack, which would certainly detract from the effect of the trick. In the method described the extra card and card No. 1 leave the glass together. The extra card makes one revolution and the thread is drawn away.

PRESENTATION OF TRICK—The performer forces three cards on the audience, duplicates of those arranged to rise first from the threaded pack. These cards are shuffled back into the pack, and in the act of exhibiting the goblet the unprepared pack is exchanged for the threaded pack back of a handkerchief or other object on the table. The prepared pack is dropped into the glass, and with the usual patter the three cards rise from the pack. If desired this form of the trick may be performed in conjunction with the penny in the glass, as described in "The Tattlings of Toto." After the last drawn card has risen from the pack the performer draws attention to the fact that only an ordinary glass is used and ordinary cards. To prove that there is no hocus-pocus about the cards he commands them all to leave the glass, which they obligingly do. Another pretty effect is to have four cards drawn (forced). Three of the cards rise, as described, and then, apparently forgetting all about the fourth card, you proceed to perform some other trick. The spectators will immediately acquaint you with the fact that a fourth card was drawn. Feign embarrassment, and say that you had forgotten all about the card, and that you are afraid it is hopelessly lost in the pack. However, you will try your best to find it, and as some of the cards are in the way you command them to leave the glass. At the word of command all the cards fly from the glass, save one, which proves to be the selected card. This effect is indescribably pretty, and goes far toward removing any suspicion that the cards are prepared in any way. Only a slight variation in threading is necessary. Let us assume that the ace of hearts is to remain in the glass. We shall begin threading with this card. With the ace of hearts in the left hand, allow the loose end of the thread to hang down as before, although in this method a little more than the length of a card is required. Now pass the thread up the face of the ace of hearts, over the top of the card, down the back of the card, etc., until all the cards but the last, or extra card, are threaded. Place the extra card on face of the pack as before, only this time with the slit edge at the top of pack instead of at the bottom, as in the previous method. Pass the loose end of thread, hanging below the pack, towards the front of the cards; draw it up over the extra card and engage the end in the slit at the upper edge. If these directions are followed every card will leave the glass except card No. 1, in this case the ace of hearts.

ANOTHER METHOD—This is the method performed by Magician Kellar, although it was not invented by him. We believe that this method of threading the pack was originated by the late Harry Stork, who was assistant to Mr. Kellar at the time the trick was produced. The method is explained just as it was described to us by Mr. Stork himself. In this method the cards really fly from the glass, sometimes to a height of six feet, and no perpendicular pull is necessary. The thread is pulled from behind the cards as in the ordinary version of the rising cards. The thread in this case must be quite coarse. All the cards must have a slit cut in the upper edge, exactly at the center. This slit should be about half an inch long. The one exception is a card that has a slit at the bottom as well as the top. This we will call card No. 1, and with it will begin the process of threading the pack. Tie a small knot in the end of the thread and engage this knotted end in the slit at the lower end of the card, the knot being on the face side of the card. The thread is now passed up the back of the card and into the slit at the upper end. Instead of the thread passing down the front of the card, as described in the first method, it is brought back through the slit, the doubled thread forming a small loop on the face of the card. The thread is now passed down the back of the card, and card No. 2 is placed on top of the thread. The thread is brought under the lower edge of this second card and passed up the back and thence through the slit at the upper edge. The thread is brought back through the slit, as before, leaving a small loop on the face of the card. The double thickness of thread prevents this loop from being drawn through the slit. In fact, a strong pull is required to release the heavy loop from the slit, and it is this tension that throws the card so high in the air. The remainder of the cards are threaded in the same manner. If desired three or four cards can be forced, as in the other method, and these cards made to rise, one at a time, after which the entire pack will fly out of the glass. The exact method of working the trick we shall leave to the ingenuity of the reader. We may add that it is necessary to use a goblet with a foot in this form of the trick; and owing to the strong pull necessary to release the cards from the looped thread the foot of the goblet must be clamped to the table, otherwise the pull on the thread will tip the glass over. One way of overcoming this difficulty is to have a slot in the table top, into which the foot of the tumbler freely slides; another way is to have three small metal arms pivoted to the top of the table, and these arms catch the foot of the tumbler in the act of setting the glass on the table. There are many mechanical methods by which this result may be accomplished, and undoubtedly the reader will prefer to devise a holder that will harmonize with his own tables.

THE RISING CARDS IN THE SWINGING HOULETTE.

In his entertaining volume entitled "More Magic," Professor Hoffmann, writing of the different methods of performing the rising card trick, says: "In yet another and very pretty form of the trick, the invention of Professor Duprez, the houlette is of glass, suspended from the ceiling by a couple of silk ribbons (some feet apart at the top), and set swinging by the performer, the cards rising as usual, notwithstanding the swinging movement of the case. The ascent of the cards, under such circumstances, seems more than ordinarily magical. The secret lies in the fact that one of the ribbons is in fact double, being composed of two ribbons laid one on the other, and sewn together at the edges, so as to form a flat tube, through which passes the motive thread, led away across the ceiling to the hands of the assistant, the cards being arranged in the usual manner. The late Harry Stork improved upon this method by using a neat metal houlette instead of a glass. So far as we know Mr. Stork was the first to use this form of the trick in this country, and he afterwards sold the apparatus to Alexander Herrmann. The swinging houlette is really one of the most beautiful and mysterious of the rising card tricks; but for some reason it has been sadly neglected by magicians. Perhaps this is so because the trick is not thoroughly understood, and also because the houlette commonly sold by magical dealers is not entirely practical. We shall describe the trick exactly as performed by Mr. Stork, and as his original houlettes are before us we can assure the reader that if he will take the trouble to duplicate them, he will have not only a thoroughly practical piece of apparatus but also an exquisite illusion to add to his programme.

In the Stork method two houlettes are used, although the audience are aware of the existence of but one. These houlettes are simple metal cases, nickel plated, and just large enough to

Fig. 23.

hold a pack of cards, see Fig. 23. There is no front nor back to the case, so that the cards are never wholly concealed from the sight of the spectators. On each side of the case, at the upper end, is soldered a small piece of wire, forming a sort of miniature handle, by which to affix the ribbons. One of these houlettes is devoid of any preparation whatsoever, and may be freely examined by the audience. The other might also be examined and no one would be any the wiser. There is a slight difference between the two houlettes, however; for the bottom of one contains a slab of heavy metal. This houlette is the one suspended by ribbons, the metal weighing it down so that when the thread is pulled there is absolutely no movement on the part of the houlette. If this weight were not used the pulling of the thread would jerk the case about, which, of course, would suggest the motive power and thus destroy the effect of the illusion. It is this slight detail that makes the trick practical, and yet it has been lacking from every houlette we have seen on sale in the magical shops.

In the actual working of the trick the prepared, or threaded, pack is placed in the weighted houlette. The free end of the silk (the best thread for the purpose is orange-colored near-silk, or Clark's Lustre Crochet cotton) is threaded through a small hole in the center of the top edge of the case — of course at the rear. Thence it passes through a small eyelet soldered on the extreme right of the upper edge of the case, the eyelet being on a straight line with the hole through which the motive power is first threaded. The free end of the silk is tied into a loop; or, better still, make a loop of very fine wire and attach the thread to the wire. The wire loop should be about an inch in length, and the point where the ends of the wire cross in making the loop should be bound with silk, so that loop and silk will slip easily when drawn through the double ribbon.

The houlette thus prepared is placed behind some object on the table. The empty houlette is offered for examination, and while it is being inspected the performer invites three spectators to draw cards, of course forcing duplicates of the cards arranged to rise from the other houlette. The spectators shuffle their cards into the pack, which is placed in the examined houlette. This

The Art of Magic

houlette is now changed for the prepared one on the table. A clever method of exchanging houlettes is to fasten the prepared case inside of the coat, and during the journey back to the table the performer drops the unprepared houlette and cards into the breast pocket and takes out the prepared case. This houlette is attached to the two ribbons that hang from each side of the room or stage; the connection is made, and, in due course the cards rise.

A word concerning the ribbons is necessary. Two ribbons are used, one of which is a double ribbon. Yellow satin ribbon, half an inch in width, is the most satisfactory kind. At the end of each ribbon is sewed a metal hook by which to hold the houlette. Both ribbons should be double so that they will look alike. Through one double ribbon runs a stout cord — oiled silk fishline is the best for the purpose. One end of the line is fastened to a dress hook of the kind illustrated in Fig. 24. This is the most

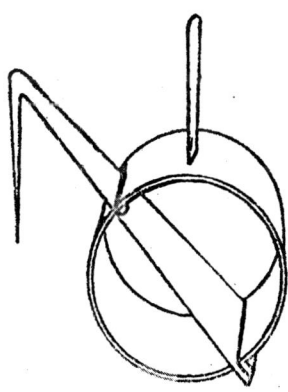

Fig. 24.

satisfactory kind of hook to use, for it will neither catch nor bind in the ribbon. In the act of fastening the case to the ribbons the wire loop at the end of the thread is engaged in this hook and the motive power is ready for operation.

As the performer will exhibit in drawing-rooms or stages of different dimensions it is advisable to make the ribbons extra long. For stage work each ribbon should be at least thirty feet long, while the drawing-room performer will find fifteen feet an ample length for each ribbon. The best as well as the simplest method of hanging the ribbons at each side of the stage or drawing-room is by means of a suspender end, about five or six inches long. One end of the suspender has a loop by which to suspend it on a convenient nail. To the other end is attached the ordinary suspender clip, through which the ribbon passes. The ribbon is adjusted in the same manner that suspenders are adjusted. When the exact length has been determined, the performer rips open about an inch of the double ribbon in front of the suspender clip, pulls the line through this opening, which should be in the top of the ribbon, passes it over a nail or hook in the wings or double doorway, and thence to the hands of the assistant. It is rather difficult to explain the exact method of hanging the ribbon but the reader will understand the modus operandi after a little experimenting.

The author of this volume makes a specialty of this form of the rising card trick. He causes four selected cards to rise, including one that rises with the back toward the audience. At the word of command the card turns around and proves to be one of the drawn cards. This effect is accomplished by means of a mechanical card, which may be purchased at any dealer of magical supplies. After the drawn cards have risen from the pack he concludes with the De Kolta rising card trick, all the cards flying from the houlette. The fact that the thread is drawn from the side of the case makes this charming effect possible. The pack is threaded in exactly the same manner as described in the first method of performing the De Kolta trick.

THE THURSTON RISING CARDS.

This trick is so named, perhaps, for the good and sufficient reason that Mr. Thurston did not invent it; but as the effect is associated with his name we retain the title. The trick in its original form, worked by a thread across the stage, made the reputation of Mr. Thurston, who certainly got all the advertising possible out of the audacious phrase, "The man who mystified

The Art of Magic

Herrmann." As the majority of our readers are familiar with this method of performing the trick, we shall not describe the modus operandi. Mr. Thurston, in his book of card tricks, describes another method of performing the trick, by means of a piece of apparatus resembling a spring tape measure, the place of the tape being taken by a black silk thread. To one side of the brass box is fastened a safety pin, with which to affix the apparatus to the performer's clothing. On the other side is a button which, when pressed, allows the thread to be drawn into the box by the internal spring. At the end of the thread is a piece of conjurer's wax. This is attached to a card, and the thread passes up over the fingers of the right hand. By pressing the button on the box the thread is reeled in and the card rises to fingers of right hand. That is to say, it does in theory. In actual practice the apparatus does not work satisfactorily, in spite of the rosy descriptions in the magical catalogues. Like the razors of the commercially minded itinerant, this kind of apparatus is made to sell. Mr. J. N. Thornton has improved somewhat on the Thurston apparatus. He has constructed a small, round tin box, japanned black, of a size to fit easily in the vest pocket. Inside the box is a wooden windlass mounted on a rubber band. The thread is wound around the windlass, the free end passing through a hole in the side of the box and terminating in a small leather button coated with wax. The simple act of drawing out the thread winds up the windlass, by twisting the rubber band, and when the hold on the thread is released the button flies back to the apparatus. While revising this volume for the press we received from Mr. Thornton an improvement upon his own apparatus. The box is the same, but the windlass is operated by a specially made spring instead of a rubber band.

This apparatus works reasonably well when the conjurer is in a dress suit, and is performing at a comfortable distance from the audience; for no matter how fine the silken thread may be there is always danger of it being seen at close quarters, and, furthermore, the windlass, in spite of all precautions, will "talk."

The Art of Magic

The ideal rising card trick is one that may be performed anywhere, at any time, and with any pack of cards. This Mr. J. N. Hilliard is able to do by an improvement on the old Alberti method.

The only apparatus used is a human hair about fourteen inches long. The exact length may be greater or less, as may be found most convenient by the performer. The hair is threaded into a needle and passed through the performer's coat just under the right lapel, near the top button. The end of the hair inside the coat is tied to an ordinary button. The opposite end carries a minute pellet of wax. When not in use the hair is drawn down inside the coat until the waxed end is concealed under the lapel. As most coats have an inside pocket on the right side, the button and hair are kept in the pocket, where the hair is out of the way and cannot be inadvertently broken. A hair thus arranged may be worn for months without danger of breaking, if the performer is reasonably careful. It is out of the way and always accessible at any moment.

This preparation made, the performer advances to the company and requests three members to draw cards, giving them full liberty of choice. When the cards are returned he brings them to be shuffled. The pack being returned, he replaces the three cards thereon. In walking back a few steps he has ample opportunity to find the wax pellet under the right lapel and draw the hair out to its full length, the button keeping the end from pulling through the coat. He presses the pellet of wax against the upper part of the back of the hindermost card, which was the last card replaced. The right hand now makes a number of passes above and below the pack. As the right hand sweeps underneath the pack it encounters the slack hair, which is allowed to pass between the first and second fingers, and is drawn up until the right hand reaches a position about ten or twelve inches above the pack.

Turning to the person whose card is to rise, the performer inquires: "What was the name of the card you chose?" "Jack of hearts" (or whatever it is), is the reply. "Jack of hearts, rise," commands the performer, and the card obediently rises to the fingers of the right hand, when it is immediately handed out for examination. This rising is accomplished by a slight upward outward movement of the right hand, which is absolutely undetectable, and which will be mastered after a few trials, although it is rather difficult to describe. The second card rises in the same manner. Mr. Hilliard varies the method of the production of the third card. He presses the pellet of wax against the upper part of the back of the card and then drops the pack into a glass, turning the deck so that the waxen pellet is at the bottom. He hands the glass to a lady to hold, and waving his hands above the glass commands the card to rise. The slightest movement of the body will cause the card to rise, the edge of the glass acting as a fulcrum. If the performer stands directly back of the glass so that his coat forms a dark background, the hair is absolutely invisible to the person holding the glass. When the card has risen nearly to its full height above the pack it is removed by the performer, who secures the wax pellet and offers the card for examination. In replacing the glass on the table he draws down the button inside the coat, which action removes both the hair and the wax pellet from sight. This method of performing the rising cards is superior to any other, we make bold to say, inasmuch as it may be done anywhere, at any time, and right under the eyes of the audience. We believe that the conjurer who once masters this method will rarely use any other, save perhaps when he wishes to present the illusion in a more elaborate and showy manner on the stage. As an impromptu trick it certainly has no peer. As a human hair is a very fragile thing and liable to be broken by an awkward movement of the hands, it is a good plan to have a fine silk thread also arranged in the coat in the same manner as the hair. If the hair breaks during the trick the performer can bring it to a successful conclusion. The presence of the thread will give the conjurer unbounded confidence. If he desires the performer may use the thread for the first two productions and employ the train for the card rising from the pack in the glass.

An amusing effect may be introduced in this method of performing the rising card trick. Run a thread through the back of the coat, between the shoulders, and pass it around to right side, below the right arm. This end terminates in a little pellet of wax and is stuck on one of the buttons of the coat. The other end is tied to the suspender on the left side. If the waxed end of the thread is attached to a card a slight pull on the thread by the left hand will bring the card on the performer's back. If this effect is added to the rising card trick, have four cards drawn, and, after three have been produced in the manner already described, draw the card onto the back and pretend to begin another trick. The audience will inform you that a fourth card was drawn, and after the usual assumption of embarrassment the card is discovered attached to the coat between the shoulders. It may be released by a slight jerk of the thread.

For a very neat method of performing the rising card trick the author is indebted to Hugall Benedict, an English wizard. The effect of his trick is as follows: Three cards are selected, marked, and returned to the pack, which is dropped into a tumbler. On being called for each card rises from the glass and floats to the performer's hand.

An ordinary pack of cards is employed, a glass tumbler, and a piece of fine silk thread, about a yard in length, to one end of which is attached a pellet of adhesive wax. To the other is tied a finger ring. Attach the waxed end of thread to a part of the ring, so that it will not be in the way. Ring and thread are placed behind some small object on the table, near the glass tumbler.

The performer offers the pack to a member of the audience to shuffle and to select any card and to mark it. This done the pack is passed to someone else, who also selects and marks a card; and so on with a third person. The performer takes back the pack and secretly palms three cards (face downwards from the bottom, in the left hand (for a good method of accomplishing this sleight see Erdnase's "The Expert at the Card Table," Page 86), and immediately hands the pack to a fourth person. He proceeds to collect the chosen cards (face downward) on the palm of his right hand, and they are apparently placed in the left hand. In reality he makes the Hellis change (see "Modern Magic," Page 33). The performer goes to the person who is holding the pack and requests him to cut the cards, and the three indifferent cards are dropped into pack, the selected cards being palmed in right hand. The gentleman is requested to shuffle the pack, and it is then placed on the table, the performer adding the three cards on top. He picks up the glass with his right hand and secretly slips the little finger of left hand into the ring. Offer the glass for examination, and, while it is being inspected, detach the wax end of thread from the ring and hold it in the right hand. Receive back glass in left hand, place it on table and take up with the right hand the pack, attach wax to top card, and drop pack into glass. The performer, standing with his right side to the audience, pretends to magnetize the cards with his right hand and in so doing obtains thread over the index finger and holds hand about nine inches above the glass, at the same time asking spectator to name the card last returned. On card being named, the performer asks the audience to watch the glass closely. Keeping his right hand perfectly still he moves his left hand rather quickly to the rear. (This movement will not be noticed as the left hand is hidden by the body and the eyes of the audience are on the glass). The jerk on the silk causes the card to jump out of the glass into the conjurer's right hand, and he immediately hands the card to the gentleman who selected it and requests him to identify the mark, at the same time removing wax and retaining same between first finger and thumb of right hand. Pack is taken out of glass with right hand and fanned out, the wax being secretly pressed on top card, which in its turn is likewise made to soar from the glass. The third card also rises from the glass in the same manner.

RESURRECTION OF THE CARDS.

This is a variation of the rising card trick. After four cards have been drawn by the audience, the performer burns them and

The Art of Magic

gathers the ashes on a saucer. "This would be a very expensive experiment," remarks the magician, "were not playing cards endowed with the peculiar virtue of the phonenix. A playing card, like that fabled bird, rises from its own ashes." He exhibits a large glass, into which he pours the ashes. The persons who chose the cards are requested to call their names, and as each card is announced it appears gradually over the border of the glass.

The glass is a large goblet with cut sides. It may be handed to the audience for examination. When the magician takes it back he wipes the inside with a silk handkerchief. As the reader undoubtedly suspects, this is not done for the sole purpose of cleaning the glass. In reality the conjurer introduces a small box into the glass. This box is rectangular and just as high as the glass and just as wide as the diameter of the glass. It is large enough to hold freely eight cards — four that are to rise and four that act as fulcrums. The cards are threaded in the usual manner. The front and back of the box are of looking-glass, so that no matter which side you turn the glass the spectator apparently sees through it. The rest of the trick requires no explanation.

Before bringing this chapter to an end we shall mention one or two ideas "touchin' and appertainin'" to the rising cards. The late Martin Chapender's method, as presented by him at Egyption Hall, may be of interest, as he was a very finished performer. He employed the familiar black thread stretched across the stage, just above the height of the performer's head.

In the wings, at each side, the thread passes over a pulley wheel, or through a round hook, and hangs about four feet down from this. At each end of the thread are attached small packets of cards — about a dozen — to act as counterweights. They keep the thread taut, but allow of it being easily drawn down and attached to a card which, when released, is drawn up by their weight. Most performers use prepared cards in this trick. That is to say, the cards that rise must have a sort of clip arrangement at the back in which to engage the thread. This method necessitates forcing duplicate cards. Mr. Chapender obviated

The Art of Magic

this difficulty by using a small contrivance known as the "Excelsior Clip," which may be bought at any dealer in office supplies, and which is described on page 54 of "Later Magic." Three cards are drawn by audience. The cards are marked and replaced singly in deck. The cards are brought to top by means of the pass, and the pack is shuffled by the performer, leaving the selected cards on top. The "Excelsior Clip" is snapped on the first card. The performer draws down the thread, engages it under the little arm of the clip, and the card duly rises to the right hand. The right hand removes the clip and the card is handed to spectator, or scaled into the body of the theater. For obvious reasons this method is not applicable to the drawing-room. At such close quarters the clip would be plainly visible to the spectators. For the benefit of those who may prefer to use prepared cards we take pleasure in describing the method of preparing the card as used by Mr. Kellar. It is by all odds the best method yet devised for attaching the card to the horizontal thread. The clip, if such it may be called, cannot be detected at a distance of even two feet. For every two cards prepared another card must be sacrificed. Cut with sharp scissors from the end of a card a piece resembling Fig. 25. This piece is glued to the back of a whole card in such a

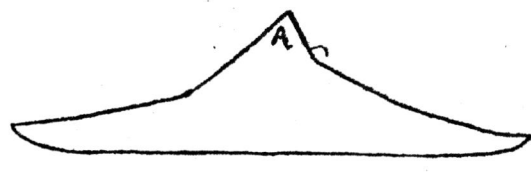

Fig. 25.

manner that the point A (in the illustration) is free to form a sort of tongue under which to engage the thread. The entire pack is prepared in this manner. With the cards thus prepared it is impossible to miss the horizontal thread, and if cards with a fancy pattern are used they can almost be handed for examination. A trial will convince the reader that this is the most practical and satisfactory method of preparing cards for this form of the rising card trick.

A correspondent, Mr. Hugh Mulloy, of Indianapolis, describes his method of performing this trick in the drawing-room in the following words: "I presume I have used for a number of years about as crude a method of doing the rising card trick as is used by any magician. I carry with me two small, brass wheels. These have sharp points and before the entertainment are pushed in the jamb at either side of an alcove or doorway, and my thread runs over these pulleys and across the door at a convenient height, the ends being properly weighted. In the center of the thread I put wax of a strong adhesive quality. When I get my cards (whether forced or not) I bring them to the top, get my thread while waving my hand, and press it with the open hand to the back of the card. Sometimes I miss it, but I have some good patter ready, and try it again. In this way I don't have much to get ready, which suits me, as I am somewhat fussy. At my own home I have the thread always ready, and then of course, all I need for the trick is a pack of cards."

Another correspondent, Morgan H. Winans, of New York, has a neat method of performing the rising card trick, in which he does away with the services of an assistant. Three chosen cards are caused to rise from the pack in a tumbler or other receptacle. The three cards are, of course, forced, and the duplicate pack is arranged as usual, with the thread passing alternately under and over the cards. The thread passes down to the floor and is attached to a small disc. This disc is made of card, blacked, or of leather, with a small tack stuck through it. (A dab of wax will do as well). Now step on the disc, which will stick to your shoe, and a slight move of the foot will pull thread causing the cards to rise.

Another excellent method of performing the trick without the services of an assistant is to have a cap made to fit over the end of the wand, matching, of course, the genuine tip. Have the thread fastened to the duplicate cap and lay it on the table. When ready to perform the trick slip the cap on to the wand and

The Art of Magic

proceed. Another clever method is to attach the thread to a handkerchief laid carelessly on the table. When about to perform the trick simply pick up the handkerchief, wipe your hands, and thrust it into the breast pocket. An improvement is to have a hook on end of thread, in which case you can use any handkerchief.

One of the prettiest effects in the line of the rising cards is known to the profession as the "Obliging Bouquet." This was one of Alexander Herrmann's masterpieces.

The effect, in brief, is this: A bouquet of real flowers is handed to a lady in the audience, and three or four cards are chosen from the pack. These cards are commanded to disappear. One by one they are then seen to rise from the bouquet while the flowers are in the hands of the lady. The secret lies in the use of a metal case just large enough to hold the cards, and the arrangement of the cards is the same as usual, with the exception that a human hair is substituted for silk. The case is placed in the center of the bouquet, in such a position that it is not visible from the outside, yet allowing the cards to have a free passage for their ascent. The greatest care must be taken in arranging the case in the flowers, although the trick is not nearly so difficult as it seems. The essentials are nerve and audacity. A thorough description of this trick will be found in Edwin Sache's admirable treatise on "Sleight of Hand," Page 202. The reader will also find the rising card trick described at length in the following standard works: "Modern Magic," page 125; "More Magic," page 91; "Trick With Cards" (Hoffmann), page 211; "Conjuring and Magic" (Robert-Houdin), page 231; "The Modern Conjurer" (Lang Neil), pages 113 to 123.

The latest and best rising card trick we know of is the invention of Mr. W. G. Edwards, who refuses, however, to disclose the secret.

In effect it is similar to the old method where the cards rise from the glass tumbler, but in this particular, and (if we must admit it) perplexing instance, any card called for *immediately* rises from the glass and falls to the table.

The Art of Magic

One redeeming feature, however, is that the trick in this form is to be presented in the act of Mr. Downs. And if at the present time we cannot give a correct explanation of this perfection of the rising cards, we can at least look on and hope, that the clever inventor of this and other bewildering effects will one day rend the vail asunder, and pronounce the "Open Sesame" that will make us "en rapport."

CHAPTER X

THE FOUR ACE TRICK.

Like the rising cards the four ace trick, in one variation or another, is a favorite with conjurers. Robert-Houdin, in his book on magic, ascribes its invention to Conus; but the historical investigations of the indefatigable Harry Houdini have impressed us with the wisdom of accepting many of the statements of Mr. Robert-Houdin with even more than the proverbial allowance of salt. However, there is nothing to be gained in controversial argument on this particular question. The salient point is that the magical eccentricities of the four aces furnish some of the very best effects in the gentle art of hocus-pocus, and the man who invented the original four ace trick, be he Comte or Conus or Old Nick himself, deserves a tablet in the Magical Hall of Fame, or at least an engrossed set of commemorative resolutions sealed with the monogram of the Society of American Magicians.

The four ace trick naturally has been improved upon since its inventor's day, although the principle remains unchanged—the dispersing of the aces and their subsequent assemblage. Every performer, of course, has his own particular method of accomplishing this effect, in which he employs his pet passes and favorite "moves;" but the following method may appeal to the amateur magician as something of a novelty. We are indebted for the idea to "Die Zauberwelt," but in the translation have added one or two original ideas.

EFFECT—Same as the old four ace trick; that is, four aces are laid face downward on the table. Three indifferent cards are dealt on each ace. One packet is selected, and the four aces are assembled in that packet.

TIME OCCUPIED—From three to six minutes, according to the amount of patter.

The Art of Magic

REQUISITES AND PREPARATION—An ordinary pack of cards, and three additional aces—clubs, hearts and diamonds. The seven aces are arranged in the pack as follows:

I. Reckoning from the face of the pack:
   Ace of hearts, the fifth card.
   Ace of clubs, the tenth card.
   Ace of diamonds, the fifteenth card.
   Ace of clubs, the twentieth card.

II. Reckoning from the top of the pack:
   Ace of hearts, the second card.
   Ace of diamonds, the sixth card.
   Ace of spades, the tenth card.

PRESENTATION OF TRICK—The performer makes the usual announcement of the four ace trick, and proceeds to take the aces from the deck, for which purpose he turns the pack face upward in his hand, by which plan he is enabled to remove the ace as arranged in order I. The performer lays these aces on the table, face downward, in the order in which they are removed from the pack. This makes the ace of spades the second, counting from left to right.

The performer then turns the pack over and deals three cards, one at a time, on each ace, from left to right. This gives you four piles of four cards each. The second pile, which has the ace of spades at the bottom, contains the three duplicate aces. The other three packets each have an ace at the bottom. You turn up each packet to convince the spectators that there is an ace on the bottom of each packet. Now force the second packet—that is, the one containing the four aces. Place the three remaining packets on the deck. It is now necessary to get rid of the three duplicate aces. The method explained in "Die Zauberwelt" is rather clumsy. Herr Willmann directs that the "card artist" must palm off each ace as he places the packets on the deck; but this method is not very artistic. A better plan is to slip each ace to the bottom of the pack as the packets are returned

The Art of Magic

to the deck. By holding the four cards of each packet fanwise in the right hand, and slipping the ace on the bottom and the other three cards on the top of the pack, the movement is as deceptive as can be desired. With the three aces on the bottom, it does not require an unusual amount of dexterity to get rid of them.

A good method of getting rid of the aces is contributed by a correspondent. He says: "My table is slightly prepared. The table itself is an ordinary one, of the kind that is commonly used for card tricks. The top is covered with black felt. Across the middle is stretched a piece of the same cloth, just a little wider than a card is long. A strip of gilt braid three-eighths of an inch wide is sewed along either edge of this piece, and similar strips of braid are arranged on the table in a rectangular pattern. The strips of braid conceal the edges of the duplicate piece of black felt.

The plan of getting rid of the aces will now be obvious. After showing each packet with an ace on the bottom the performer replaces the packets on the table, moving them forward, during which operation the ace on the bottom is slipped under the felt flap at the center of the table. The trick is now practically done. The three packets (containing three cards only) are placed on the deck, which is given to a spectator to hold. Then in the most magical manner possible the three aces "leave the pack" and join the ace of spades on the table, while the three "indifferent" cards return to the pack—at least that is what the spectators imagine, if you have performed the trick in the proper manner and with appropriate patter.

SECOND METHOD — The four aces are placed on top of the pack by a spectator. The conjurer shifts three to the bottom, and deals an ace and three indifferent cards, separately, on the table. Three indifferent cards are dealt on each supposed ace. The three aces at the bottom are shifted to the top, and the performer takes up four cards, holding them so as to appear as one card. Pick up two or three other cards in same hand, as if you were looking for some particular card; then replace cards on top of the pack and deal the three aces on the ace on table. If this is done carelessly the spectators will be convinced that you have dealt three indifferent cards on the ace, and the subsequent assemblage of the aces will have all the effect that can be desired. The feature of this method is the four card "stall."

THIRD METHOD — Cover three aces with cloth of the same color as that used on your table. At the outset these cards are on the table where, under artificial light, they can not be detected by the keenest eye. You must remember the order of the suits. Hand four aces to the audience for the purpose of having them marked. Take back one ace (the ace of clubs for sake of illustration), and in turning toward the table make the bottom change, leaving the ace at the bottom of pack and placing the indifferent card on the cloth-covered ace of clubs on the table. On top of this card deal three indifferent cards, exhibiting them to the audience. Repeat the maneuver with the next two aces (say hearts and spades). At this juncture you have three aces on the bottom of the pack. Shift these to the top. Now place the ace of diamonds on the table, and on this ace deal the three aces from the top of pack. You can now pick up each packet and show an ace at the bottom. In replacing the packets shove them forward, leaving the cloth-covered aces at the rear of the table. The packet containing the four aces is forced, the other three packets are returned to the pack, and the trick is brought to the usual conclusion. This is a very mysterious trick, and will prove valuable to the amateur who is obliged to exhibit his tricks frequently before the same audiences. The most satisfactory method of preparing a cloth-covered card is to soak it in warm water, when it may easily be split. When the two halves are dry cover the *back* with cloth, and turn the cloth around the edges, gluing it to the inside. The cloth should turn about an eighth of an inch. Now glue the front and back together and dry under a heavy weight, or, better still, in a letter-press. By turning the cloth in this manner, and gluing it between the two halves of the card the edges cannot ravel. Consequently a card prepared in this manner will last for years.

The Art of Magic

FOURTH METHOD—The feature of this method is that the four aces are laid face upward on the table, three indifferent cards being dealt, also face upward, on each ace. This is a beautiful and mystifying trick; and, as will be explained later, is admirably adapted for a stage performance.

Prepare six aces (two hearts, two clubs and two diamonds) by splitting them and gluing indifferent cards to their backs. The ace of spades is not prepared. Place three of the prepared aces on the bottom of the pack, the indifferent side down. Then place nine miscellaneous cards beneath, and under these place the other prepared aces (ace side down) and leave the unprepared ace of spades at the bottom of the pack.

In presenting the trick, the performer deals the aces (the ones at the bottom of the pack, of course) face upward on the table, placing them side by side, the ace of spades occupying the last position. Now deal three cards face upward on each ace, which operation gets rid of the nine indifferent cards originally placed between the two sets of prepared aces. The three prepared aces, the indifferent side face up, are dealt on the unprepared ace of spades. Pick up each packet, and spread the cards, showing one ace and three cards. In closing the packets turn over the ace under cover of the indifferent cards. When you exhibit the packet with the ace of spades on the back, bring this unprepared ace to the front and turn the three cards under cover of the ace. The aces are now with the ace of spades, and there are no aces in the other piles. By the familar system of elimination the spade pile is forced, and the remaining packets being returned to the pack. The pack is handed to a spectator, the three aces commanded to join the ace of spades on the table and the three indifferent cards to return to the pack. After the magic formula has been pronounced this transposition is found to have taken place. Although there are three prepared cards in the pack the performer need have no hesitation about inviting a spectator to look through the pack in order to convince himself that the aces are really gone. He will never think of looking at the backs of the cards.

The Art of Magic

In order to make the trick suitable to the stage the performer utilizes a piece of apparatus familiar to the readers of Mr. Downs's book on coin manipulation. This is a small triangular-shaped contrivance covered with black velvet. It stands on the performer's table, and the cards are laid against the outer face so that they are always in full view of the spectators.

FIFTH METHOD—This method is adapted to a small audience, and is excellent for impromptu work. It is one of specialties of the very clever Nate Leipzig. Four aces are shown; each one is marked by a spectator; and they are then laid face downward on the table, side by side, three odd cards being dealt on each ace. As usual the four aces assemble in one heap.

The basis of this trick is the old and familiar sleight known as the top change, which, at this late day, needs no explanation. Lay the four aces on the table, face downward. Hold the pack in left hand and with left thumb push three cards over the edge in readiness for the change. With the other hand pick up one of the aces and hand it to a spectator with the request that he or she will mark it. Receive the card back in right hand, and, sliding this card under another ace, pick up this second ace and also offer it to be marked. This card is received back in the right hand, on top of the first ace, and the two, held together as one card, are slipped under another ace. This third ace is offered to another spectator to mark, and is received back in the right hand on top of the other two aces. The three aces in right hand, held as one card, are now slipped under the fourth ace, which is likewise tendered to a spectator. While the fourth ace is being marked the performer exchanges the three aces in the right hand for the three indifferent cards on the top of the deck. This sleight is accomplished as he turns to lay the pack on the table. Receive back the fourth ace in left hand on which you immediately drop the three indifferent cards from the right hand. You now have a packet of four cards, one an ace (at the bottom) and three indifferent cards. Hold this packet so that the ace is visible, although not verbally calling attention to the card. Place the four cards face downward on the table as usual and deal three

The Art of Magic

indifferent cards on each supposed ace, and the three aces on top of the ace. The trick is then brought to the familiar conclusion, the four aces assembling in one packet. This is a very fine sleight of hand experiment, and the reader is strongly advised to add it to his repertory; for it is convenient at times to have more than one method of accomplishing this popular effect.

SIXTH METHOD—This is also one of Mr. Leipzig's specialties, and we shall explain the trick as worked by this accomplished card artist, in whose hands it is a veritable mystery.

Offer the four aces to a spectator with a request that they be marked, after which he is directed to place the ace of spades on the bottom of pack and ace of hearts on the top, the performer holding the pack in his own hand. The performer makes the double-hand pass, thus bringing ace of spades and ace of hearts to the center, and, lifting up the ace of hearts, he inserts the little finger between it and the lower part of the pack. Opening the pack at this break the performer requests the spectator to place the ace of clubs and the ace of diamonds in the center of pack. When this is done drop the ace of hearts on the two aces just replaced in the pack, and, closing up the cards, insert little finger between the ace of hearts and the ace of spades. Now make the shift, with an exaggerated move of the arms, so as to attract attention. This shift brings the ace of spades back to the bottom of the pack and the ace of hearts to its original position on the top. All is the same as before except that under the ace of hearts, at the top, are the ace of clubs and the ace of diamonds. The chances are that if the pass is made in the manner suggested some one in the audience will remark that the aces have been juggled away, or at least there will be suggestive smiles on the faces of the spectators. Quietly ask the audience to name the position of the different aces. They will probably answer that the ace of spades *was* on the bottom, that the ace of hearts *was* on the top, and that the ace of diamonds and the ace of clubs *were* in the center. "Correct," replies the conjurer, turning over pack, so as to show the ace of spades. "The ace of spades *is* on the bottom, and (turning up top card) the ace of hearts *is* on the top, just as they were placed by this gentleman (indicating the spectator). And the other two aces are in the center of pack." The conjurer does not offer to show that the ace of clubs and the ace of diamonds are in that position, which is not necessary; for the other two aces being in their original position the spectators are satisfied that everything is as it should be, which is an illustration of the psychology of this fascinating art. The performer now shifts the two bottom cards to the top, so that the ace of spades is the second card from the top. "Would you believe," observes the conjurer, "that I could make the four aces fly from this pack? Really, it is a very simple matter. I have only to click the pack four times like this (clicking the lower corner of the pack with the little finger of the left hand) and the cards obey. See!" He shows that the ace of spades has left the bottom of the pack, and, by turning up the indifferent card on top, shows that the ace of hearts has also obeyed his command. Now comes the boldest and yet the most successful and convincing move of the whole trick. Observing that the ace of clubs and the ace of diamonds have also left the pack, the performer deliberately spreads the cards, one by one with the left thumb, face upward, before the eyes of one of the spectators. At the outset the cards are spread deliberately, the movement being accelerated after the center of the pack has been reached, while toward the last the cards are spread briskly. At the same time the performer holds the cards nearer to the face of the spectator, so that when the end of the pack is reached the cards are so close to the spectator's eyes that he is not able to see that the last six cards (four of them aces) are not spread at all, but are held as one card. The performer does not give the spectator any time to reflect. Turning abruptly he repeats the operation before the eyes of a second spectator. A third demonstration is not necessary, as the audience is convinced by this time that the aces really have left the pack.

Now for the reappearance of the wandering aces. Get rid of the top card either by the shift or a false shuffle. Hold pack in left hand, the face of the cards toward the audience. The position of pack is much the same as in the first position for executing the Charlier one-hand pass, with the single exception that the left thumb instead of resting on the upper edge of the deck extends over the face of the bottom card, as in the conventional position for dealing. The right hand now grasps the pack at the lower ends, between the thumb and first finger. The back of the right hand is toward audience, but the bottom card of the pack is not for an instant hidden from the eyes of the spectators. The ostensible reason for the right hand approaching the pack is to square up the cards; but the real reason is to obtain possession of the top card of deck (the ace of spades). This is accomplished by the four fingers of the left hand pushing the top card downward until it is in a position to be palmed by the right hand. This operation is invisible, as the sliding of the card is masked by the right hand. A trial before a mirror will convince the conjurer of the practicability of this move, which in the hands of its inventor is an exceedingly subtle sleight. The right hand is now moved away from the left, and is then suddenly brought palm down on the face of the pack with a resounding slap, the right hand being immediately drawn back. The effect to the audience is that simultaneously with the noise the ace of spades appears on the face of the pack. The sudden and mysterious appearance of the card has a bewildering effect. Mr. Leipzig makes the three other aces appear in the same manner; but in less skillful hands such a proceeding is more or less dangerous, to say nothing of it violating the cardinal rule of conjuring,— namely, never to repeat a trick before the same audience. The reader is advised to produce the other aces by means of the various methods for producing what is know as the "color change." If he has faith in his skill he may produce the last ace in the same manner as he did the first. This trick is one of the very best of the four ace series, and, as this is the first time it has been explained in print, the reader will no doubt add it to his list of accomplishments.

SEVENTH METHOD—This effect differs radically from the conventional four ace trick, but for obvious reasons is included in this chapter. In good hands it forms a satisfactory and mystifying experiment.

EFFECT—The performer secures the assistance of two gentlemen from the audience. A pack of cards is handed to them with a request to remove the four aces and the four kings, and, if they so desire, to mark them. Two ordinary envelopes are examined; one is marked "Kings," the other "Aces," *in large letters*. The performer takes the envelope marked "Aces" and in it places the four aces, in full view of the spectators, seals it, and hands it to one of the gentlemen. In like manner he places the kings in the other envelope, which is held by the second volunteer assistant. A little patter and the gentlemen are requested to open the envelopes, when it is found that the aces and kings have changed places.

TIME OCCUPIED—About five minutes—the exact time, of course, depending upon the amount of patter in which the performer clothes the experiment.

REQUISITES AND PREPARATION—A duplicate ace and king, prepared by gluing to their backs cloth of the same color as that on the performer's table, preferably black or dark green. The prepared cards are on table. In addition to the feked cards, an ordinary pack of cards, two envelopes, and a lead pencil are used.

PRESENTATION OF TRICK—Invite two gentlemen to assist you and offer the cards to them, asking them to take out the aces and kings, and mark them with the pencil. Hand the envelopes to them, and while they are examining them take back the cards. Get the ace and king corresponding to the feked cards to the front of their respective piles, taking especial pains that the audience shall take note of the card at the bottom of these piles. Now lay the two piles of cards on the table, putting the pile of aces on the feked king and vice versa. Now call for the envelope marked "Aces"; take up the kings with the feked ace in front, and apparently place them in the envelope. In reality, after showing the ace at the bottom, the cards are turned with their backs to the spectators, and the four kings alone go into the envelope, the feked card slipping down behind on the outside.

The Art of Magic

As soon as the feke is safely out of sight behind the envelope bend back the flap so that the audience can see that the four cards, which they imagine to be the aces, are really placed inside the envelope. The feked card is held behind the envelope with the thumb of the left hand, and is palmed in that hand in the act of raising the envelope to the lips to moisten the gum on the flap. The envelope is then handed back to one of the gentlemen, and the performer has an opportunity to dispose of the palmed card. The movements are then repeated with the other cards; a little patter follows; and the assistants are requested to open the envelopes, when the cards are found, to all appearances, to have changed places.

The weak point in this trick is the repetition of the movements. This is easily avoided by the performer laying down the envelope first used, ostensibly to pull back his sleeves a little, but really to dispose of the feked card without palming. He is then able, in sealing the envelope, indirectly to call the attention of the audience to the fact that his hands are empty, which makes it easier to palm the second cloth-covered card without detection.

The reader who is curious to delve into the history of the four ace trick and become acquainted with its innumerable variations, may find the following references of interest: "Secrets of Conjuring and Magic" (Robert-Houdin) page 260; "Modern Magic," pags 79, 80 and 93; "Tricks with Cards" (Hoffmann) page 107; and "The Modern Conjurer" (Lang Niel), page 113.

CHAPTER XI

CARD TRICKS WITH APPARATUS AND IN COMBINATION WITH OTHER OBJECTS.

The tricks described in this chapter are primarily intended for performance in the drawing-room, although they require the aid of mechanical appliances or apparatus. One or two of the tricks described, notably the cards appearing on the plate glass, are also suitable for presentation on the stage; but as a rule card tricks are rather unsuitable for the modern large theater, as the spectators in the rear of the auditorium, or in the balcony and gallery cannot see the cards. Consequently much of the effect is lost. In a small theater, of course, conditions are more propitious.

One of the most serious problems the amateur conjurer has to solve is that of apparatus. At first thought this would seem an extremely simple affair. There are numerous manufacturers of and dealers in magical supplies, and their imaginatively illustrated catalogues, all so much alike, are positively alluring. The student is captivated by the cunningly contrived descriptions of tricks and illusions, and he soon begins to squander his money on various contraptions. We use the word "squander" advisedly; for as a general rule the apparatus one purchases from professional dealers is not worth the money expended on expressage. There are two kinds of magical apparatus; the kind that works and the kind that does not. Generally speaking, the amateur buys the kind that does not. The professional conjurer, of course, has no such problem to solve. He knows what he wants and where to get it. In most cases the professional magician has his appliances constructed by skillful workmen who know little or nothing of magic, and we advise the reader to do likewise. In every city or town are skillful machinists, metal workers and

The Art of Magic

cabinetmakers, who can turn out apparatus superior to anything that can be bought at most magical repositories; and the student who knows what he wants will have little difficulty in getting together by this means a collection of practical appliances for, and accessories of, magic that should, with reasonable care, last a lifetime.

Of course there are some things that cannot be obtained outside the conjuring shops, but the student should, if possible, do his purchasing in person. In this way he will secure a better quality of goods for his money.

A list of reliable dealers in magical apparatus will be cheerfully furnished by the publishers of this book on request.

The student is advised not to rely too much on the use of apparatus. Mechanical appurtenances should be used sparingly and only in tricks that require dexterity and address. It cannot be gainsaid, however, that in a performance of even a half hour duration the effect is enhanced by the occasional introduction of a neat looking piece of apparatus which is not too suggestive of mechanism. The novice may imagine that no particular skill or adroitness is necessary in handling apparatus; but nothing could be farther from the truth. As a matter of fact, almost as much practice must be devoted to a mechanical trick as a feat of pure sleight of hand; for even the best made aids to conjuring have a habit of not working just at the critical moment; and, therefore, every detail of the trick must be carefully practiced and rehearsed.

CARD, ORANGE AND CANDLE.

This trick is one of the specialties of Mr. John Northern Hilliard, and while there is nothing absolutely new involved in the experiment, the combination of effects is entertaining and mystifying.

EFFECT—A card is drawn and torn in eight pieces, one of which is retained by a spectator. The seven pieces are burned and the ashes passed into an orange held by a spectator. The orange is cut in half, and the restored card is discovered inside

The Art of Magic

the orange. One corner of the card is missing, and the piece held by the spectator exactly fits the torn section. The conjurer asks a lady if she would like to take the card home as a souvenir; but, as the card is limp and soggy with orange juice, she naturally declines. The performer says that he will dry the card. He loads the card and its corner into his magic pistol and fires at a candle that has been burning on his table during the experiment. The card appears, dry and completely restored, in the flame, and is handed to the lady as a souvenir of the performance.

Time Occupied—About ten minutes.

Requisites and Preparation—An ordinary pack of cards; a conjurer's pistol; a plate containing three oranges, one of which is prepared; an envelope; and a mechanical candlestick. This is an ordinary looking brass candlestick, plain or nickel-plated. The foot is weighted with a piece of lead, a cavity being left between this and the foot proper for the purpose of concealing a card. To the top edge of the candlestick is hinged an arm of iron wire, the hinge being provided with a strong spiral spring with a tendency to keep the arm in an upright position behind the candle. On the other end of the arm is a metal clip for holding a card, which, when the arm is in position, will appear to be in the flame of the candle. The flame, of course, is extinguished by the force of the shock. To prepare for the trick load the arm with a duplicate of the card that is to be found in the orange. A small metal button keeps the arm in position, which is released by a thread in the hands of an assistant. The orange, which should be of the large navel variety, is prepared as follows: Remove the pip and save it for future use. Now with a sharp pointed instrument, about the diameter of a lead pencil, puncture the top of the orange in the exact spot from which the pip was taken, exercising more or less care not to break or cut the surrounding skin. The tough, fibrous core may now be removed, which will afford space enough to accommodate a card rolled cigarettewise. Before rolling the card should be soaked in water for a few moments, otherwise when produced from the orange it will have a creased and cracked appearance suggestive of folding. As a card inside an orange would naturally be soaked, the preliminary wetting makes no difference in the denouement of the trick. The moistened card is rolled up tightly as possible, when it is gently forced into the orange through the small hole at the top, the operator taking care that the hole is not enlarged or the skin of the orange abraded. Push the card well into the orange, and fill in the hole with the tough white fibrous substance from another orange. Then with a little adhesive wax attach the pip to its proper place, when a microscopical examination will not reveal anything wrong with the fruit. If the "building up" process, so to speak, has been done properly, the spectator may even remove the pip without being any the wiser. The performer is advised to mark the prepared orange so that he may readily know which globe contains the card. The simplest way is to remove the pips from the two unprepared oranges. Their absence will not be remarked by the audience. Of course the card in the orange must have a piece torn from one corner, and this piece must be concealed either on the person of the conjurer or in some readily accessible place, say under the envelope on the table. This envelope should be as small as practicable. The performer has another envelope similar to the one on the table, but made of flash paper. This envelope contains several small pieces of flash paper, so that when the envelope is held in front of a light the spectators will see what they suppose are the pieces of cards. This duplicate envelope should be placed under the performer's vest, or in some convenient pocket, where it may be readily "ringed," or changed, for the ordinary envelope. On the table, in addition to the articles described, there should be a fruit plate, a knife, and a magician's pistol.

PRESENTATION OF TRICK—The performer brings forward a plate containing three oranges arranged in triangle form, so that the prepared orange will be at the apex. Request a spectator to select an orange, and the chances are that the center one (the orange at the apex) will be chosen. Allow the orange

The Art of Magic

to be examined, and then place it on the table at the foot of the prepared candlestick, the candle of which should be burning throughout the experiment. Request a lady to draw a card, forcing a duplicate of the card in the orange, say the queen of clubs. Have the queen torn in eight pieces and place the pieces in the unprepared envelope. The performer in picking up this envelope gets possession of the corner torn from the card in the orange. Placing the eight pieces in the envelope the performer starts to seal the top down, but bethinks himself that there is no way to identify the mutilated card. Accordingly he takes out one of the pieces, really, of course, bringing out the duplicate piece, which has been concealed in his fingers. Handing this piece to the spectator who drew the card, the performer seals the envelope, and, in turning toward his table, exchanges it for the envelope made of flash paper. He holds this in front of the candle, to prove that the pieces are still there; but with apparent carelessness he moves the envelope too close to the flame. The envelope disappears in a flash. The performer pretends to be disconcerted; but finally professes to believe that the contents may have passed into the orange. The orange, on a plate, is handed to a spectator, who cuts it open and finds the card. The orange should be cut open at right angles to the position of the rolled up card, so that when the fruit is divided into halves the card sticks up in one half. The piece retained by the spectator is matched to the missing corner.

Having demonstrated by this apparently honest method that the card is the same one the spectator destroyed, the performer asks a lady if she would care to take the card home as a souvenir. She naturally answers in the negative. "It *is* rather soggy," replies the performer, "but that is easily remedied. Do you know how to launder cards? No? Well, I'll give you an idea of the process." The conjurer loads the wet card and the dry corner into his pistol, and fires at the candle. The restored card immediately appears in the place of the flame and is tendered to the lady as a souvenir of the performance.

This is one arrangement of the trick, which, of course, is

The Art of Magic

susceptible to many variations, and the student with any originality will introduce novelties of his own. In the present form, however, the trick has always caused unbounded amazement wherever performed. The idea of the card being introduced into the orange previous to the presentation of the trick never enters the minds of the spectators, and, therefore, they are astounded when it is discovered. Even if one of the more acute of the spectators suspects the preparation of the fruit, the torn corner method of identification, effectually disposes of that theory.

THE CARD IN THE FRAME.

One of the most effective of card-apparatus tricks is that of a chosen card appearing in a frame. Sundry frames for obtaining this effect are on the magical market, ranging from the cumbersome and suggestive picture frame supported on a brazen pillar and enclosing a background of black cloth whereon cards and sundry articles are made to appear, down to the simple glass mounted on a wire frame, on the cardboard mount of which a chosen card appears. The simplest of all frames was invented by Professor Field of Royal Aquarium celebrity. Its only drawback is that after placing the frame and cardboard mount together the frame cannot be shown empty, but has to be covered with a handkerchief. This defect is remedied in the frame about to be described, which is the most perfect apparatus of the kind ever devised. The performer who adds this piece of apparatus to his collection will never use any other card frame. The trick is equally good for stage or parlor.

EFFECT—A small frame is taken apart and shown to be devoid of any trickery, the parts being examined by the audience. It is then put together, and, after once more being shown empty, is wrapped in a piece of newspaper. A drawn card is torn into several pieces, one of which is retained, and the pieces are loaded into a pistol and fired at the frame. A spectator removes the newspaper covering, and the restored card is discovered inside the frame—that is to say, the card is restored with the exception of one corner. The frame is taken apart and the card handed to spectator, who, upon experimenting, discovers that the piece he retained exactly fits the mutilated corner.

TIME OCCUPIED—Five to seven minutes, according to amount of patter.

REQUISITES AND PREPARATION—An ordinary pack of cards; a conjuring pistol; two sheets of newspaper; and a card frame. This frame will need a detailed description. The frame proper is innocent of preparation and resembles the illustration, see Fig. 26. It is made of mahogany, or ebony, highly polished, though

Fig. 26.

of course any other wood will do equally as well. The most convenient size is about ten inches by seven. The frame itself is one inch wide and three quarters of an inch thick. The frame has a wooden back, kept in position by a tongue of wood turn-

The Art of Magic

ing on a pivot, after the manner of a photographic printing frame or the drawing slates of the top shop. The space behind the glass is filled by a sheet of white cardboard. The card to appear is at the outset stuck on the hinder side of the cardboard with a minute piece of conjuring wax, just as in Professor Field's trick. The frame, however, has an important addition. This is an oblong piece of thin copper of a size to fit loosely in the front of the frame. The two sides and one of the ends of the copper slab are turned slightly so as to hold a piece of glass backed with white paper so as to resemble the cardboard mount in the frame proper. By turning three sides only of the copper, feke the glass, should it be broken, may be easily removed, and another piece slipped in. The turned over pieces are japanned to match the wood of the frame and the back of the copper feke is painted black.

It is obvious that when this feke is fitted into the front of the frame the latter will appear empty. We advise the reader to have the inside of the frame beveled, in which case the edges of the feke will be invisible, seemingly forming a part of the beveled frame. The frame may be bought of any dealer in such materials, and any metal maker will turn out the copper feke in a few moments. A glazier will cut the requisite glasses for a few pennies.

The actual preparations are as follows: The various parts of the frame are on the table. As the top of the feke is the same color as the table top it will not be visible in an artificial light—that is to say, if the spectators are sitting at some distance from the table. In order that the trick may be performed without risk in a small room we have devised a better way of concealing the feke. The two sheets of newspaper are folded in four and placed over the feke. The frame is lying on the papers, the front of the frame being downward. The glass, the wooden back and the cardboard mount are also lying on the table in plain view of the audience. To the under side of the cardboard mount is affixed with a minute pellet of wax a duplicate of the card you intend to force—let us say the king of spades, as a black card shows up to better advantage in the frame. One corner of the card is missing, and this piece is concealed in some convenient pocket ready for use. A pack of cards, with a king of spades on top ready for forcing, and a conjurer's pistol complete the arrangement.

PRESENTATION OF TRICK—Call attention to the simplicity of the frame, carrying it among the spectators for examination. Returning to the table you remove the folded sheets of newspaper with the left hand, at the same instant placing the frame over the feke, which is now rendered absolutely invisible, even at a distance of two feet if the inside and rear of frame are painted black. The papers are unfolded and hung over a chair standing near the table. The most important part of the trick is now accomplished. You have, in the most natural manner in the world, succeeded in getting the feke into the frame. Now call attention to the glass, holding it up so that all may see through it, remarking, as "our Mr. Ellis Stanyon" would say, that you hope the audience will not see through the trick as easily as they see through the glass. Place the glass in the frame and casually pick up the cardboard mount. We say "casually," advisedly, for the reason that the performer must be as nonchalant with this article as he was with the glass. On the success of convincing your audience that there is nothing unusual about the cardboard mount depends the success or failure of the trick. On the hinder part of the cardboard, it will be remembered, is the card destined to appear in the frame, and consequently the mount is exhibited with the unprepared part toward the audience. It is held upright between the tips of the first and second fingers in front and the tip of the thumb behind. The arm is upright. The performer now lowers the arm vertically, apparently showing the opposite side of the cardboard. As a matter of fact, however, he at the same time gives the arm a half-turn, the second finger, moving behind the cardboard, taking the place of the thumb, which is now extended and takes no further part in the artifice. The effect on the spectators is that you have shown both sides of the cardboard, whereas in reality it is the same side of the card-

The Art of Magic

board which is again exhibited. At first thought the move may seem audacious, but it is perfectly practical and absolutely deceptive. Still holding the cardboard between the extended first and second fingers (the first finger on top and the second finger underneath) drop the cardboard mount on the glass in the frame. Now exhibit the back of the frame in exactly the same manner as you did the cardboard and going through the same movements as before only with this exception, that in this case you actually do exhibit the front and hinder part of the piece of board. As the hinder part has a "button," or cross-bar, the spectators, convinced that they have seen both sides, will have no suspicions concerning the cardboard. The back is put in its place and made secure.

Having assembled the frame the performer picks it up with the feke front in position and calls attention to the fact that the frame is unprepared, rapping with fingers or wand on the front (the glass part of the feke) to prove that everything is status quo. He may even go down among the audience to exhibit the frame, but in our opinion this is rather overdoing matters. Holding the frame in the left hand, the front toward audience the performer takes the two sheets of newspaper in the right hand. He now lays the frame face downward on the table, and holding a sheet of newspaper in the left hand and one in the right he shows both sides of each sheet. He then takes both sheets in the right hand. "I am going to wrap the frame in one of these papers," says the performer, and suiting the action to the word he picks up the frame with the left hand, leaving the feke on table, and at precisely the same moment drops both sheets of the paper over the feke. Without an instant's pause the frame is laid on the paper, is wrapped up in the top sheet, and handed to a spectator for safe keeping. The other sheet remains on the table concealing the feke. The performer should practice so as to perform these different moves without hesitation, as the subterfuge may be used to excellent advantage in many ways. The performer now proceeds to force the proper card. It is torn up, one piece retained (it is really the corner from the card in the frame that is handed to the spectator) and the other pieces are rammed into the pistol and fired at the frame. The spectator removes the newspaper, and the restored card is revealed between the glass and the cardboard mount. The performer assists the spectator to take the frame apart and removes the card from the mount himself. If the right amount of wax is used there will be no telltale smudge on either the card or the mount.

We have been somewhat prolix in describing this effect for the reason that it is one of the finest card tricks in which apparatus is used, and the apparatus is so simple that the amateur magician may readily have it constructed for an insignificant sum. It is by all odds the best frame trick ever invented, and the most ingenious apparatus of its kind since Bosco, or whoever it was, invented the sand frame. The trick combines just enough of the mechanical with the proper amount of sleight of hand to make an ideal conjuring trick, and we predict that once the reader has added this trick to his programme he will never discard it. The author wishes that he knew to a certainty who invented this frame; for it would be a source of gratification to give credit to the clever man who conceived the idea. All the author is reasonably certain of is that the frame came originally from England, and that it was introduced into this country by J. Warren Keene. In the original form a sheet of celluloid was used for the feke. This material may do tolerably well for the stage, where the spectators are at a goodly distance from the performer; but it is not satisfactory for the close quarters of the drawing room. The feke constructed of glass and copper is our own improvement, and has proved eminently satisfactory. For stage work a larger frame should be used and three cards made to appear instead of one. For drawing-room purposes one card is preferred; for without the torn corner method of identification the trick loses much of its effect.

The magician Hornman works the card and frame trick with a mirror instead of ordinary glass. A framed mirror, six by eight inches, is exhibited to the audience, back and front, the performer holding it so that the spectators may see the reflection of their faces. The frame is then placed on the table and covered with a handkerchief. A selected card is placed in a pistol and fired at the frame, and the handkerchief falling from the frame reveals the restored card.

The acute reader has already guessed that two mirrors are used. One is stationary in the frame, the other slides in a groove. The space between the two mirrors is about the thickness of a card. The card to appear is affixed by a dab of wax to the stationary mirror, and the other mirror is put in its place in front. The frame may be casually exhibited. In returning to the table the sliding mirror must be disposed of. One way is to drop it into a servante, in the act of covering the frame with a handkerchief; or a slit can be cut in the table through which the mirror may slide. Another way is to dispose of the mirror in a chair servante, doing away with the use of the table. In this method, which, in our opinion, is preferable, the covered frame may be stood upright against the back of the chair. The dropping of the handkerchief at the report of the pistol is accomplished by means of a silk thread to one end of which is a small hook — a bent pin will do the trick as well as anything. In the act of covering the frame the hook is engaged in the handkerchief. The assistant does the rest; or, if no assistant is convenient, the free end of the thread may be attached to the pistol, and in the act of firing the performer himself pulls the thread. We have given merely the skeleton of the trick. The performer, of course, will utilize the torn corner effect and invest the trick with appropriate patter.

THE VALLADON CARDS ON GLASS.

We give the above title to the following trick for the reason that it is generally associated with Mr. Valladon, although we are not aware that he is the inventor of the really excellent combination.

EFFECT — Three cards are drawn, replaced, and the pack shuffled. The pack is magnetized (in a Pickwickian sense, of course) and caused to adhere to a sheet of plate glass suspended

The Art of Magic

from a large metal stand. On a small table or tabouret in front of the hanging glass is a lighted candle. The performer offers a pistol to one of the audience and requests him to shoot at the pack on the glass. The spectator does so and the shot extinguishes the candle. The performer then fires at the candle and his shot relights it. He also fires at the pack on the glass, and at the report all the cards fall to the floor with the exception of the three drawn cards, which attach themselves to the glass in the manner depicted in Fig. 27.

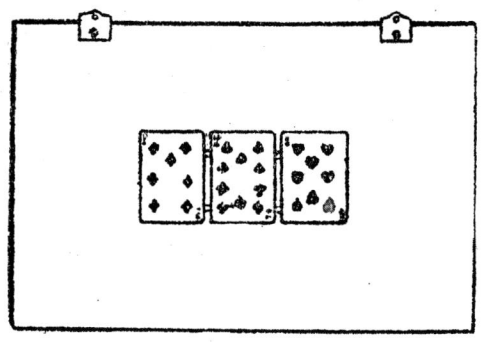

Fig. 27.

TIME OCCUPIED — Seven minutes.

REQUISITES AND PREPARATION — A sheet of plate glass and a framework from which it is suspended; a mechanical candlestick; a pistol; two packs of cards; a mechanical folding card, or rather three cards arranged so as to fold and expand at the option of the performer; and a peculiar "sucker" device. We shall describe each item separately.

As the plate glass and frame before us as we write were made for stage presentation we shall base our description on its dimensions, although the reader may have it constructed of any size he may desire. The frame, as shown in Fig. 28, is seven feet high (including bases) and three feet three inches wide. It is constructed of gas-pipe nickel plated, and each side is made of two rods, for convenience in packing. As a matter of fact, the whole frame work may be taken apart. From each corner of the

The Art of Magic

frame depends a stout chain twenty-six inches long. The sheet of plate glass, which hangs from these chains, is nineteen inches long by seventeen inches wide. Two nickel plated metal loops, two inches long, are riveted through the glass at the upper part, and it is into these loops that the hooks at the end of the chains are engaged. The frame and glass should stand at the rear of the stage, or room, so that the apparatus will be out of the way. The candle, extinguished or lighted at the desire of the performer, is not really a candle, but a miniature lamp concealed in

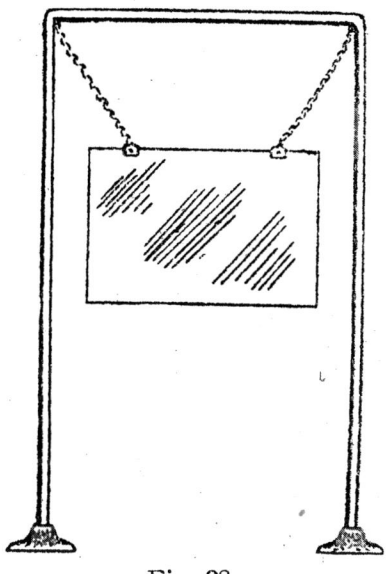

Fig. 28.

a metal tube japanned in imitation of the real article. This tube is screwed in the candlestick so as to form one continuous piece. The lamp arrangement inside is raised or lowered by means of a string in the hands of an assistant. The round wick of the lamp resembles the wick of a candle. The lamp is filled with a slow burning oil and the wick raised just sufficiently to give a small flame. When the spectator fires the pistol at the cards on the glass the assistant releases the string, which allows the flame to drop out of sight. By reversing the operation the candle is relighted. This is the only part of the apparatus that cannot be

The Art of Magic

made by the reader or under his supervision. The plate glass will be furnished by any dealer in such supplies, and he will drill the holes for the metal loops. The frame work will be made by any metal worker at slight expense. The trick, of course, may be presented without the obedient candle; but as this feature adds more or less comedy to the performance, the small investment will not be regretted.

The three cards that appear on the glass are specially prepared. Let us assume that these cards are the seven of diamonds, the ten of clubs and the eight of hearts. Each card is really of double thickness. That is to say, two cards are glued together. Between each double card is laid crosswise two strips of flat elastic each seven and a half inches long, or just a trifle longer than the width of the three cards, so that between each card there is about one-twelfth of an inch space. The construction of the cards is shown in Fig. 29. In the illustration the

Fig. 29.

space between the cards is made larger than it really is, in order to show the position of the elastic. The card glued on the rear of the seven of diamonds is face downward—that is to say, its face is on the back of the seven. The card on the back of the middle card, the ten of clubs, is arranged the same, but the opposite is true of the card glued on the rear of the eight of hearts. In

The Art of Magic

other words, these two cards are glued back to back. You now have three cards hinged together by two strips of flat elastic. A still further preparation of the center card, the ten of clubs, is necessary. Take a playing card (any one will do) and cut out a rectangular piece two inches long and a half an inch wide. Care should be exercised to remove this piece from the center of the card. The card so cut will look like Fig. 30. The card so

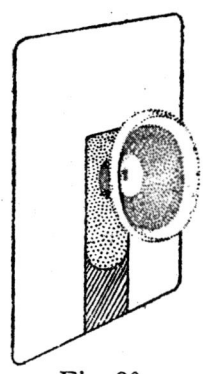

Fig. 30.

treated is now glued face downward to the back of the middle card. The lower part of the card—that is to say, the part below the slot, is glued entirely to the card; but the upper part, in which the slot is cut is glued around the edges only. Properly prepared the back of the middle card has a slot in which you can slide the piece of apparatus shown in Fig. 31. This is an ingen-

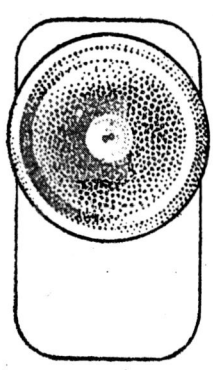

Fig. 31.

ious application of what is commonly known as the "sucker." The little hollow cone or rubber cup is an inch and one-eighth in diameter. The metal apex is brazed to a small piece of thin metal two inches long and an inch and one-quarter wide. The four corners of this small metal plate are rounded. The "sucker" is fastened to the plate about three-quarters of an inch from the top, as shown in the illustration. This apparatus slips readily into the slot arrangement on the hinder part of the three prepared cards. With the sucker in place fold the seven of diamonds onto the face of the ten of clubs and then fold the eight of hearts onto the front, when the reason for gluing the third double card back to back will be apparent, for the front of the folded cards will be a face card. Before folding the hinged cards, however, another piece of apparatus is necessary. This is illustrated in Fig. 32. It consists simply of a thin

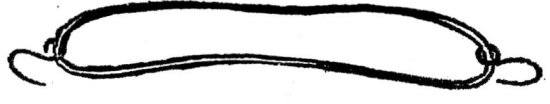

Fig. 32

rubber band, three inches long at the ends of which are two small hooks. These hooks are made of ordinary pins. File the head off a pin and with a pair of pincers bend the pin in the shape of Fig. 33, which is much larger than the hook actually is.

Fig. 33.

Before folding the cards engage one hook in the upper part of the outer side of the eight of hearts, see A in Fig. 29. The elastic is now stretched across the rear of the three cards and the other hook engaged at the outer edge of the seven of diamonds, see B in the same illustration. Now fold the seven of diamonds on middle card, and then the eight of hearts. The tension of the elastic will be so strong that you cannot release the grip of the fingers. On top of the packet of folded cards place an ordinary deck, of course, face upward, and over the bottom edge of the pack slip a little clip. This clip, see Fig. 34, is made of a strip

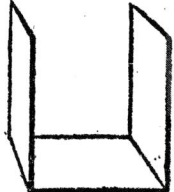

Fig. 34.

of thin brass a trifle less than an eighth of an inch in width and japanned white to match the white space in the front card of the pack, which should be an ace—clubs for preference. To this clip is attached a long thread that runs to the hand of an assistant. The lips of the rubber sucker are moistened with glycerine.

The prepared pack lies on the table behind some convenient object, say a handkerchief. The thread runs from the clip through a small screw-eye in the floor exactly beneath the center of the glass plate, and thence to the assistant. Allowance must be made for an adequate amount of slack. On the table is the conjurer's pistol and a pack of cards, with the three cards to be forced on top. If the student is not certain of his ability to force three cards, a forcing pack may be used. In front of the hanging glass is the table or tabouret on which the candle is burning.

PRESENTATION OF TRICK — Force three cards (in this case the eight of hearts, the ten of clubs and the seven of diamonds), have them replaced and the pack shuffled. Return to the table and lay the pack in front of the handkerchief. Pick up the pistol and hand it for examination. While the spectators are inspecting the weapon, return to the table and pick up the prepared pack, at the same time covering the other pack with handkerchief. Patter a little about the power of mesmerism, and pretend to mesmerize the cards. Press the pack firmly and steadily against the plate glass, where it will adhere, taking care that the slot in the hinder part of the folding card points downward, so that when the assistant pulls the clip off the folding card will not be moved. Ask for the name of the three selected cards, and announce that you will cause them to jump from the pack. Request a spectator to fire at the pack. He does so, and the candle is extinguished. In reality the assistant releases the tension on the string and the flame drops out of sight. Take the pistol and fire it yourself, when the candle is relighted. Fire again, this time aiming carefully at the plate glass. At the report the assistant pulls the thread attached to the clip; the clip falls with the loose cards to the floor; the folding card opens and the three chosen cards are revealed in a row on the glass. The effect is very pretty and mystifying. It is the tension of the elastic band that causes the opening of the cards, and this same tension keeps the cards pressed tightly against the glass. The elastic band would not perform this function, however, owing to the manner in which the cards are folded, were it not for the initial propulsion given by the elastic hinges.

CHAPTER XII

FANCY FLOURISHES WITH COINS, USEFUL SLEIGHTS, AND ADDITIONS TO THE MISER'S DREAM.

The author assumes that the reader is aquainted with the conventional sleights and passes applicable to coin tricks, such as are described in the standard works on conjuring, and also with the method of presenting the coin-catching deception known as "The Miser's Dream," as described by myself, the inventor, in "Modern Coin Manipulation." We cannot do a greater service to the reader than open this chapter with a description of one of the most illusive coin passes in the whole range of coin conjuring. We cannot claim that this pass is original, or even new; but it is not generally known to the profession. The sleight was a favorite of the late Harry Stork, and it is a specialty of an esteemed correspondent, Mr. T. J. Crawford. The salient feature of the pass is that the coin is vanished after it has been unmistakably placed in the palm of the hand in plain view of the spectators; and if the movements are once acquired it is not possible for the keenest observer, a close range, to locate the vanished coin.

The spectators see the coin beyond question placed in the palm of the left hand, but the fact that the tips of the first finger and thumb of the right hand never release the coin does not occur to them. The position in Fig. 35 shows the coin actually lying in the palm of the left hand. Now the fingers of the left hand begin to close upon the coin, and when they have curved just enough to hide the coin from view, the middle, third, and little fingers of the right hand extend into the palm under the curved fingers of the left hand as in Fig. 36. The right hand now moves away from the left, while left continues the closing process; and the coin, instead of being in the closed left hand, is still held between the tips of the first finger and thumb of the right hand, and concealed from the view of the audience by the three extended fingers. The deception is so complete that there

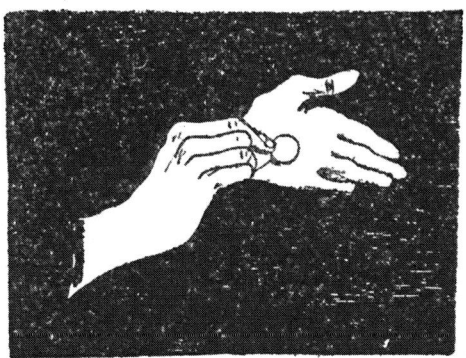

Fig. 35.

is never a doubt but that the coin was actually deposited in the left hand, which is now closed; and while all eyes are focussed upon this hand the three extended fingers of the right hand place the coin securely in the right palm, and the hand assumes a

Fig. 36.

natural position. The left hand is now slowly opened, the fingers carefully separated, and the coin is gone.

In the written description these various positions will seem separate and distinct, and difficult to accomplish; but with a certain amount of practice, they will very soon blend into a single movement; and no easier, simpler, or more deceptive method for vanishing a coin can be acquired.

"One of the features of this pass," writes Mr. Crawford, "is that it is not confined to a single coin. The limit depends entirely upon the performer's ability. I am able to palm twelve half dollars successfully; but half this number is always sufficient to fill an audience with amazement. The coins, of course, are vanished singly, being noiselessly placed in the palm of the right hand. After all have been singly vanished — the stack being in the palm of the right hand — both hands may be shown absolutely empty by executing the change-over palm.

THE HILLIARD PASS — This is an illusive pass and may be used to advantage in a series of fancy sleights with coins. The performer stands with his right side toward the audience, the right arm extended so that the hand, the palm, which is turned toward the audience, is on a level with the eyes. The fingers should be separated, and on the tip of the extended thumb is the coin about to be vanished. To accomplish this the fingers of the left hand encircle the thumb — the back of the hand toward the audience — as if to grasp the coin. The instant the left hand masks the thumb the coin is backpalmed between the first and second fingers. The left hand closes about the thumb, and is then drawn off the digit. The left hand is held closed as if containing the coin, and as the inside of the right hand is facing the audience the spectators can have no suspicion that the coin is not in the closed left hand. In the simple movement of turning over the right hand the coin is reversed palmed and produced at the performer's pleasure.

THE WRIST PALM — This is an exceedingly mystifying diversion with a coin. The performer places a half dollar in the palm of the right hand, see Fig. 37. The hand is held so that the palm is parallel with the floor. A spectator is asked to feel the coin. The movements are repeated, and when the spectator feels again in the performer's palm he is surprised to discover that the coin has disappeared. The performer slowly turns his

The Art of Magic

hand over, and the coin is revealed in the palm. A glance at Fig. 38 discloses the secret. When the conjurer repeats the

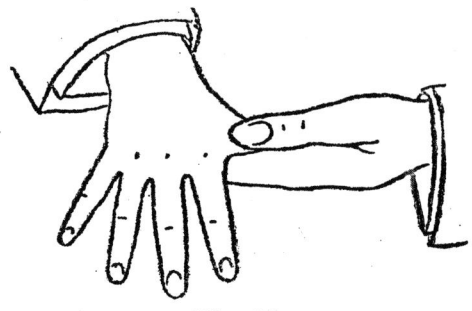

Fig. 37.

movement of putting the coin in the palm he really "palms" the coin on the wrist, as depicted in the illustration. The hand may then be held as shown in Fig. 37. In turning the hand over the coin is adroitly caught in the palm. At first the student may declare that the accomplishment of this sleight is an impossi-

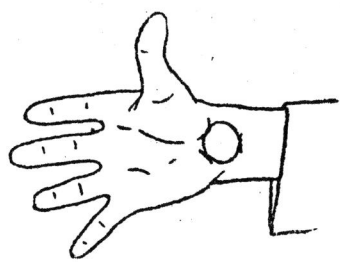

Fig. 38.

bility; but in this as well as all other branches of conjuring practice will achieve the desired result. For the encouragement of the student we may say that this trick is an especial favorite of Mr. Downs.

THE COIN ROLL — This effective and difficult flourish will be appreciated by the reader who makes a specialty of coin manipulation. In effect a coin rolls or travels around the hand, from finger to finger. At the outset the coin is held between the

The Art of Magic

thumb and the first finger near the base as depicted in Fig. 39. The coin is now allowed to fall over the top of the first finger and its opposite edge is caught between the first and second fingers at

Fig. 39.

their roots. The coin then falls over the second finger and is caught between the second and third fingers, as depicted in Fig. 40. The coin then rolls over the third finger and is caught

Fig. 40.

between the third and fourth fingers. The coin is then allowed to slide down between the third and fourth fingers until it hangs underneath the fingers as depicted in Fig. 41. For the sake of

Fig. 41.

The Art of Magic

clearly illustrating the movement the coin is depicted hanging between the third and little fingers. In actual practice, however, the tip of the thumb keeps the coin from falling to the floor. The coin is then carried by the thumb, underneath the hand, see Fig. 42, back to its original position, as depicted in Fig. 39, and

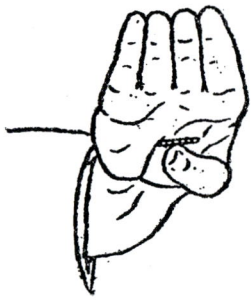

Fig. 42.

the rolling movement over the top of the fingers is repeated. At first these different movements will be slow and awkward, but as the student attains proficiency the coin will roll over the fingers rapidly and without a cessation of movement. The manipulation is beautiful and effective and is well worth the time spent in acquiring it. The illustrations depict the fingers of the right hand manipulating the coin, but there is no objection to the left hand being used if it comes more natural to the student. A few performers are skillful enough to execute this flourish with both hands simultaneously, and the two coins rolling in opposite directions has an effect that must be seen to be appreciated.

THE COIN THROUGH THE KNEE — The effect of this sleight or flourish is as follows: The performer exhibits a half dollar in the fingers of the right hand. Taking the coin in the left hand it is passed into the left knee; thence it passes down the performer's leg, and is reproduced from the bottom of the trousers. The manipulations are as follows: The coin is held between the thumb and second finger of the right hand, in the position for "le tourniquet" or the "French drop." The coin is apparently taken into the left hand and the left foot is placed on a chair. The right hand throws coin up the left trousers leg, and at the

The Art of Magic

same instant the fingers grasp the front of trousers, at the crease, and twist the cloth around the leg, so that the coin will not fall out. The right hand holds the trousers leg in this manner — which exactly resembles the fold of the trousers when wearing a bicycle trousers guard. The left hand, all this while, has been tightly closed above the left knee. The hand is now brought down upon the knee with a resounding slap, the performer loosens his grip on the trousers, and the coin falls to the floor. Neatly performed this will prove a very effective interlude.

THE TRAVELING COIN — This is a subtle and mysterious method of causing a coin apparently to travel invisibly from the right to the left hand. At the outset a coin is concealed in the right hand. Two coins are held in the left hand between the thumb and second fingers, in exactly the position for the "French drop." The right hand apparently takes one of the coins from the left fingers. In reality, however, the undermost coin is allowed to drop into the palm, or, better still, to the base of the left fingers, and the coin in the right hand is produced at the finger tips. The audience sees one coin held in the left hand — and one in the right hand. The coin in the right hand is vanished (by any palm the performer elects), and simultaneously the coin in the left fingers is allowed to drop upon the concealed coin. The audible click of the two coins adds materially to the effect of the illusion.

DOWNS'S LATEST METHOD FOR "THE MISER'S DREAM." This is an entirely new production of coins at the finger tips, and is one of the most puzzling and indetectable features of Mr. Downs's performance of "The Miser's Dream." The hand is shown empty, back and front, the fingers wide apart, and yet a dozen or more coins are produced, one at a time, or in a fan, at the finger tips.

At the outset a dozen coins are palmed in the edgewise manner described by Mr. Downs in his book on coin manipulation. The hand holding the coins — the right hand — is lowered, the stack is dropped to the third joints of the fingers, when it is crotched between the thumb and first fingers, as depicted in Fig.

43. Of course the hand is not held so that the coins are visible, as depicted in the illustration, which shows the exact method of holding the coins. In the actual presentation of the trick, the

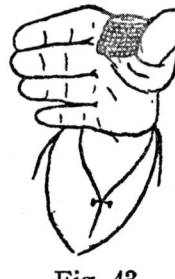

Fig. 43.

hand is held as in Fig. 44, the palm toward the audience. The hand may now be shown back and front and the fingers separated, without any risk of exposing the coins.

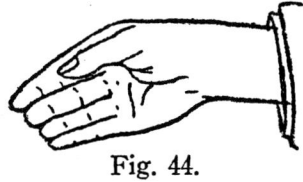

Fig. 44.

To produce the coins, one at a time, at the finger tips, the bottom coin is slipped out by the second finger, see Fig. 45, and is caught by the tips of the first finger and thumb as depicted in Fig. 46. It is then dropped into the hat. This method of pro-

Fig. 45.

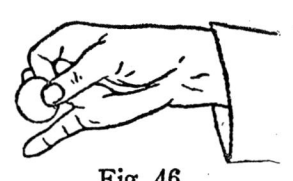

Fig. 46.

ducing coins is the most brilliant and bewildering of the many subtle moves in the act known as "The Miser's Dream."

CHAPTER XIII

COIN TRICKS WITH AND WITHOUT APPARATUS.

THE SYMPATHETIC COINS.

This is one of the finest coin tricks in existence, and as an impromptu or after dinner trick has no rival.

FIRST METHOD — This was one of Yank Hoe's specialties, and we shall describe the trick exactly as he performed it, afterward describing an alternative method of our own.

EFFECT — A borrowed handkerchief or napkin is spread over the table. Four half-dollars are laid on the handkerchief so as to form the corners of a square. Two of the coins are covered with small squares of paper. The four coins eventually come together under one of the papers.

TIME — About two minutes.

REQUISITES AND PREPARATION — A handkerchief or napkin; four half dollars (they may be borrowed and marked); and two squares of stiffish paper — the quality of paper used for magazine covers is the proper thickness. These squares should measure about four inches by four.

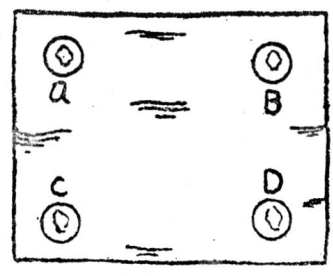

Fig. 47.

PRESENTATION OF TRICK — The four coins are placed on the handkerchief in the manner shown in Fig. 47.

A, B, C and D are the four coins. The effect of the trick will be enhanced if a handkerchief of dark color is used, as the

The Art of Magic

silver coins show up better by the contrast. The performer exhibits the two squares of paper, calling attention to the fact that the experiment is more in the nature of an optical illusion than a feat of magic. Of course, this is not so; but it is not wise to inform an audience in advance as to the exact nature of a trick. The successive covering of the coins, hereafter described, may be accounted for by means of patter based upon the science of optics. Standing behind the table and holding a square of paper in each hand, revealing the hand otherwise empty, the magician covers the coins marked A and B, covering A with the paper in the left hand and B with the paper in the right hand. Observing that by covering these two coins, the other two coins are visible, he quickly shifts papers so as to cover the coins C and D, observing at the same time that the two front coins are visible. He now covers C and B, calling attention to the fact that A and D are visible, and then quickly shifting the papers, covers A and D, the paper in left hand covering A and the paper in right hand covering D. Now while the left hand holds the paper over A, the right hand shifts paper from D to B, and while talking to, and looking straight at, the audience (asking them, for instance, if they can see the two rear coins) the fingers of the right hand (under cover of the paper) pick up coin B. This movement, it must be understood, is made without moving the paper, nor should there be the slightest visible movement of the right hand. The sleight will be facilitated if the right thumb presses down on the left edge of coin, which slightly tilts the right edge into the finger tips. The eyes of the performer, it is scarcely necessary to say, must never for an instant glance at the right hand during the picking up movement. Should the performer forget himself in this respect the audience will instantly suspect the removal of the coin.

Now comes the crucial move of the trick. It is not a difficult move, and, if made properly, the whole operation is covered. While the right hand holds coin B under the paper, the left hand removes paper from coin A, and holds it squarely in front of the right hand. Under cover of this paper, the right hand carries

The Art of Magic

paper and coin away, and as the right hand moves away, the paper in left hand is allowed to fall on table, where coin B is supposed to lie. The right hand moves over to the left side of the table, and in the act of covering coin A with paper, the coin in right hand is laid on table near A. Of course you must not let coin B clink against coin A in this operation. At this stage of the experiment, you have two coins under the paper at A, although your audience believe that there is one coin under each of the papers. It will be understood that all these moves are made quickly and to the accompaniment of lively patter.

Now for the second part of the trick. Grasp the lower left hand corner of the handkerchief with the left hand, the *fingers well underneath* and the *thumb above*. Take the coin C in the fingers of the right hand. Hold it up high, so that all may see that you actually hold a coin. The left hand lifts up the corner of the handkerchief and the right hand carries the coin under the handkerchief and apparently pushes it toward the front of the table until it is directly under the paper at A. A slight upward movement is made with the fingers of the right hand; there is an audible clink of two coins coming together; and removing his right hand from beneath the handkerchief, and showing it unmistakably empty, back and front, the performer daintily picks up paper at A, and exhibits the two coins. If these movements are made as described, and the clink of the coins is audible, the effect to the audience is that the coin really passed through the cloth. Of course, it did no such thing. As you passed the right hand under the handkerchief, you left the coin between the first and second fingers of the left hand. There must be no hesitation in the execution of this movement. The right hand must transfer the coin to the left without pausing the fraction of a second, the fingers of the right hand, held as though they contained the coin, pushing slowly forward until they are under the paper cover at A. Now, if an upward movement is made with the fingers, one of the coins will be thrown upon the other, causing the illusive clink.

The right hand is now withdrawn and lifts the paper cover.

The Art of Magic

At the same moment the left hand, holding the coin between the first and second fingers, releases the handkerchief and takes the paper cover from right hand. The coin is now concealed under the paper in the left hand, which replaces the paper cover over the two coins, being careful not to allow the coin to clink as it is released from the fingers. As there are three coins now under the paper at A, the process is repeated with coin D. When the paper in left hand is again placed over the coins at A, there are four coins under the cover, although the audience is convinced that there are only three. In order to pass the coin B (apparently) under the paper at A you must vary the procedure. Simply bend over and blow briskly under the paper at B. The effect is as if you blew the coin from B under the paper at A. Lift up this paper and exhibit the assembled coins.

SECOND METHOD — Invariably an encore is demanded when this trick is presented, and unlike most sleight-of-hand effects, the effect may be repeated before the same audience. As a matter of fact, its performance by means of the second method leaves the audience more mystified than ever.

In this method the magician uses five coins instead of four; but of course the audience is unaware of the existence of the extra coin. Conceal the fifth coin in left hand, and arrange the four coins as before. In laying the papers over A and B you do not take away B, as in the first method, but allow the extra coin in left hand to join the coin at A. The trick now proceeds as before, except after passing the last coin, B, under the handkerchief you must get rid of it in some manner. It is easy enough to slip the coin into the pocket while lifting up the paper at A, because all eyes are attracted to this part of the table. We have been at some pains to describe this trick in detail, because it is really worth the attention of the most fastidious sleight-of-hand artist. It is simple in theory, but the amateur will discover that it must be worked with a delicacy of touch and breezy patter, in which case the illusion produced is perfect. Don't be misled by the apparent simplicity of the trick and present it without the requisite amount of practice, or you will regret your temerity.

The Art of Magic

THE COIN THROUGH THE HAT.

Nothing could be simpler than this trick, but it seldom fails to produce unbounded astonishment.

EFFECT — A coin is placed on the performer's knee. He covers the coin with the crown of a borrowed derby. The coin disappears and is found to have passed through the crown into the hat.

TIME OCCUPIED — A minute.

REQUISITES AND PREPARATION — A borrowed coin — any denomination; a duplicate coin palmed in right hand; and a derby hat.

PRESENTATION OF TRICK — Borrow a derby and secretly insert palmed coin in rim. You are now able to show freely the inside of the hat and the hands back and front. In the act of sitting down the performer introduces the coin into the hat. He

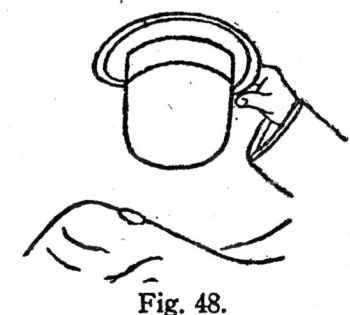
Fig. 48.

requests a spectator to place a coin on his knee, as illustrated in Fig. 48. He covers the coin with the hat for an instant, takes

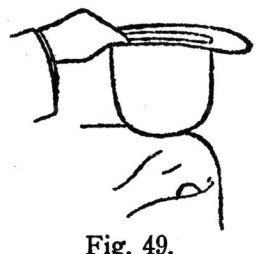
Fig. 49.

the hat away, and shows that the coin has vanished. He then produces the coin from the hat. As a matter of fact, the coin

The Art of Magic

merely slid into a fold made in the knee of the trousers. The illustration, Fig. 49, shows the kind of fold required.

THE EXPANSION OF TEXTURE.

This is a marvelously effective coin trick and calls for cleverness of manipulation and neatness of address. It is the invention of Jose Antenor de Gayo, Marquis de Orighuela, who is famous on the Continent as "L'Homme Masque," the "Masked Man," and of whom we have had occasion to speak before in this volume. He is the inventor of many subtle and bewildering tricks with coins, cards and other small objects, and "The Expansion of Texture" is his favorite experiment as well as his masterpiece. It is suitable for presentation anywhere — in the drawing room or on the stage.

EFFECT — Two marked half dollars and a handkerchief are borrowed from the audience. One of the coins is placed in the performer's pocket; the other is wrapped in the handkerchief by the spectator who volunteers to act as the conjurer's assistant. The handkerchief never leaves the assistant's hands; but nevertheless the coin is passed from the conjurer's pocket into the handkerchief, and eventually both coins are magically removed from the handkerchief.

TIME OCCUPIED — About five minutes.

REQUISITES AND PREPARATION — Two half dollars and a handkerchief, all of which are borrowed from the audience. No duplicate coins are used.

PRESENTATION OF TRICK — The conjurer borrows a handkerchief — as large a one as possible — and two half dollars — After the coins have been marked he hands the handkerchief and one of the half dollars to the volunteer assistant, the conjurer holding the other half dollar in his uplifted right hand, so that every one can see it.

When you are both standing on the stage, turn your face squarely to the audience, the assistant standing a little to your left. Show him the half dollar piece in your hand and ask him to remember the mark. Then remark: "I am going to put this piece in my pocket for a little while." Suiting the action to the words, thrust the hand containing the coin into the trousers pocket. The coin is not left in the pocket, however, but is palmed and the hand withdrawn. In order to hide the coin, pick up your wand, which should lie on a table or chair near by. From now on this stick will assist you in concealing the essential manipulations.

Wand in hand, advance toward the assistant and address him as follows: "Now, sir, with your own hands cover the coin with the handkerchief, so that the money will lie about in the center. Observe, please, ladies and gentlemen, that I have nothing to do with the operation. Now hold the covered coin between the thumb and finger tips of the right hand." The four ends of the handkerchief hang down, and you request the assistant to hold the ends together in his left hand, in order that there can be no deception or trickery on your part. When he has the four ends in his left hand, command him to let go with the right. When he has done so you remark: "As you see, we have a little pocket in which there is imprisoned a marked half dollar." While saying this strike the imprisoned coin with the wand, so that every one can hear the sound. Continue: "In order to be more secure, also hold the four ends with the other hand (the right hand, which is free)." When the assistant does this you strike the coin once more with the wand and take hold of it with the left hand, the thumb turned upwards. The wand is placed under the left arm. Push the coin towards the hand of the assistant, at the same time bringing the coin palmed in the right hand under the handkerchief in the exact position that the imprisoned coin occupied. This coin is now held by the fingers of left hand and the assistant and spectators will not dream but that it is the same one that was put in the handkerchief by the volunteer assistant. Strike the coin with the wand and call attention to the impossibility of any one tampering with the money while the representative of the audience holds the ends of the handkerchief in such a tight grip. Replace the wand under the left arm, and seize with the right

The Art of Magic

hand the coin that is actually inside the handkerchief, and ask the assistant to grasp with the left hand the coin that is apparently in the handkerchief but which in reality is concealed by a fold, directing him to hold it with the thumb on top and the fingers underneath.

You now address the assistant something as follows: "Well, sir, you are certain you have possession of the coin, are you not? Very good. You haven't had your hands off this handkerchief during the experiment, have you? I advise you to hold tight, however, for you can never tell what advantage I will take of you if you relax your vigilance even for an instant." Pass the right hand under the handkerchief, the palm upwards, and request the assistant to open his right hand so as to show the audience the interior of the handkerchief. As you help to open the handkerchief at the ends, throwing the ends over the assistant's hands, the first half dollar (the one the assistant wrapped in the handkerchief) drops into your hand and is palmed. The instant this is accomplished, take the wand in the right hand and strike the coin the assistant is holding, and then show very distinctly, one after the other, the four ends of the handkerchief. Neither the assistant nor anybody else will suspect, at this stage of the trick, that there has been any hanky-panky work. This demonstration over, allow the four ends of the handkerchief to hang down again, and request the assistant to assume his first position — that is to say, he holds the coin in the right hand and the four ends of the handkerchief in the left hand. You now take hold of the coin with your left hand, allowing the assistant to hold the ends of the handkerchief with both hands.

You are now master of the situation. The half dollar originally wrapped in the handkerchief is palmed in your right hand, and the coin apparently put in your pocket is on the outside of the handkerchief concealed by a single fold of the cloth. You strike this coin again with the wand and say: "Well, this is what I intend to do. I shall not only try to get this dollar out of the handkerchief, but I shall first command the coin which I

The Art of Magic

put in my pocket (pointing to pocket with wand) to leave the pocket and join the coin inside the handkerchief." You replace the wand under the left arm, thus bringing the right hand toward the left, which is holding the coin in the fold of the handkerchief. The palmed half dollar is now joined to this coin under the handkerchief. This delicate move is accomplished as follows: The coin under the handkerchief must lie on the three fingers viz., the middle finger, the ring finger and the little finger. The first finger bends a little backward and leans on the edge of the first coin. One edge of the second coin touches the first coin, and the opposite edge is held by the first finger. The two coins, of course, are covered by the handkerchief. The thumb, which is on top of all, holds everything securely.

You now pretend to remove the coin through the pocket. Apparently holding it in the closed right hand say: "One, two, three, pass!" at the same time draw away the first finger of the left hand and press with the thumb against the other fingers, and by this maneuver the two coins will come together with a loud click. The exact position of the fingers in executing this move is rather difficult to describe; but if the explanation is actually followed with coins and handkerchief, the reader will soon get the idea, which produces a complete illusion. Immediately the two coins come together — being careful to hold the handkerchief so that the pieces of silver cannot fall out — you enlarge the folds on top and shake the handkerchief so that everybody may hear the jingle of the two pieces.

Having effected this surprising result, you further address the audience: "Ladies and gentlemen, having passed one coin into the handkerchief, I shall attempt a still more difficult feat. I shall remove the two coins, one at a time, and you will observe with what delicacy the handkerchief will close its textures after the pieces have passed." You draw the first piece through the handkerchief fold, and hand it to the assistant to verify the mark. Then draw out the second piece, and also offer it for identification. Now, in order that nobody may get any clue to the modus operandi, open the folds of the handkerchief with

The Art of Magic

both hands — under the excuse of wanting to restore the texture — so that the handkerchief forms an empty bag. This done, you beg the gentleman who was so kind to asist you to open the handkerchief and examine the texture.

This experiment produces a wonderful effect, but the student must not attempt to produce it in public until he has mastered every detail and clothed every move in appropriate patter. Cleverly done, and with the proper address, there is not a coin trick that can surpass it. We have described the trick exactly as it is performed by its accomplished inventor; but, of course, it is susceptible to variation, and the student is advised to alter the trick to conform to his own personality, arrange his own patter, and compose a little plot to give verisimilitude to the experiment.

While on the subject of coins mysteriously passing through the meshes of a handkerchief, we may acquaint the reader with a particularly neat and effective method of apparently causing three or four coins to disappear. Spread a handkerchief over the palm of the left hand. Apparently place a coin in the center of the handkerchief, but really palming it in the right hand, the left hand closing as if it really contained the coin. Pick up second coin and apparently drop it in to the handkerchief, but in reality allow the palmed coin to drop upon the coin on the fingers, after which you repalm the two coins. If this sleight is properly executed the spectators will be convinced that the two coins are in the handkerchief in the closed left hand. Repeat the operation with a third and even a fourth coin. Then turn the left hand over, grasp the handkerchief with the hand in which the coins are palmed, shake handkerchief, allowing the coins in the hand to rattle. The coins are then vanished from the handkerchief and produced at the pleasure of the performer.

THE BEWITCHED NICKEL.

This is the fanciful title of a clever impromptu trick. The effect is as follows: The performer borrows a nickel and places it in the palm of the spectator's hand. The hand is then closed,

The Art of Magic

and upon being opened the nickel is discovered to have changed to a penny.

The only requisites for this trick are a nickel, a penny, a nerve and audacity. When the performer borrows the nickel he has the penny palmed in his right hand. A spectator is asked to hold out his right hand, palm upward. The performer places the nickel on the upturned palm. "Now, sir," says the conjurer, "I want to see how quickly you can close your hand. Ready, one, two, three!" At each count he lightly taps the spectator's palm with the finger tips of the right hand. At "three" the spectator closes his hand. "Oh, dear, not half quick enough," complains the conjurer. "Let us try again." This time the counting is a trifle more rapid. As the performer is about to say "three," he drops the penny from the right hand into the spectator's hand, as near to the root of the second and third fingers as possible, while at the word "three" the finger tips of the right hand tap the spectator's palm, which causes the nickel to fly into the conjurer's hand, where it is palmed. This time the spectator closes his hand very quickly, and the exchange of coins is not noted. He is accordingly very much surprised, upon opening his hand, to discover that he holds a penny instead of the nickel. This trick is simple in design, but demands neat execution, and the student will find that a good deal of practice is demanded before he is certain of executing the change in the desired manner. The main point to observe is that the penny in the performer's palm must be dropped a fraction of a second before the nickel is removed. It will be remembered that each time the conjurer counts he taps the spectator's palm. The exact time to drop the penny is the instant the hand is raised after striking the spectator's palm on the beat of "two." This trick is not new; but, so far as we are aware, this is the first time an explanation of it has appeared in print.

THE DISAPPEARING DOLLARS.

The effect of this trick is as follows: Four dollars, dropped by the audience into a small china vase, mysteriously disappear.

The Art of Magic

The vase is about eight or ten inches high, and has an opening large enough for a dollar piece to drop through, but too small to allow the hand to be inserted.

The conjurer asks four gentlemen each to drop a coin into the vase, which he holds at the upper end. Then he shakes the vase several times so that everybody can hear the coins rattle, "One, two, three." At the word "three" the coins disappear, and the vase is handed for examination.

The secret consists of a little black cloth bag, the opening of which is attached to a small wire ring. To this bag is fastened a black thread about 25 inches long. The other end of the thread is attached to the coat under the right arm. In the beginning this bag is concealed in the right palm — the hand that holds the vase. Invite several persons to try to put their hands into the vase. And in showing them that you cannot get your own hand through the opening drop the little bag into the vase, allowing it to slide to the bottom. The working of the trick will now be clear. The four dollars really fall into the bag. After shaking the vase several times, holding it at the upper part, extend the right arm. The thread becomes taut and pulls the bag of coins into the right hand. The bag is concealed in the hand and the vase handed out for examination. The coins may be reproduced at the option of the performer.

THE FREE AND UNLIMITED COINAGE OF SILVER.

This is the nonpareil of after-dinner tricks and smartly worked has a bewildering effect. Mr. Downs saw it performed by an itinerant conjurer in a Viennese cafe, and was so charmed that he purchased the secret, which is now given to the profession.

EFFECT — A half dollar is exhibited in the performer's hand. A spectator is asked to select one of the objects on a dinner table. The coin disappears and is found under the object selected. A number of objects on the table are lifted in turn, and under each one a coin is found.

TIME OCCUPIED — From three to six minutes.

The Art of Magic

REQUISITES AND PREPARATION — Four half dollars, three of which are palmed in the right hand at the beginning of the experiment.

PRESENTATION OF TRICK — The conjurer calls attention to three objects on the table, say a napkin, a salt cellar and a cruet. In handling the objects he slips a coin under each, a la the cups and balls. One of the three objects is selected, and the performer, holding a half dollar in the right hand, apparently takes it in the left hand, and, holding this hand above the article, commands the coin to pass under it. The left hand is shown empty, and the performer lifts up the article with the right hand, revealing the coin. He takes this coin in the left hand and in replacing the article the coin in the right hand is introduced underneath. In the same manner coins are found under the other two articles, and as there is always one coin palmed in the right hand the performer, by the mere act of lifting up any article on the table, for the ostensible purpose of showing that there is nothing under it, can introduce a coin under it by the mere act of replacing the article. The production of coins under six or seven articles will be sufficient.

COIN, GLASS AND CONE.

An admirable impromptu trick especially adapted to presentation at the dinner table. The effect is not new, but the author has added sundry original ideas that practically make a new trick out of an old one.

EFFECT — The performer shows an ordinary drinking glass — small size preferred. A piece of newspaper is compressed around the glass so as to form a cover. The performer borrows a half dollar or he may use a coin of his own. The coin is dropped on the table and covered with the glass. The glass is then covered with the papershape, and on top of this the performer places a plate. The plate is distinctly heard to click against the glass and the sound naturally convinces the spectators that the glass is still under the paper. The performer eventually removes the plate and strikes the paper shape a heavy blow. The paper is crushed to the table, and the glass has disappeared, to be reproduced elsewhere.

TIME OCCUPIED — Two or three minutes.

REQUISITES AND PREPARATION — A glass, a half dollar and a half sheet of newspaper. This newspaper is really double, and in the center, between the two sheets, is waxed the half dollar — an imitation coin will serve the purpose just as well as a genuine half dollar. When this paper is pressed over the glass, the coin is naturally on top. The reason for this will be explained later.

PRESENTATION OF TRICK — Borrow a half dollar. Place it on the table, in front of where you are sitting, and then cover the coin with the glass, mouth down. Cover the glass with the newspaper which you press on all sides so that the shape fits snugly over the glass. Lift glass and cover and call attention to the coin, which, you say, will be made to disappear and fly invisibly into a spectator's pocket. As you carefully replace the covered glass with the right hand, make a feint with the left, to give the impression that you have removed the coin. The spectators will immediately inform you that the coin is no longer under the glass. Feign embarrassment, and after a little acting, calculated to work the audience up to a pitch of excitement, raise the covered glass. The coin, of course, is still on the table, and all eyes are focused upon it. Taking advantage of this, the performer, holding the covered glass near the edge of the table, allows the glass to drop into his lap. He immediately places the paper shape over the coin, the audience, of course, entertaining no suspicion that the glass is not inside the paper cover. In order to make doubly sure on this point, we originated the little artifice of the coin waxed between the double sheet of paper. If this cover is made as described, the coin will be in the top of the shape. In placing the plate on the shape, a loud click will be made, and it is this sound that convinces the audience that the glass is under the cover. Consequently they are genuinely startled when the performer raises the plate and deliberately strikes the supposed tumbler a blow with his fist. The paper is crushed to the table, and the glass, which the audience expect to see splintered into a thousand pieces, has vanished. The performer may reproduce the glass from under the table, or from a pocket of a spectator, or from his own pocket. The most effective way, however, is to allow the glass to drop to the floor. If this movement is perfectly timed, the effect is that the glass is actually driven through the table. If this method is adopted, the glass should be allowed to slide down the performer's legs before dropping to the floor, so that there will be no danger of the glass being broken.

Another method of concluding the trick is by utilizing a very useful contrivance known as the "bag servante." This is a black bag, or cotton net, the opening of which is sewn to a strong wire ring about five inches in diameter. To this wire are fastened two stout black elastics, the other ends of which are sewn to the back of the performer's vest. When about to perform the trick the conjurer secretly pulls down the net and draws it through between his legs, preventing it from slipping back by holding it with his knees. The glass is dropped into this bag, and as the performer rises from his chair the bag and glass are drawn up behind his back under cover of the coat. This apparatus is very useful in many table tricks, where fruit, or tumblers, or any reasonably small objects are to be vanished. It is particularly effective in this trick, as the performer is enabled to rise from the chair before striking the blow, which action negatives any suspicion that he may have the glass in his lap or under the table. The performer can place his hand under his coat and apparently reproduce the glass from his pocket. Some performers palm the glass and reproduce it from a spectator's pocket. The borrowed coin remains under the crushed paper, and as it is not vanished, it can be returned to the owner, the performer explaining that he struck such a heavy blow that the glass vanished instead of the money. The crushed paper shape is crumpled together and twisted until the coin breaks through. The coin is palmed and the paper ball tossed carelessly on the table.

The Art of Magic

THE TRAINED HALF DOLLAR.

This is a rather novel adaptation of one of the oldest of coin tricks, yclept the "Animated Coin." The performer uses a folded newspaper, see Fig. 50, which is prepared as follows: Underneath the lower part (a) you glue a little pocket (b), also made of newspaper. This pocket should be large enough to hold a half dollar. The pocket opens to the right. In the pocket place a half dollar (c), to which is attached black silk thread (d), the other end of which is held by an assistant behind the scenes. Or, if no assistant be employed, the thread may be attached to the back of a chair standing near the table.

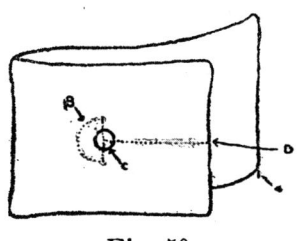

Fig. 50.

On the table stands a large glass. On the table near the glass is the prepared newspaper with a coin in the pocket. In presenting the trick, first draw attention to the glass, rattling the wand inside to prove that it is unprepared. Then exhibit the paper on both sides, turning it quickly so that the pocket will not be noticed. Now lay the paper over the glass, so that the pocket is directly over the opening of the glass. In order to make all secure you place a book over the paper.

The performer borrows a half dollar, has it marked, and apparently throws it at the glass. At the same moment, assistant pulls the thread, and the coin falls into the glass. As the audience both see and hear the coin fall, the effect is all that can be desired.

The coin now begins to dance in the glass, a la "Animated Coin," or it answers questions. In order that the thread may move freely, the performer pushes the book a little to the left

The assistant then manipulates the coin as the performer may dictate.

To conclude the trick, performer seizes the paper with his left hand, and with the fingers of the right hand clutches the rim of the glass. At the same moment the assistant pulls on the thread and the coin rises into the performer's fingers. The coin is now exchanged for the borrowed and marked coin, which is duly returned to its owner.

THE NEW FLYING COIN.

An effective impromptu trick, in which a half dollar passes invisibly into a handkerchief in a glass which is held by a spectator. On the performer's table is a half dollar and an ordinary glass tumbler. He has a duplicate half dollar palmed in right hand. Borrowing a handkerchief he shows it on both sides, taking care not to expose the palmed coin, and while carelessly rolling the silk into a small ball introduces the coin. The handkerchief is dropped into the glass and a spectator requested to hold the same. Picking up the half dollar the performer causes it to vanish by means of any of the numerous passes. Ask a person holding a glass to pull the handkerchief out slowly, and the half dollar will make its appearance.

THE COIN THROUGH THE HAT.

This is more in the nature of an interlude than a trick, but may be introduced to advantage during an experiment in which a silk hat is an accessory. Prepare a thin coin by gluing to one side of it a piece of black silk, such as is found on silk hats. When this is thoroughly dry, clip away the superfluous silk almost flush with the edge of the coin, leaving just enough margin to press down over the edge to conceal the rim. Now if this prepared coin be placed on the top of a silk hat it will be invisible at a short distance, as the black matches the silk of the hat. Take up an unprepared coin in the right hand and pretend to snap it through the top of the hat from the inside. This is done by snapping the finger against the inside crown of the hat

The Art of Magic

directly under the prepared coin. This will "flip" the coin into the air and cause it to turn over, showing the unprepared side. It is understood that the hat is held in one hand with its mouth turned straight down. In removing the prepared coin from the hat, exchange it for the unprepared one, which is still in the right hand.

THE TRANSMUTATION OF METAL.

This is a very old trick — at least the principle is ancient — but the following method of performing it is new. In its modern guise the trick is a favorite with such well-known performers as Mr. Leipzig and Nelson Downs.

EFFECT — Six copper coins (English halfpence) are stacked on the back of a spectator's hand. The coins are covered with a small paper cone. The cone is removed and the six copper coins have changed mysteriously into a like number of silver dimes.

TIME OCCUPIED — About two minutes.

REQUISITES AND PREPARATION — The principal apparatus consists of a half dozen halfpence fastened together by a rivet running through the whole thickness of the pile. The centers of five of the coins are drilled out to within about an eighth of an inch from their edges, leaving a mere rim of metal. The top penny is intact. When this prepared stack is placed on a table or on the hand, with the complete coin upwards, it has all the appearance of a pile of ordinary halfpence, the slight lateral play allowed by the rivet aiding the illusion. Some manufacturers use two rivets in joining the coins, but as this arrangement does not admit of the lateral movement, we advise the reader to use the kind we have described. The cut out portion of the stack should be large enough to conceal six dimes. You must also have a paper cone to fit over the prepared stack and six unprepared halfpence. The paper cone is two inches and a half long and one inch wide at the base. In order not to have to make a new cone every time you present the trick, instruct a wood worker to turn out a solid wooden cone of the exact size required, and keep the paper cone on this wooden shape. Thus

The Art of Magic

you can always carry the cone and pence in your pocket, prepared to present the trick at any moment.

The actual preparation of the trick is as follows: The paper cone on the wooden shape is in the right coat pocket, and the prepared stack of halfpence, with the six dimes inside, are either in the vest pocket on the left side or in the left trousers pocket.

PRESENTATION OF TRICK—You begin by drawing attention to the six unprepared halfpence, and while the spectators are inspecting the coins you take the opportunity to get the prepared stack in the left hand, where it is concealed between the first and third phalanges of the second and third fingers. Taking the unprepared coins in the right hand you pretend (Pass 6, "Modern Magic," Page 151, or the Downs Click Pass. "Modern Coin Manipulation," page 73, are the best for the purpose) to transfer them to the left hand. The fingers of the left hand make a movement as if reducing the coins to nothingness, while the right hand goes into the right coat pocket, leaves the coins there, and brings out the paper tube. At this point you pretend to overhear some one saying that the coins are not in the left hand. "What's that, sir?" you ask. "Not in my left hand? Oh, really now, I wouldn't deceive you in such a bold manner. Yes, they are really there." You open the hand, and exhibit the stack of coins, and owing to the lateral play allowed by the rivet, the stack exactly resembles the pile of separate coins. Continue: "Since you are so suspicious, I will perform the trick in a different manner. I will let you hold the coins yourselves." Request a spectator to hold out his hand, palm downward. Stacking the prepared coins with the right hand you place them carefully in the volunteer assistant's hand, guarding against a premature appearance of the ten-cent pieces. Now place the paper cover over the coins. Saying, "One, two, three! Pass!" you remove the cover, squeezing with the fingers and thumb so as to lift up the hollow pile with it, disclosing the dimes. The paper cap is jerked carelessly forward in the direction of the audience, or simply dropped to the floor, the prepared coins falling into the curved fingers of the right hand; and while everyone's attention is concentrated on the dimes, the stack is dropped into a convenient pocket. Presented in this manner, the ancient trick of the cap and pence is worthy of the attention of the most fastidious performer.

SUBTRACTION OF MONEY.

This idea may be used to advantage in the well-known trick entitled "The Multiplication of Money." After the coins have passed into the hands of a spectator, he is requested to count them openly and carefully into your right hand. After he has done this you pour them back into his hand, showing your own empty. You then request him to close his hand and hold it "high up." Stepping back a few paces you command one of the coins to leave his hand and fly to you, immediately showing a coin at right finger tips. The spectator counts his coins and finds them one short.

This clever trick, one of Mr. Hardin's novelties, is based upon the backhand palm. While the spectator is counting the coins into your outstretched righthand you secretly push one coin down with the thumb between the second and third fingers, backpalming it by the edge. You apparently pour all the coins back into the assistant's hand. However, you have one of the coins backpalmed, and this is the one produced at the finger tips in the manner described.

EVERY MAN HIS OWN MINT.

This effective trick is also essentially an impromptu feat. You roll up your sleeves and exhibit a half-dollar on the extended left hand. You offer your right hand for examination to prove that you have absolutely nothing in it. Now you pick up with the right hand the coin which is in your left, immediately closing the left. Next, you put the coin in your outside coat pocket. Then you open the left hand and another coin appears on the palm as if by magic. You take this coin also with the right hand and put it in the pocket, again closing the left hand. Upon opening it another coin appears. You repeat this many times.

The Art of Magic

Finally you ask some one to take the coins from the pocket, but upon examination the pocket is found to be quite empty.

This trick demands more or less skill. When you come forward the left hand is open, holding the coin on the palm Between the second and third fingers of the same hand is another coin backpalmed by the edge. After the right hand has been examined, you pick up the coin from the left and hold it up a moment in the right as if to exhibit it more fully. Then you place it back again. In doing this you carry off in the right hand the second coin from the back of the left hand, and palm it. Now you pick up the first coin again, but in the act of doing so you drop the palmed coin into the left hand, at once closing it. The right hand openly puts the coin into the right outside coat pocket, immediately palming it, and bringing out the hand apparently empty. Now upon opening the left hand the other coin is discovered. You keep on repeating these movements many times, finally taking the coin from left hand *without leaving* the palmed right-hand coin. You pretend to put this coin into the pocket, really palming it in addition to the one you already have concealed in the right hand; and bringing out the hand you invite anyone to take the coins from the pocket. Of course they find it empty.

NEW COIN CATCHING.

Attach a coin to a piece of fine black silk thread, the free end of which tie to your lowest vest button. Produce the coin at the finger tips and drop it into a metal tumbler held in the left hand. Show your right hand unmistakably empty and pass it quickly over the tumbler so that the thread comes between the forefinger and the thumb and the coin rises to your palm ready for the next production. The movement must be executed with lightning-like rapidity, and the thread must be sufficiently strong.

A NEW COIN COMBINATION.

This effective coin trick is contributed by a valued correspondent, Yogi B. Girindrashekhar, of Calcutta, India, a Hindu

The Art of Magic

magician of originality and skill, who performs modern tricks with coins and cards and kindred objects instead of causing assistants to vanish into thin air or commanding mango trees to shoot up into ambient space. "In connection with this trick," writes the Yogi, "let me describe an entirely original method of substituting a coin or coins. The coin to be substituted is placed in the palm of the left hand, near the root of the middle finger, in full view of the audience. The other coin is held in the right hand, palmed in the ordinary way. After making any suitable remark, pass the right hand over the coin. As the palms cross each other, drop the substitute in the palm of the left hand and in its place carry away the original coin. The effect to the eyes of the audience is that you have simply passed your hand over the coin. Indeed, this change is so much illusive that I have used it with great success in carrying out a number of successive changes, from a pice to a rupee, thento an ivory ball, and so on, the last change being from a porcelain cat to a live mouse, the articles named being palmed and pocketed during the time the attention of the audience is engaged in the change that has just been accomplished."

Now for the trick, which is a novel adaptation of an old coin effect that in its day was a decided favorite. The performer borrows a number of coins (from fifteen to twenty) in a hat, the mouth of which is covered with a handkerchief. A gentleman is asked to take out any coin, mark it and return it to the hat, which is then well shaken, in order that the coins may be thoroughly mixed up. The performer now dips his hand into the hat and takes out a coin, which is not likely to be the chosen one. It is placed inside a handkerchief and the gentleman is requested to hold the same. Another gentleman is now asked to remove the marked coin from the hat, and after he has done so the performer places the coin in the palm of the left hand and commands it to change place with the unmarked coin inside the handkerchief. The command is instantly obeyed.

The secret is simple. After the coin has been taken from the hat and marked, the magician requests the spectator to hold it as tightly as possible, in order that "the radio-active principle may not escape," but in reality that it may become heated to the body temperature. When the coin is returned to the hat the performer rapidly locates it by the sense of touch, as it remains considerably warmer than the other coins. The magician, while mixing the coins, palms the heated one, and at the same time produces an unmarked coin, which, however, he changes for the marked coin while placing it inside the handkerchief. The marked coin which the other gentleman removes from the hat was secretly dropped in by the performer. The conclusion of the trick will not require any explanation.

THE DOWNS COIN WAND.

This is a wand of polished brass tubing, one-quarter inch in diameter, and about eighteen inches long — some performers may prefer a wand either shorter or longer than the size given, but eighteen inches is the most practical size for the drawing-room. On the stage Mr. Downs uses a wand almost thirty inches long. A glance at Fig. 51 will give a general idea of the appearance of the wand. A is the brass tubing, one end of which is threaded to receive a small knob, C, which gives a finished appearance to the apparatus. The other end of the tube is split in four places, D, each slit about three-quarters of an inch long. These four pieces are bent in so as to form a spring clip, which prevents coins, cards, or other articles coming off until the performer wishes. The articles to be produced are prepared by putting in a pin, E, of smaller gauge than the slot in the wand, about one-quarter of an inch long and with a head larger than the slot. A coin prepared with pin is shown in Fig. 52. The articles to be produced are put on the knob end of the wand, at C, after which the knob is screwed on. In the case of coins, a number can be loaded on before the performer introduces the wand to the audience. To produce a coin (or any other article) at tip of wand, lower the end D, at the same time releasing the coin from the hand that holds the knob end of the wand, thus causing it to slide down, the pin traveling freely in the slot, until it is clutched

The Art of Magic

by the spring D, which now allows the wand to be raised at any angle with the coin attached. The movement of the coin down

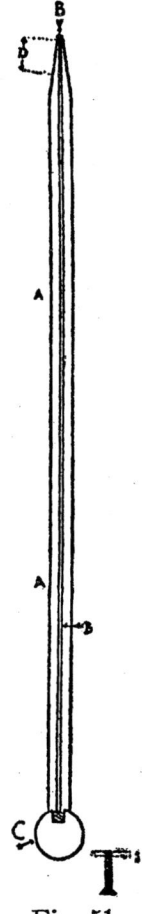

Fig. 51.

the wand is quite invisible, especially if, after the coin is released from the right hand, the wand is raised with a quick upward

Fig. 52.

jerk, the effect being that a coin is actually plucked out of the air by the tip of the wand. If the performer wishes, the knob C may be removed and the wand used as follows: After showing both hands empty, the performer procures by the ordinary means known to conjurers (from back or front palm, vest, pochettes, etc.), his load, and while drawing the attention of the audience to the "unpreparedness" of the wand (the slot B being invisible at a short distance), the prepared article is slipped upon the wand at the open end, which is covered by the performer's palm. Billiard balls, imitation eggs, oranges, lemons or other small articles, if prepared with pins as described, may be produced at the tip of the wand; but the most appropriate use for the wand is in the act known as "The Miser's Dream" (see Mr. Downs's "Modern Coin Manipulation"). The effect of this act will be enhanced by catching two or three coins at the tip of the wand, actually taking them off and tossing them into the hat, which, for the time being, is resting crown up on the table. We may mention in conclusion that this wand is patented in Great Britain, the patent number being 11,901.

THE NEW COIN WAND.

This is an adaptation of the Downs coin wand and is a decided novelty. It is a solid nickeled wand, very slender, about twenty-four inches long, and it may be offered freely for examination. Receiving it back, the performer waves it in the air, and a half dollar, or other silver coin, appears mysteriously at the tip. The coin thus produced is visibly taken off the end and dropped into a hat — if the performer is working the money-catching trick.

The wand is innocent of preparation or mechanism, save for a slight — almost unnoticeable — bulge at one end. The secret is in the coin. Instead of a pin, as in the Downs wand, a small ring is soldered to the center of the coin. This ring is just large enough to travel freely on the wand. In actual practice the wand is worked exactly as with the Downs wand. The coin is dropped from the right hand, an upward sweep of the wand

The Art of Magic

producing it at the very tip, where the slight bulge prevents the coin from flying off the end. This bulge, however, is not pronounced enough to prevent the performer readily taking the coin off. This wand is really a most ingenious piece of apparatus, and owing to the fact that it can be rigorously examined is preferable to the Downs wand for parlor use. The latter apparatus is more effective on the stage, however, for the reason that the pin is soldered near the rim of the coin, which allows it to poise at the very tip of the pointed wand, an effect that cannot be obtained with the wand just described.

A NEW COIN SPIDER.

This spider was invented to enable the performer not only to show both back and front of the hand empty, but also to open the fingers while the palm is toward the audience. It is undoubtedly the nearest approach to perfection to which the spider idea has been brought. Fig. 53 shows the back of the hand with

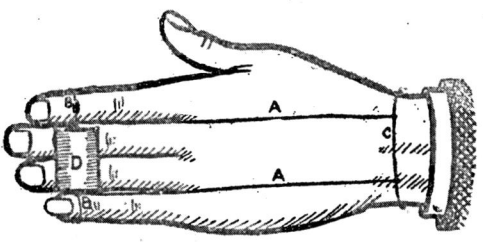

Fig. 53.

the apparatus attached. AA are two very fine wires affixed to the first and fourth fingers by the fine wire rings B B. The other ends of the wire are fastened to another wire encircling the wrist, C, with a little catch. D is an ordinary coin holder arranged to hold a dozen coins, which is attached to the wires by two minute rings. From the position depicted in the first illustration, it will be evident that the holder can easily be transferred to the front of the hand in the ordinary way, and the back of the hand shown to be empty. It will be equally clear that if reversed again the palm can be exhibited. If the hand be held in a somewhat upright position, the coin holder will slide of its own accord along the wires to the point C, thus enabling the performer to open his fingers as shown in Fig. 54. When requir-

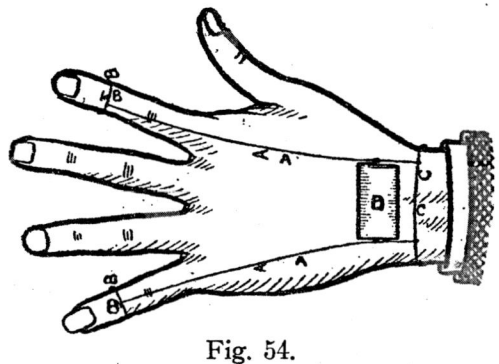

Fig. 54.

ing the coins, the fingers are closed and the holder is allowed to slide back to the finger tips, from whence they can be produced at will. If desired, the wires can be painted flesh color; but this is really quite immaterial, as they cannot be seen at a distance of a few feet. The holder, of course, must be painted the same color as the hand.

CHAPTER XIV

A COIN ACT AND A COIN LADDER.

The following description of methods and apparatus, embraces nothing particularly new, but rather a combination of several good things and improvements upon several heretofore weak points of construction and operation. For the material used in this chapter the readers are indebted to Mr. Carl Anderson, a clever and original magician.

EFFECT—A hat is borrowed and placed on the table, opening toward the audience. The performer rolls up both sleeves and, showing both hands actually empty, picks up the hat, turns out the sweat band and proves the hat to be without preparation.

Holding the hat in the left hand, he reaches into the air and catches, one at a time, twenty coins, dropping them into the hat, after which he again shows both hands empty, and pours out all the coins onto the table. He now picks up one or more coins and after several passes, places them back with the other coins on the table.

Picking up the hat with the left hand and holding it under the front edge of the table, he tilts the table forward when the coins are seen and heard to fall into the hat.

Standing on his center table or on the floor, is a coin easel as shown in Fig. 55. In appearance this easel consists of a black stick with two rows of brass-headed tacks driven part way in; supporting it on each side are legs of brass tubing, and at the back is a third leg. The top is a circular piece of board from which depends a heavy gold fringe.

Placing the hat containing the coins upon the lower end of the black stick, the performer steps away from the coin easel, and, clapping his hands, commands the coins to leave the hat, which they do, travelling tick-tack, tick-tack downward between

The Art of Magic

the brass tacks and into the glass. After a dozen or so coins have fallen into the glass, the performer again claps his hands, calling the coins to "hurry up." They immediately respond and travel down the easel at an accelerated speed.

When the last coin has fallen into the glass, the performer picks up the hat, turns it over, thereby showing it to be empty; and returns it to the owner.

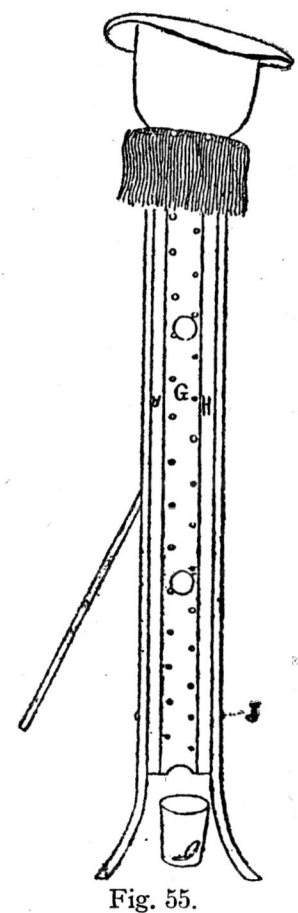

Fig. 55.

Before the construction of any of this apparatus is undertaken, the size and kind of coins to be used should be decided upon. The T. Nelson Downs palming coins, will be found satisfactory. As the edge is higher than the center they stack evenly. They also have a permanent glitter.

The Art of Magic

THE COIN DROPPER.

The coin dropper, shown in Fig. 56, consists of a piece of brass tubing, the inside diameter of which is slightly larger than the coins, allowing them to work up and down without binding. The length of the dropper should be about an inch less than

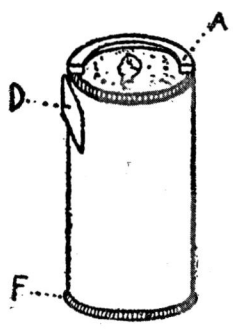

Fig. 56.

the breadth of the palm. Inside one end of the tube a thread is cut, into which is screwed a solid brass cap, with a shoulder, the outer edge of which is milled. One-half the circumference of the other end of the tube is fitted with a semi-circular piece of brass (A) about one-eighth of an inch across its face and one thirty-second of an inch deep; this should be fastened in place by "sweating" so as to leave the inside of the tube smooth. The remaining half of the circumference is now filed down below the under edge of A to a depth equal to one and one-half times the thickness of a coin. Inside the tube is a spiral spring similar to the one shown in Fig. 63 (b), but in length when expanded, the same as the outside measurement of the coin dropper.

To one end of the spring a brass disc the size of a coin is soldered. With the spring and disc in place, the pressure of the spring holds the disc against the under side of A, in Fig. 57, and when a coin or coins are placed between the top of the disc and the under side of A the top coin is held firmly in place, and cannot drop out until forced by the tip of the first finger.

The Art of Magic

Fastened to the outside of the tube at right angles to the open side of and a little below A is a piece of brass (D) one-half by one and one-quarter inches.

In operation the coin dropper is filled with coins, and thumb-palmed in the right hand by grasping the milled edge (F) in the crotch of the thumb and the hand. As the borrowed hat is passed up it is received sideways, crown downward, and the coin holder placed between the hat crown and the inside edge of the brim, the milled edge holding it in place.

That hat is now placed upon the table, and the sleeves rolled up, after which the hands are shown empty and the hat picked up with the right hand, the left hand, which holds the coin dropper, coming up under the side farthest from the audience. Removing the coin dropper and giving the hat a quarter turn brings the apparatus inside the hat, where it is easily turned so that the plate (D) rests against the sweat band. The position of the dropper is horizontal; the little finger is placed across the end of the cap (F); the second and third fingers are around the dropper; and the thumb is outside the hat, thus leaving the first finger in position to push the top coin downward and out of the dropper, allowing it to fall into the hat. The coil spring immediately pushes the next coin into position, and the move is repeated.

For those who are particular in regard to details Mr. Anderson suggests the following slight improvement to the dropper: Cement to the inside surface of the cap (F) a piece of rubber on which the lower end of the spring will rest. This will prevent it "talking." The outer face of the brass disc on which the coins rest is also covered in the same way, but in this case the diameter of the rubber should be less than the disc, so as to prevent any binding on the inside of the tube. In the next chapter will be described the only practical and satisfactory method of applying rubber to metal surfaces.

The various moves for catching the coins and apparently dropping them into the hat are so fully covered in "Modern Coin Manipulation," as well as in other treatises on magic, that

The Art of Magic

we shall not take up the space to describe this part of the act in detail. The construction of the apparatus is what mostly concerns the reader. The first piece is

THE TABLE.

The small side table or stand upon which the coins are turned out of the hat, is the well known "well top," around which a drape about eight inches deep is hung, Fig. 57. The

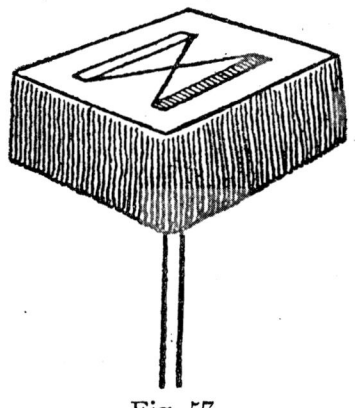

Fig. 57.

table top is about thirteen by fifteen inches and three-quarters of an inch thick. One inch from the edge of a long side a slot is cut three inches long and one and one-half inches wide. The top is covered with black felt which is cut and turned in around the "well." This "well" is concealed by an inlaid design. The shaded portion of the design in Fig. 57 shows the "well."

Standing at the side of the table, the performer grasps the rear edge with the right hand, at the same time placing the hat against the front edge. By tilting the table forward the coins slide into the "well," although the spectators imagine the money falls into the hat.

THE COIN EASEL.

This apparatus, illustrated in Fig. 55, consists of a black stick thirty-one inches long by three inches wide and seven-eighths of an inch thick. The face (G) is two and one-quarter inches wide and the balance of the width is equally divided and beveled at the edges (H-H). Two rows of brass-headed tacks are driven part way into the stick, the rows being two and one-

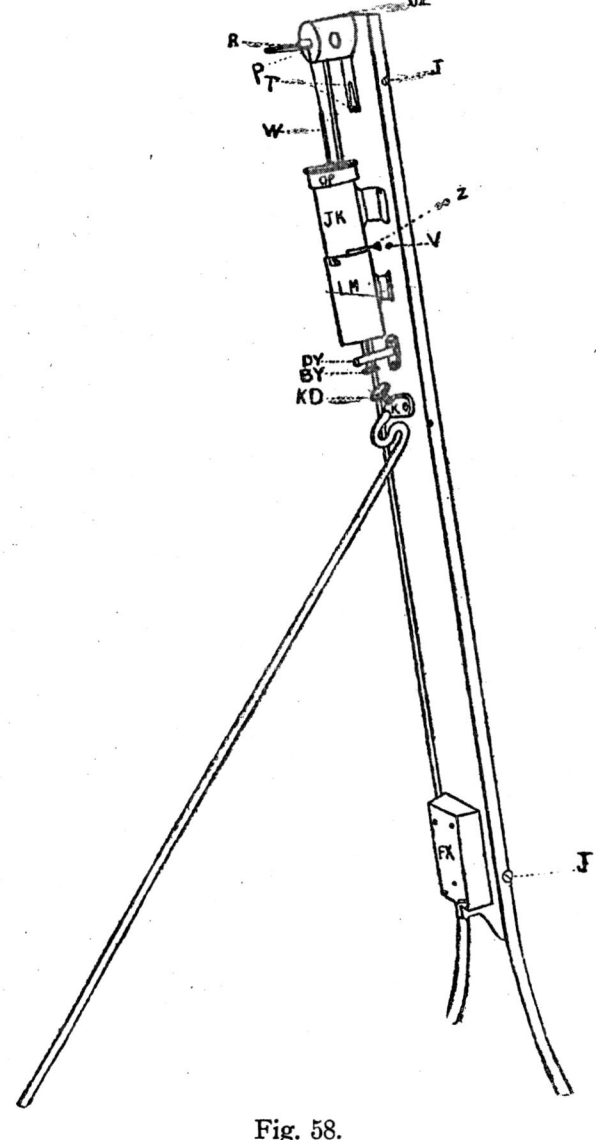

Fig. 58.

quarter inches apart and each tack separated from the other by two and one-quarter inches. The tacks in the two rows are not set opposite each other, but alternately, as shown in Fig. 55.

The Art of Magic

At each side of the stick is a piece of brass tubing made fast by screws at (J-J). At the back is a third leg of one-quarter inch steel rod fitted into a socket as shown at (K) in Fig. 58. The rod is made fast by a thumb screw (KD). The angle at which the easel stands is, of course, determined by the length of the third leg. The proper angle for the easel is twenty degrees from the perpendicular.

The top, shown inverted in Fig. 59, is five inches in diameter and one-half inch thick, made of soft wood, into which two pegs

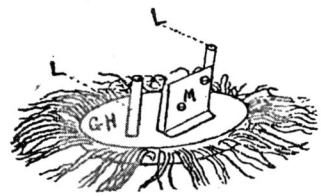

Fig. 59.

go inside the tubing which form the legs, thus holding the top in place.

Between the pegs, a peculiar shaped piece of tin (M), is fastened; to this tin, two brass tacks are soldered, in the correct position to bring them in line with the rows on the stick. The purpose of this tin mask will appear later on.

The coin holder (O), referring again to Fig. 58, is a piece of brass tubing, two inches long and of the same diameter as the coin dropper illustrated in Fig. 56. One end of this tube is closed with a brass plate, in the center of which is set a brass collar (P) through which the rod (R) works; on the end of the rod, inside the tube, is a disc slightly smaller than the coin, as illustrated at (AB) in Fig. 60. When the tube is loaded with coins and the rod and disc (R) and (AB) are moved forward the coins are forced out, *one at a time*. A brass plate (CD) one-half by two and one-half inches, is soldered to the tube near the open end.

On the side opposite the plate (CD) an inverted "L" shaped piece is fastened (EF) in which a "V" shaped slot is cut; the distance between the face of (EF) and the mouth of the tube should be one-sixteenth inch greater than the thickness of the stick (G) in Fig. 55.

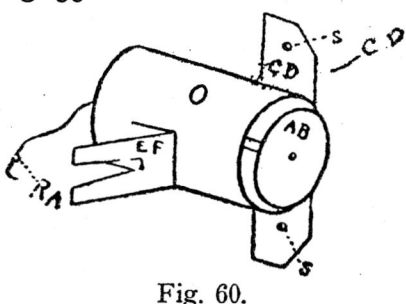

Fig. 60.

At the top of the stick, or face of easel, an "U" shaped cut is made, in which the dropper (O) fits, see Fig. 58; and at each side of this opening, and on the top edge of the stick, a brass nail (UZ) is driven and the head filed off, leaving the nails one-quarter inch above the surface. Near each end of the brass plate (CD), Fig. 60, two holes (S-S) are drilled to receive these nails, while on the back of the stick, see Fig. 58, near the top, is a large and a small round-head screw (T). These screws engage the "V" shaped slot in (EF), Fig. 60, which, with the nails at (UZ), see Fig. 58, keep the holder firmly in place; but like the rest of this apparatus, is instantly removable *for* packing without the use of any tool.

With the coin holder loaded and in position the top, Fig. 59, is put on, the piece of tin (M) masking the mouth of the coin dropper, but not resting on it, as one-fourth inch of each side of the plate (M) is turned at right angles, thus forming a chute down which the coins fall on to the tacks, after leaving the dropper, the fringe partially hiding them until they are fairly started on their zigzag journey. This gives a perfect illusion of the coins falling through the bottom of the hat and traveling down the easel.

We now come to the most interesting portion of the apparatus. The motive power of the coin dropper, Fig. 58 (JK), is a tube filled with fine dry sand, which is allowed to escape into

The Art of Magic

the cup (LM) through a slot in the bottom of (JK) controlled by the lever (Z). Through the cap (OP) a rod (W) projects; and fastened to the end of this rod inside the tube is a disc, as illustrated at (RS) in Fig. 63. Between this disc and the inside of the cap (OP), in Fig. 58, a coil spring (B), Fig. 63, is compressed and held until the cap is fastened in place. The disc prevents the spring forcing its way into the sand; but as the sand runs down, the spring slowly expands forcing the disc (RS), Fig. 63, downward, thereby drawing with it the rod (W). This rod in the motor is connected with the rod (R) of the coin holder, see Fig. 58, by a piece of black fish line and small hook (RA), see Fig. 60, running through the eye at (P), in Fig. 58.

The speed at which the sand is allowed to run determines the interval of time between the starting of the several coins on their zig-zag journey down the easel.

Fig. 61 gives an end view of the tube (JK) which is three inches long and of the same diameter as the coin holder. Exactly one-half inch from the lower end of (JK) a bottom is set in, in

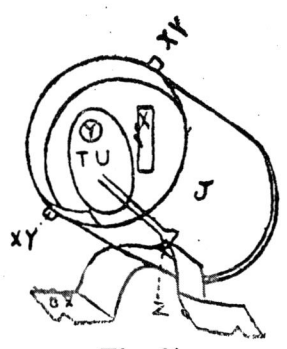

Fig. 61.

which a slot (X), one-half by one-eighth inch, has previously been cut. A pear-shaped piece of brass (TU) loosely riveted at (Y) covers or opens the slot (X) when moved by the lever (X) to which it is fastened. A portion of the tube (JK) is cut away to allow the lever (Z) to be moved far enough around to close the slot (X). Projecting above the surface at (XY-XY) are two rivets made to engage the slot (AX-AX), see Fig. 62.

The Art of Magic

This cup (LM) into which the sand runs, is three inches long and in diameter fits tightly over (JK), as in Fig. 58. The Cap (OP) has a thread cut on the inside and screws onto the top of (JK) which is threaded to receive it.

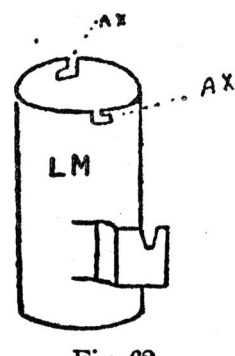

Fig. 62.

In a parallel line to the lever (Z) a piece of sheet brass one by three inches is fastened, and bent to form two feet, as shown in Fig. 61 (BX). On the sand cup (LM), see Fig. 62, is fastened a similar piece, but forming only one foot, which is on the side opposite the lever. Each of these three feet has a "V" slot cut from the *top downward*. Three screw-eyes are placed on the back of the stick to engage these slots, the motor is placed against the stick with the opening in each slot immediately under a screw-eye; the motor is then moved upward until the screw-eyes are wedged in the slots, when the screw-eyes are given a quarter turn. As soon as the spring inside the motor is in action, its tendency is to pull the whole motor upward, hence the position of the "V" slots and the screw-eyes. Under the sand cup, Fig. 58, is a post (DY) with a thumb-screw (BY) threaded through it near the outer end. This is turned upward until it binds against the bottom of the sand cup, and prevents the motor falling before the spring is in operation.

In Fig. 58 (FX) is a piece of lead made fast to the easel to overcome its top-heaviness. By attaching a black fish line to the lever (Z), threading it through an eye at (V) and through another eye in the table top, and thence running it off to an

The Art of Magic

assistant, the coins, when this line is pulled, will commence falling, and later will fall at greater speed, when, at the command of the performer, the assistant pulls the lever wide open. To prevent corrosion, all parts should be nickel plated, but not polished, and then painted black on the outside. The cost of materials for the construction of the various pieces of apparatus described is slight. The principal item is labor. The reader possessing mechanical ability will find little difficulty in construct-

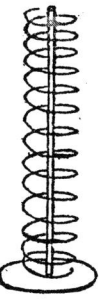

Fig. 63.

ing, or having constructed under his supervision, a perfect and satisfactory piece of apparatus, if the minute details of construction are closely followed. Except the spring in the coin dropper and in the motor, neither of which lift (both expanding without interference) gravity, the one dependable force used in magic, is the cause of all the effects.

To the audience the easel is simple in appearance, and too slender and fragile in construction to suggest concealed machinery. The black stick brings the bright coins into bold relief, while the musical cling-clang of the coins dropping into the glass, together with the others zig-zagging down the easel, please the eye and ear far better than the larger and more expensive coin ladders designed for the stage.

CHAPTER XV

TRICKS OF THE TRADE.

This chapter is one of the most valuable in the volume. The author can say this much freely, without being accused of egotism, for it is none of his work. They have to thank Mr. Carl Anderson and Mr. W. G. Edwards for compiling the following list of practical hints:

1. Before painting or cementing on metal, especially brass, the metal should be soaked for at least an hour in a saturated solution of sal soda, and then rubbed clean and dry with a soft cloth. This removes the grease that is always found on new metal and which otherwise would cause the paint to scale off.

2. Cloth cannot be glued to traps or other metal surfaces. Use the rubber cement with which tires are cemented to bicycle wheels. After preparing the metal as described in the previous paragraph, spread a thin coat of the cement on the metal and allow it to stand between twenty and thirty minutes, or until it becomes "tacky." Then apply the cloth or other similar material. When applying sheet rubber to metal, coat both the metal and the under surface of the sheet rubber.

3. To prevent warping, table tops should be three-ply, that is to say, three pieces of wood, each piece about a quarter inch or less in thickness, laid one upon the other with a coating of glue between; but the grain of one piece should run across the grain of the piece placed next to it.

4. Both sides of a table top, and especially around traps or "wells," should be painted with a dead black paint containing neither varnish nor dryer. If the felt covering is torn or burnt the table top thus prepared will not show.

5. Felt for table tops should be shrunken before using. Wring out, in cold water, a white cloth of the same size as the

The Art of Magic

felt. Spread the felt on the wet cloth and roll the two pieces up together and let the bundle stand for three hours, after which hang the felt up to dry. When the felt is quite dry press out any wrinkles. If not properly shrunken, the action of the air or the glue will, in time, shrink the cloth away from the trap or "well;" and cloth not prepared in this way is more liable to show spots.

6. The "Anderson Inlaid Top" differs from the original "well-top" table in two respects: No circular designs are used. Circular patterns may lead to the impression that there is "a hole in the table," due to the natural idea of a hole always being round.

The designs are made with ribbon, Figs. 57 and 64, cemented

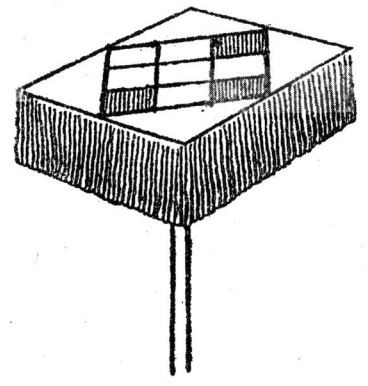

Fig. 64.

into the felt top. The absence of all tacks and thick braid permits coins, cards and, of course, larger objects to be moved into the "well" without picking them up. The shaded portions of the designs represent the "wells."

Prepare the wood top of the desired size, as described in paragraphs 3 and 4. Lay out the design on the wood with a scratch-awl, allowing for the width of the ribbon; then cut out the portion of the design intended for the "well." Next cover the surface of the wood with liquid glue and apply black felt, which has been prepared as described in paragraph 5. Cut the felt diagonally from corner to corner of each well, turn it in and

The Art of Magic

tack in place. Again lay out the same design, using tailors' chalk. Prepare the ribbon as follows, using satin-faced bright yellow ribbon, about three-eighths inch wide.

Place the ribbon face down on a smooth surface; cut into narrow strips thin sheet rubber sometimes called "mending tissue" and which is used by tailors; lay the rubber on the ribbon and moisten at intervals of every three or four inches. With a warm flat iron touch quickly one of the moistened spots on the rubber, and it will adhere to the ribbon. If the iron is too warm, or the motion of touching the rubber is slow, the rubber will melt. A good deal of practice is necessary to learn the proper temperature for the flat iron. Prepare the necessary amount of ribbon in one piece, and trim off the surplus rubber at the edges. Lay the prepared ribbon between the chalk lines indicating the design on the table top; over it place a damp cloth and press with a flat iron which should be hot enough to make the cloth steam. The rubber now melts, immediately cementing the ribbon to the felt. Cut off the ribbon and repeat until the design is completed. Do not cut the ribbon in strips before applying as it shrinks when steamed.

7. Various kinds of silk and silk handkerchiefs are sold as "Liberty" silk, but none of them is as thin or springy as the real article. Genuine "Liberty" silk can always be told by the price, which is about three times the price charged for China silk. As it is not made in strong colors, it is advisable to purchase the white and dye to the desired shade.

8. There are three kinds of sheet brass: soft, half-hard and hard. In appearance all three look the same; but the two latter are best adapted for springs. Brass has a grain the same as wood, and the way of the grain makes the most permanent spring.

9. Use only soft or half-hard brass for the manufacture of articles bent at sharp angles, as hard brass will in time crack.

10. "Pan" velvet has more sheen, and is, therefore, more pleasing to the eye than the ordinary velvet used for table and other drapes.

The Art of Magic

11. The thinness of ordinary brass tubing prevents the cutting of a deep thread, which is the only kind that will wear. Cut the thread on a short piece of brass rod and solder the other end of the brass rod inside the tubing, leaving the portion with the thread projecting the required length.

12. The "Lighted Candle from the Pocket" and similar effects require a wax match in the place of the candle wick. To prepare, cut off the wick and insert a hot needle in the center of the candle. As the wax softens, quickly withdraw the needle and put in the wax match, which the cooling wax will fasten in place.

13. For the "Obedient Candle" and similar lights use sweet oil.

14. A handy servante for a glass of water, is made by bending a stiff wire into a ring and fastening the other end of the rod to the under side of the table. If before bending the wire is covered with small rubber tubing, it will prevent the glass "talking." Of course the glass must be one that tapers, else it will fall through.

15. Small black fish line is more dependable than black thread.

16. The best wax for magic purposes may be purchased at any drug store. It is called "Diachylon Plaster" (or lead plaster). Its usual form is a round bar about one inch in diameter. Cut out from the center a small piece, and work it between the fingers a few moments, when it will be found "tacky," but will come off clean and in one piece from the card or other object.

When paint is "tacky" rub it with a cloth wet with ammonia.

One coat of varnish never cracks.
Two coats of varnish seldom crack.
Three coats of varnish often crack.
Four coats of varnish always crack.

Did you know that the juice of an onion will clean gold paint and make it look like new?

To paint on tin, scratch the surface to be decorated with

The Art of Magic

a piece of sandpaper, apply a coat of thin shellac varnish, then paint the desired color. This will prevent the paint from shelling off, as it often does on the "painted flesh color apparatus" you purchase.

Varnished apparatus may be made to look like new by washing with a mixture of a pound of wheat bran boiled in a gallon of water.

CHAPTER XVI

TRICKS WITH EGGS.

Conjurers, as a rule, are partial to eggs, and in one guise or another the product of the industrious Penelope of the barnyard may be found in every well regulated magical programme. Cards or rings or gloves are passed mysteriously into eggs; from eggs the conjurer produces yards upon yards of ribbon or showers of confetti; eggs are caused to disappear and reappear in the most bewildering manner, or to transform themselves into handkerchiefs and other objects with equal facility. There are hundreds of egg tricks known to the profession; every work on conjuring, pretentious or otherwise, discusses the subject at more or less length; and while the author dares not indulge the hope that everything explained in this department will be a novelty to each and every reader, they do believe that they have contributed an interesting chapter to the History of Humpty Dumpty.

TO BALANCE AN EGG ON A TABLE.

The difficulty of accomplishing this effect with an unprepared egg is that the yolk, which is heavier than the rest of the contents, is held suspended near the center, and consequently the egg is top heavy. If the egg is well shaken beforehand, so as to break up the yolk, the center of gravity will be lowered, when the egg may be balanced on its larger end. A much simpler and, we venture to think, decidedly better method, inasmuch as an unprepared egg may be used, is to place a grain of salt on the table. Place the larger end of the egg on the minute piece of salt, pressing down so that an almost invisible hollow is formed in the particle, when the egg will stand up as straight as in the experiment of the Genoese navigator. A still more startling feat is to balance an egg on the rim of a tumbler. The effect is obtained

The Art of Magic

in exactly the same way. A grain of salt is placed on the rim (which must be flat) and the egg is balanced on the minute particle of salt. Although the skeptically inclined may be disposed to believe that a second grain of salt is essential in order to believe this explanation, we assure the reader that if a glass with a perfectly flat rim is used the apparently impossible feat will become possible.

While on the subject of balancing we may describe a particularly neat method of balancing a glass of water, a feat that may logically precede or follow the two just described. A glass is partially filled with water and balanced on one edge. This looks for all the world like a feat of skill, but without a knowledge of the secret one might practice until Doomsday with no better result than spilling the water on the tablecloth. The secret is absurdly simple. Before presenting the trick slip a match or toothpick under the tablecloth, or under a napkin, and tilt the glass over it. The result is that the glass will remain on its front edge, as if balanced. Care must be exercised to use exactly the right amount of water. A few trials will determine the proper amount which is, roughly speaking, one-fourth of a glassful. In presenting this trick before a large company the reader is advised to attach the match or toothpick to a piece of thread. If any undue curiosity is manifested, and there is a desire on the part of the skeptical to peep under the tablecloth, the performer can instantly withdraw the "apparatus." Although absurdly simple this little trick is one of the best described in this book, and the reader is earnestly advised to present it on suitable occasions—after dinner or at a banquet.

EGG CHANGED INTO CONFETTI.

A very effective interlude in a series of egg tricks is to take an egg in the left hand, wave a fan in front of it and lo! a shower of confetti powders the air.

The secret is simple. Blow an egg, making the hole at one end rather large. When the egg has been rinsed and dried, fill it with confetti, and conclude by pasting a piece of paper over the hole. While fanning the egg is crushed in the left hand, and the confetti is wafted into the air. The fragments of the eggshell fall to the floor with the confetti. Select a white egg for the experiment. This egg may be used to advantage in the "Japanese Egg Trick," which is described in this chapter.

A NEW IDEA IN THE VANISHING OF AN EGG.

The author is indebted to Mr. Max Holden for this pretty and mysterious vanish, which is as follows: After an egg has been produced, the performer places it in a thin paper bag, and, on holding this before a candle, the shadow of the egg is seen on the bag. The bag is then crushed, and all traces of the egg are found to have disappeared.

For this trick nothing is necessary except an egg, a bag, and an oval shaped piece of cardboard. The cardboard shape is placed in the bag, and it is this that causes the egg-shaped shadow. When the egg is apparently placed in the bag it is in reality palmed. After the shadow is shown the bag is crushed, and the egg reproduced as fancy dictates. Mr. W. G. Edwards performs a similar trick with a brilliant ball, by pasting a piece of red glazed paper in the bag.

THE EGGS FROM THE MOUTH.

The feat of producing a number of eggs from the mouth of the performer's assistant is very old. Bellachini made it a

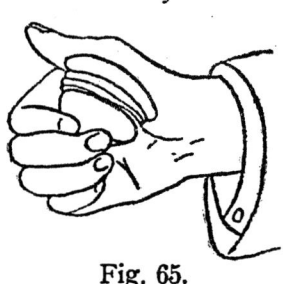

Fig. 65.

special feature of his programme, and sundry conjurers since his day—Hellis, the Hermanns, and others of minor note—have presented this effective, if somewhat repulsive, illusion. The old

The Art of Magic

method is so well known that we will not venture to describe it, but will content ourselves with a brief account of the latest and best method. The eggs in this instance are made of thin india-rubber and have a tiny hole in each end. This admits of their being crushed quite flat as illustrated in Fig. 65. Six or more of these eggs may be placed in the mouth at once. As the eggs are pushed between the lips, one by one, see Fig. 66, the air,

Fig. 66.

rushing into them through the two holes, fills them out to their proper shape. The eggs, on being released, fill out instantly, and the illusion is perfect.

THE CONJURER AS CHICKEN FANCIER.

This is a laughable and mysterious experiment. In effect it is as follows: The performer borrows a derby hat, and, after proving it empty, places it crown downward over a small pillow on the seat of a chair. On lifting the hat an egg is seen in the improvised nest. The performer repeats the operation until six eggs appear, one at a time, in the nest, and concludes by producing a hen from the hat.

The requisites and preparation for this trick are as follows: A chair with an opaque back to which is hanging a bag containing a small hen; on the seat of the chair a small pillow, which is pressed in so as to form a slight hollow or nest; six eggs concealed on the person of the performer, one in the right trousers pocket; one in the left trousers pocket; three vested (right, left and center); and one in bend of left arm.

Borrow a hat and deposit it on the seat of the chair while you pull up your sleeves. The left hand pulls up the right sleeve first, and in pulling up the left sleeve the egg in the bend of the arm is palmed in the right hand. Pick up the hat and press the egg in the outside rim. The hands and hat may now be shown empty, and in the act of setting hat down on pillow the egg is shifted inside the hat and allowed to drop into the nest. In the act of lifting the hat to show the egg, the left hand palms another egg, and the movements are repeated. When the eggs on the left side are exhausted the performer moves to the other side of the chair, so that he can manipulate the hat with the left hand and palm the eggs in the right hand. When the last egg has been discovered in the nest, the performer casually passes the hat behind the chair and loads the bag holding the hen. In the act of returning the hat to its owner the hen is produced, much to the astonishment of the wearer and the amusement of the spectators. The conjurer brushes the hat with a handkerchief, both inside and out, carrying away the bag under the handkerchief.

JAPANESE EGG TRICK.

We do not know whether this pretty trick is of Japanese origin or not; but it is so charming and illusory that it inevitably suggests the graceful and dextrous jugglers of the Land of the Rising Sun.

In effect the performer takes a cigarette paper, or any small piece of tissue paper, rolls it into a little ball, moistens it between the lips, and then, placing it on a fan, makes the little ball jump and roll to the accompaniment of lively music (in case the amateur is fortunate enough to have an accompanist). The pellet suddenly puffs out and gradually becomes larger and larger, eventually assuming the form and color of an egg. The conjurer shows that the egg is solid and unprepared. Then he waves a

The Art of Magic

fan in front of it, and lo! the egg disappears in a shower of confetti.

The secret is decidedly ingenious. In the first place, the conjurer must heed the advice of the immortal Mrs. Glass, of rabbit stew fame, and procure an egg. This egg should be an ordinary one—the more ordinary the better. Do not be extravagant in the purchase of this necessary article. We give this advice for two reasons: First, one should always practice the virtues of economy and buy as low as possible; second, this experiment will not be successful with a newly laid egg, for the simple reason that the inner skin is thicker and more resilient in an old egg than a fresh one. The egg best adapted for the purpose should be about two weeks old. It is the egg's inner skin that is used for the trick. In order to get this skin soak the egg over night in white wine vinegar (sometimes twenty-four hours, the exact time depending on the age of the egg), so that the shell may be entirely dissolved. Before immersing the egg in vinegar shake it thoroughly, so that the yolk will be broken. The necessity for this will soon be apparent.

When the shell is dissolved, wash the egg; and when the white skin, which is now the egg's only wrapper, is quite smooth, perforate the small end with a pin, and carefully remove the contents, taking especial pains not to enlarge the hole more than is absolutely necessary. In order to simplify this operation the egg is shaken before it is immersed in the acid bath. When the egg is empty dip the skin in the water, and by pressing the skin between the fingers, so that the water goes in and out, the inside is thoroughly cleansed. In this condition the little "apparatus" is ready for use. The skin may be preserved for an indefinite time if kept in a solution of water and alcohol. With ordinary care one skin should last an entire season.

Before presenting the trick the egg-skin, which must not be dry, is rolled into a small ball, and in this shape it cannot be distinguished from a pellet of cigarette paper. The egg-skin ball is concealed in the mouth. It is easily exchanged for the paper ball when the latter is put between the lips as if to moisten it.

The Art of Magic

The little ball is now placed on a fan, and if made to jump about, it will gradually assume its original form, on the same principle that a flattened rubber ball swells into shape when it is tossed between the hands. The effect of the supposed pellet of paper visibly changing into an egg is indescribably pretty, although the effect will be heightened if the egg-skin is jounced to a jocund two-step or sprightly gavotte.

The concluding part of the trick will now be clear to the reader. An egg, loaded with confetti, is vested on the left side, or concealed in any manner convenient to the conjurer. While the eyes of the spectators are focused on the dancing egg-skin the egg loaded with confetti is palmed in the left hand. This hand now grasps the inflated egg-skin, which is compressed and concealed behind the natural egg. This egg is passed rapidly around by the performer to satisfy the spectators that it is unprepared. The egg actually does not leave the conjurer's own hand, although if carefully prepared it will withstand an ordinary examination.

The student is advised to use nothing but white wine vinegar in preparing the "apparatus" for this trick. Although ordinary vinegar and acetic acid will dissolve the shell equally as well, they discolor the egg skin. Probably the first egg or two that the reader prepares will not be a success, owing to the fact that proper care is not observed in removing the contents of the egg from the skin. Patience and perseverance will overcome the difficulty, however, and the experimenter will be rewarded with the prettiest of all egg tricks.

THE LATEST EGG, HANDKERCHIEF AND GLASS TRICK.

A favorite combination trick is that in which an ordinary egg, marked with a pencil, and dropped into a glass and covered with a paper cylinder, changes places with a handkerchief held in the performer's hands. The usual method of accomplishing this effect is by means of bottomless tumbler. The author takes pleasure in presenting a comparatively new and superior method of accomplishing this effective combination. The bottom-

The Art of Magic

less glass is retained in this method, but it is used in conjunction with a dainty and ingenious piece of apparatus — a miniature table, illustrated in Fig. 67. This table, which is nickel plated

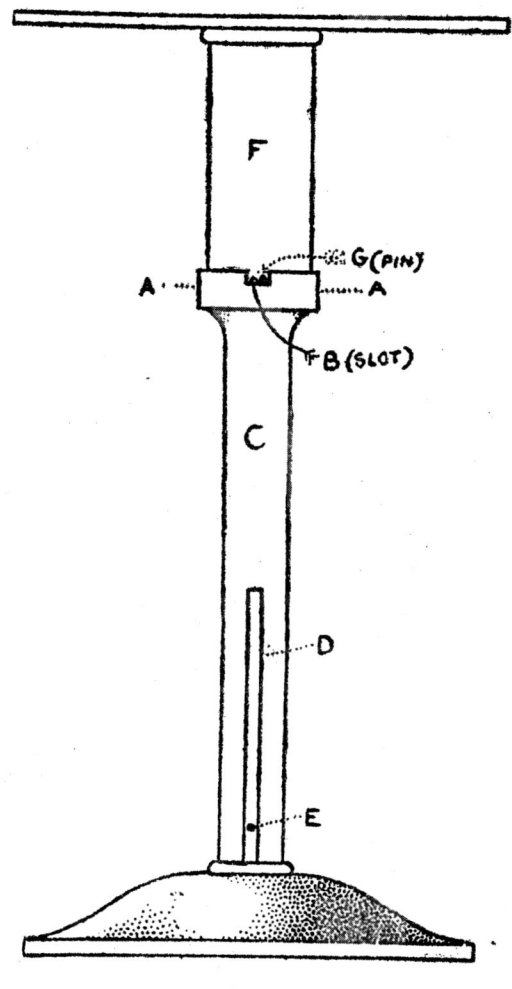

Fig. 67.

throughout, save for the top, which is covered with a figured felt, is sixteen inches in height and the base and top measure five inches in diameter. The standard is composed of two parts. The lower part, nine inches long, is made of half-inch tubing, to the top of which is brazed a cup-shaped attachment as shown in A

The Art of Magic

in Fig. 67, made of metal one-twelfth of an inch thick. The diameter of this flaring cup at the top is one and one-twelfth inches. The cup, bulging in this way, provides an inside collar or rim, about one-eighth of an inch wide. One side of the cup is slotted for a bayonet catch, see (B) in Fig. 67. Fitted inside the tube (C) is a piston seven and one-half inches long, the top of which normally rests inside the cup (A). A slot, two and a half inches long, is cut in one side of the tubing, shown at (D), and by means of a small projecting stud (E) the piston may be raised. The upper part of the leg or standard (F) is made of tubing a trifle less than an inch in diameter, and is just large enough to fit snugly in the cup (A), a small pin (G) being brazed to lower end of the tube which fits in the slot (B). This part of the leg is permanently attached to the underside of the table top, being threaded into a metal plate which is fastened by screws to the wood. The table top is sawed out of quarter-inch stuff, painted black on the under side, and the top is covered with the very best quality of figured felt. A black felt with green figures gives the best results. A circular hole is cut through the top corresponding to the diameter of the metal tube. The felt is cut to correspond with the hole in the table top, save that the circular piece is not entirely removed, a hinge of cloth being left so that the small circular piece of felt forms a flap, or trap, which covers the hole. As the felt is figured the line of this cloth trap cannot be seen at a distance of three feet.

To prepare for the trick the two parts are fitted together, as in Fig. 67, and a small liberty silk handkerchief is pushed into the upper part (F), and the felt flap, or trap, is smoothed down flush with the top. The apparatus thus loaded should stand on one of the regular tables. A duplicate handkerchief lies on the table beside the little stand. In presenting the trick, an examined and marked egg is placed in the bottomless glass, after which the glass is covered with a large handkerchief. In the act of placing the covered glass on the little stand the egg is allowed to fall into the palm of the left hand. This hand adjusts the handkerchief, which should be large enough to fall down as far

The Art of Magic

as the slot (D), and at the same time the right hand moves the stud upward, the piston forcing the concealed handkerchief into the glass. Taking the duplicate handkerchief from the table, holding it in the left hand so that the egg is concealed, the performer announces that he will pass it into the glass. Placing the two hands together, and standing with the left side to the audience, the arms are moved up and down, and under cover of this movement the handkerchief is worked into the fingers of the left hand, the egg eventually becoming invisible. The egg is then transferred to the right hand and passed to the audience for examination. The left hand, in which the small silk handkerchief is concealed, whips the large handkerchief off the glass, and in laying the handkerchief cover on the table the palmed handkerchief is dropped into a servante, or simply hidden under the larger handkerchief. The left hand now jerks the small silk handkerchief out of the glass, and with a synchronal movement the right hand carries the glass away. The glass is not lifted from the table, but is taken off with a sliding movement, so that the bottom edge will level the felt flap flush with the top. This flap, of course, was raised by the action of the handkerchief being pushed by the piston into the glass, and as it is not heavy enough to fall back by itself, the sliding movement of the glass is an important detail. If the performer works with an assistant he can simplify the trick by having the latter manipulate the piston. There is another form of handkerchief stand designed for use on a regular piston table. In this case the table is only a foot in height, and the tubing (which forms the standard) is of uniform size from base to top—five-sixths of an inch in diameter. The standard itself is ten and one-half inches in length, and the lower end of the tube screws into the base so as to bring the bottom of the piston, which works inside the tube, flush with the bottom of the base. In other respects the table is the same as the one described. The advantage of this design is that the handkerchief may be loaded into the glass by the assistant pulling a string attached to a piston concealed in the regular table. This piston operates the piston in the little stand and the handkerchief is forced into the glass without any work on the part of the performer. Undoubtedly this is the cleanest method of presenting the trick.

'EGGSAMPLE."

We are indebted to Mr. W. G. Edwards for the trick of the above title, and in his hands it forms a complete illusion.

EFFECT — An ordinary playing card transforms itself into an egg of the Simon Pure variety.

PRESENTATION — Show hands empty. Take a playing card from table and hold at finger tips of right hand. Vanish and appear card once by means of the back hand palm. Under cover of this sleight, produce and palm the egg in left hand. Now with the left side of body presented to spectators commence a rubbing movement of the left hand over the right. On the third or fourth movement quickly back palm the card and leave the egg in its place at the finger tips of the right hand, making a slight upward movement with both hands as the change is made. The appearance of the egg is so unexpected that the knowing ones are completely fooled. The egg is then taken from the right hand and held exhibited with the left, the right hand reaches to table, takes up wand to tap the egg to show its solidity, and of course leaves the card on the servante, or behind some object on table.

CHAPTER XVII

TRICKS WITH BALLS

Within the last decade the magic of billiard balls has become popular with both the amateur and the professional conjurer. The idea of using billiard balls for conjuring purposes originated, we believe, with the late Bautier De Kolta, to whose ingenious brain the conjuring fraternity is indebted for many useful sleights and illusions. It is a far cry, however, from the clumsy hinged shell of De Kolta to the single hand production of four billiard balls; and it was this surprising trick that gave the impetus to the vogue for billiard ball manipulation.

As most recent works on conjuring contain the orthodox explanation of the single-hand production of four billiard balls—that is to say, three solid balls and a half shell—we shall not take up any space in explaining the trick, but will begin this chapter with the explanation of a method of achieving exactly the same effect without the use of the half shell. This method demands more than ordinary skill in maniuplation and will require many hours of patient practice on the part of the neophyte. The result is well worth the labor, however, and used in combination with the manipulations that follow, forms a really startling opening to a brilliant series of billiard ball tricks.

EFFECT—Four solid billiard balls appear, one at a time, between the fingers of the right or the left hand.

TIME OCCUPIED—About three minutes.

REQUISITES AND PREPARATION—A magic wand and four solid balls. Two balls are in a contrivance known as the "Downs bag" on the left side, and the other two are vested. This bag is in reality a long cloth tube stitched down the inside of the coat. The diameter of this tube is just large enough to hold comfortably a billiard ball. Around the lower end is sewed an elastic which keeps the balls from falling through, but which allows of a ball being pressed out by the fingers of the left hand.

PRESENTATION OF TRICK—Begin by casually showing the hands empty. Pick up the wand with the right hand, the left hand palming a ball from the Downs tube. Make the "change over" and conclude by producing the ball from the tip of the wand. The "change over" and production of ball from the wand are old sleights and undoubtedly familiar to the reader.

The ball is now placed on the doubled-up fist of the right hand. The left hand comes up to take the ball (back of left hand and right side of body to audience) from the right hand, which it really does. The left hand fingers are now opened and closed, as if making the ball smaller; and while this is being done the right hand makes a move toward the right trousers pocket.

Pretend to overhear a remark that you did not really take the ball in the left hand, and eventually open the left hand, showing the ball there.

The ball is again placed on the right hand fist, and this time as the left hand approaches the right the ball is allowed to drop into the right hand where it is palmed. The left hand is closed, as if it really contained the ball; once more the fingers are "worked"; and finally the hand is exhibited empty. The performer remarks that when a ball disappears in that fashion it always appears in the trousers pocket. The right hand accordingly reaches into the trousers pocket and apparently brings out the ball, but in reality the ball is left in the pocket. The right hand stimulated, placing a ball in the left hand.

The performer coughs slightly, explains that billiard balls are good for a cold, and apparently places the ball is his mouth, pushing his tongue into the cheek so as to make it appear that the ball is really there. The lump in the cheek is then touched with the finger, the ball apparently swallowed, and one of the balls produced from the vest.

This ball is also placed on the top of the right hand, and in turning (right side to audience) the left hand palms the remaining ball from the tube.

The Art of Magic

The left hand with the palmed ball approaches the ball on top of the right hand. The left hand apparently takes the ball from the right hand, really letting it drop into the right hand.

Performer now casts a quick glance at the left hand and says: "I beg your pardon. Not there?" Opening the left hand and showing the ball which he again places on top of the right hand. "Really I would not deceive you that way." While saying this the ball that was on top of the right hand is back-palmed, which is accomplished by throwing back the thumb and holding the ball between the thumb and the back of the hand. The other ball is held on the palm of the hand by the third finger tip. The hand is now turned over, palming the ball that was held by the finger, and letting the back-palmed ball fall into place between the first finger and thumb. If this move has been done neatly, and the proper patter and misdirection used, the hand will appear to contain only the one ball. As the majority of readers will be unable to perform this sleight, owing to the formation of the hand, they will have to omit this part of the trick. In this case proceed as follows: Instead of placing the ball on top of the right hand for the last time (after performer says "I beg your pardon—not there?") the right hand (which has a ball concealed in the palm) is turned with the back toward the audience (the left side is toward audience) and the left hand places the ball between the thumb and first finger on the right hand. The right arm is extended. The hand is now lowered a trifle, and during this movement the ball between the thumb and first finger is rolled up between the first and second fingers, and on quickly raising the hand the palmed ball is allowed to fall, or rather roll, toward the finger tips. If done correctly the ball will be caught between the first finger and the thumb. This move is almost impossible to describe, but practice will soon demonstrate that an upward and inward swing of the arm, bringing the hand toward the body, will throw the ball into the proper position. The ball does not actually fly through space, but rather rolls along the inside of the hand, the first finger and the thumb forming a sort of track. The student should practice this move assiduously until he can produce the ball at the tips of the thumb and the first finger without any appreciable move of the arm; for unless he masters this essential part of the manipulation he may as well skip this chapter, as the majority of tricks described herein depend absolutely on this basic sleight. Skillfully executed, the sudden appearance of the ball from the palm is startling, and infinitely more effective than the production of a solid ball from the shell.

The two balls are knocked together, in order to prove their solidity to the audience. One ball is now held in the right hand and one in the left. Stand with the left side of the body toward the audience and toss the ball from the left hand into the air several times; then turn so that the right side of the body is toward the audience and toss the ball from the right hand into the air, meanwhile *vesting the ball which is in the left hand*. At the same time the other ball is palmed in the right hand. Now make a half turn to the right (left side of body toward audience) and drop the palmed ball from the right hand into the left and casually show the right hand empty. The right hand then reaches into the trousers pocket and produces the ball left there earlier in the trick. While this is being done the left hand palms a ball from the vest, at the same time holding a ball at the finger tips.

One ball is now held in the right hand and two balls are in the left hand (one being palmed). The left side is toward the audience. Knock the balls together, and as the ball in the left hand is placed between the first and second fingers of the right, the ball in the left palm is palmed in the right hand (during the instant that the left hand places the ball in the right fingers). The back of the right hand, of course, is turned toward the audience.

The ball held between the first and second fingers of the right hand is rolled up between the second and third fingers by rolling the ball *over* the second finger to the third finger. This will bring the second finger down behind the first ball which is rolled up between the first and second fingers, while the ball in

The Art of Magic

the palm is propelled, by the movement previously described, into the place occupied by the first ball — that is to say, between the thumb and the first finger. The three balls are then knocked together to prove their solidity.

The ball held between the first finger and the thumb is now apparently swallowed (really palmed in the right hand), and the remaining ball is produced by the left hand under the vest.

Now turn with the right side of the body toward the audience and knock the ball in the left hand against the two visible balls in the right hand.

Transfer the ball from the left hand to the right, depositing it between the first finger and the thumb, and in turning so that the left side faces the audience transfer the ball from the right palm to the left palm.

The performer now holds the right hand, with the three balls in it, high in the air, back of hand toward the audience, and allows the ball held behind the first finger and the thumb to fall into the right palm, which move is exactly the reverse of the method of production. The ball in the left hand is produced from behind the left knee.

This ball is knocked against the ball in the right hand (back of right hand to audience) and in making a half turn to the right the ball is transferred to the left palm.

Knock the balls together once more and place the visible ball held in the left fingers between the first finger and thumb of the right hand, at the same time transferring the ball in left palm to the palm of the right. This maneuver is in reality the "change over" palm.

The back of the right hand is now toward the audience, and the ball between the second and third fingers is rolled *over* the top of the third finger so that it is held between the third and fourth fingers; simultaneously with this movement the ball between the first and second fingers is rolled *over* the top of the second finger and is held between the second and third fingers; and the ball held between the first finger and thumb is rolled *under* the first finger and is held between the first and second fingers; while the palmed ball is jerked or rolled into the place of the first ball—that is to say, between the first finger and the thumb. This movement is extremely difficult — without doubt the most difficult sleight in the whole range of conjuring. Probably in the beginning the student will despair of ever mastering it. Patience and practice, however, will in time be rewarded by a mastery of the move, and the student will be qualified to take up the following brilliant series of billiard ball manipulations, which form a natural sequence to the trick just explained. It may encourage the reader to know that the author of this book performs the trick exactly as described.

PASSING FOUR SOLID BALLS FROM HAND TO HAND.

The only preparation necessary in this trick is to vest a shell on the left side.

After the four-ball production the balls are held in the fingers of the right hand. The shell is finger-palmed in the left hand. The ball between the first finger and the thumb of the right hand is transferred to the first finger and the thumb of the left hand, during which operation the finger-palmed shell is slipped over the ball.

The ball held between the third and fourth fingers of the right hand is placed between the second and third fingers of the left hand; the ball held between the second and third fingers of the right hand is placed between the third and fourth fingers of the left hand; the ball held between the first and second fingers of the right hand is placed between the first and second fingers of the left hand. The fingers of the right hand are thus brought behind the ball in the shell. This ball is finger-palmed in the right hand.

The right hand is held below the left. The left hand is now turned over, palm to the audience, slipping the shell on the first solid ball and showing the three balls. At the same time the ball that was finger-palmed in the right hand is brought into view by the aid of the thumb. The eyes should look at the three

The Art of Magic

balls in the left hand for an instant and then shift to the one in the right hand.

The ball in the right hand is tapped against the balls in the left hand. As the right hand passes the ball held between the first and second fingers of the left hand it finger-palms the shell. The left hand is then turned over (back toward the audience), and the ball in the right hand is placed between the first finger and the thumb of the left hand.

The left hand is again turned over (palm of left hand toward audience), and the ball held between the third and fourth finger is taken in the right hand, at the same time slipping the finger-palmed shell onto it. The shell and ball are held between the first finger and thumb of the right hand as one. Turn so that the left side is toward the audience. The right and the left hands are now held about a foot and a half apart and are lowered and raised in the air several times. The third time, the left hand makes a kind of an over-hand throw and palms the ball that was held between the first finger and thumb, at the same time the ball that was in the shell in the right hand is brought into view.

The right hand is now brought towards the left (also make a half-turn of the body to the left), and the shell in the right hand is slipped over the ball palmed in the left hand, and these are knocked against the two in the left hand.

Another ball is rolled into position for vanishing in the left hand, and the balls in the right hand are each rolled down one finger lower, which brings the shell-covered ball between the first and second fingers. Now stand directly facing the spectators with both hands extended as far as possible from the sides. Now make a motion of throwing a ball from the left hand into the right (at the same time making a half-turn to the right), immediately turning the right hand over and apparently showing the ball. (By aid of the shell).

Slip the shell over the ball palmed in the left hand the same as before, and repeat same movements for the production

The Art of Magic

of the fourth ball in the right hand (in reality three solid balls in a shell). The solid ball in the left hand is palmed.

Straighten the balls in the right hand and then put the left hand down to the left knee. Turn the right hand quickly over and exhibit only three balls, the ball between the first and second fingers being shelled. *At the same time* turn the left hand and produce the palmed ball. This ball is then changed for the ball and shell in the right hand.

The right hand, with the three balls in it, is then raised to the mouth and the ball between the thumb and first finger is apparently swallowed (really palmed), and the left hand reaches under the vest and produces the ball and shell as two balls.

Now slip the shell over the ball palmed in the right hand and hold ball and shell between thumb and first finger of the left hand.

Two balls are now shown in each hand, and the left hand is placed behind the back. The right hand now makes several motions towards the chest, and at the third movement one of the balls is palmed. The left hand is brought quickly from behind the back with apparently three balls in it.

Slip the shell over the palmed ball the same as before and knock the balls together. The right leg is now raised and the single ball in the right hand is palmed as a throwing motion is made towards the knee.

The left hand now reaches down to the shoe and produces the ball by drawing the hand from the heel to the toe, and when nearly to the toe the hand is raised in the air.

The balls are now placed, one at a time, between the fingers of the right hand, during which operation change the shell (held between the first finger and the thumb of the left hand) for the ball palmed in the right hand. The shell is then dropped into the vest servante, or into any convenient pocket. This trick mastered the student will be prepared to undertake what we may truthfully say is the ne plus ultra billiard ball tricks, the

The Art of Magic

COLOR CHANGE WITH FOUR SOLID BALLS.

This trick follows naturally the one just described. In order to present it you must have four white balls in the Downs tube on the left side. If the student desires to make the three tricks herein described into a consecutive series of billiard ball effects, the tube can be made long enough to hold six balls; the two red ones used in the first trick (the production of four solid balls) and the four white balls used for the color change.

At the conclusion of the last trick the four red balls were held in the right hand. The left hand palms a white ball from the bag and takes the ball held between the first finger and thumb of the right hand and knocks it against the three balls in that hand. The left side is toward the audience. The ball is then replaced in the right hand, during which operation the ball in the left palm is transferred to the palm of the right hand, the back of which is turned toward the audience.

The left hand now takes the wand and with it taps the ball held in the right hand between the first finger and thumb. At about the fourth stroke the red ball between the first finger and the thumb of the right hand is dropped into the left hand, and the white ball in the right palm is produced in its place, as in the "One to Four Production with Solid Billiard Balls." If this movement is properly executed the effect to the audience will be that the tapping of the ball with the wand caused the change in color. The right hand is not stationary during the change but moves with a sweep toward the left hand, and when the left palm covers the ball the latter is dropped and the palmed ball produced. The movements of the two hands must be exactly timed, a desideratum that will be obtained by practice.

The ball palmed in the left hand is dropped onto the servante in the act of laying the wand on the table, and another white ball is finger-palmed in the left hand from the bag.

The right hand is held with the palm toward the audience, and the left hand, covering for an instant the red ball between the first and second fingers, palms the ball. The right hand is now turned over so that the back of the hand is toward the audience. By keeping the left hand *motionless* this move will bring the finger palmed with ball into the place of the red ball. This is a very effective color change.

The ball in the left hand is vested as the right hand is raised in the air, and as the eyes of the audience are on the right hand (on the ball that has just changed color) the movement of the left hand will not be noticed. The left hand then squeezes a third white ball from the tube.

This ball is transferred to the palm of the right hand in the act of showing that the balls in the right hand are solid— that is to say, by knocking them together.

The left hand may now be shown back and front, after which it is passed over the third ball in the right hand, moving downward over the rest of the balls several times. At about the third or fourth time it quickly finger-palms the third ball, and the move for the production of the third ball, as described in the "One to Four Production with Solid Billiard Balls," is made.

The finger-palmed ball is dropped onto the servante, while the right hand knocks the third ball on the table in order to prove its solidity.

Another white ball is palmed in the left hand from the bag.

The red ball held between the third and fourth fingers of the right hand (the fourth ball) is taken in the left hand between the first finger and the thumb, and the right hand is turned over so that the palm is toward the audience.

The visible ball in the left hand is now apparently taken back in the right hand, but in reality it is the ball that was palmed in the left hand. The left hand is held over the ball and strokes it a few times and finally it is shown to have changed color. The ball in the left palm is disposed of on the servante or in the performer's pockets.

THE TRAVELING BALLS.

A favorite trick with magicians who are partial to the manipulation of billiard balls is to wrap a red and black ball each in a piece of paper and cause them to change places. The old method by which this effect is accomplished is to wrap each ball in a sheet of paper prepared by pasting two pieces of newspaper together by their edges, a loose layer of glazed paper being placed between the two. The red ball is wrapped in the sheet prepared with black paper; and the black ball in the sheet containing red paper. Each parcel is handed to a spectator for safe keeping, but before doing so the performer, in showing the balls for the last time, so that the audience may know the relative position of each ball, tears the outer layer of each sheet, the glazed paper being visible. The balls are then made to change places with the greatest of ease.

The following is a decided improvement upon the old method of working the trick. Exhibit a red and a black billiard ball and announce that you intend to perform the trick in two different ways, invisibly and visibly, so that the spectators will be able to present the experiment if they be so minded.

While you are talking wrap the two balls separately in a sheet of paper. Each sheet has a hole in the center through which the audience can see the ball. Two spectators are requested to assist in the experiment, and to place themselves on opposite sides of the stage or room. The man on the right holds the red ball and the man on the left holds the black. "One, two, three!" The papers are unfolded and the balls have changed places. The trick is then repeated in order that the spectators may see the actual transposition of the colored globes.

We shall describe the invisible transposition first. The two balls are not prepared. As in the old trick the whole secret lies in the preparation of the papers in which the balls are wrapped. These papers are prepared as follows: Take a piece of strong white wrapping paper, ten by fifteen inches, see (A) in Fig. 68. With a pair of sharp scissors cut a piece (B) out of the center, about as large as a twenty-five cent piece. Take a piece of glazed red paper or silk (C), about three inches square, and of the same color as the red ball. Strengthen this paper by pasting it on a piece of linen, and fasten to one of the edges (D) the end of a piece of white thread (E). This thread must be very thin

The Art of Magic

and strong, for which reason silk is preferable to cotton. A little above the hole (B) paste a strip of linen (H), in order to strengthen the paper. Pass the thread through one end (F) and let it come back at the other end (G) and then fasten the end to the red paper at (J). At the other side of the paper the thread will form a ring whose use will be explained later. When you

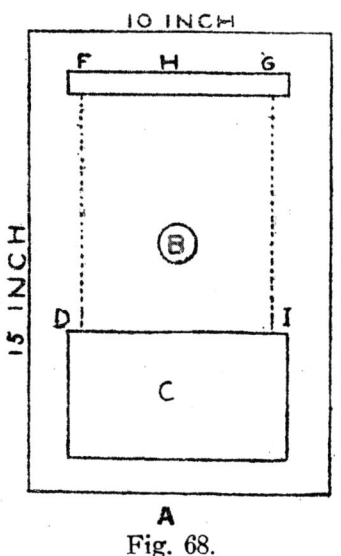

Fig. 68.

have arrived at this stage of the preparation, take a second piece of paper, fifteen by ten inches, and paste it to (A) by the edges only. This second sheet also must have a hole corresponding with (B) in the prepared sheet. Prepare another sheet in the same manner save that a piece of black glazed paper is used instead of the red.

In the actual presentation of the trick, casually show the two balls, knocking them together to prove their solidity, and then as casually exhibit the two sheets of paper, showing both sides of each sheet. Remark that you are going to wrap each ball in a sheet of paper, and in order to convince the spectators that there is nothing in the experiment that savors of hanky-panky, you have cut a hole in each paper so that the ball is always in sight. Pass the wand through the holes, this diversion being accom-

The Art of Magic

panied by appropriate patter, and hold the red and black balls separately behind the holes so that the audience can see each one through the aperture. Wrap the red ball in the sheet that contains the black paper, and wrap the black ball in the sheet containing the red paper. While wrapping up a ball cover the hole with the fingers of the left hand, and with the thumb and index of the right hand, which holds the ball, draw quickly on the thread outside the sheet. This raises the sheet of colored paper so that it covers the hole. Wrap the ball rapidly in the paper and give the package to a spectator, bidding him to stand at the right of the stage or room. Of course, he holds the package so that the audience cannot see the hole. Now wrap the other ball in the second paper in the same way, and give to the same person to hold. If you exhibit the two packages to the audience they will see the red ball in the package that really holds the black ball, and vice versa.

At this stage of the experiment request a second gentleman to assist you, and he is stationed on the left side of the stage or room. Take the package that really holds the red ball and give it to the assistant on the left, saying, "I herewith give you the black ball, while the other gentleman (pointing across the stage with wand) holds the red one." While talking you once more exhibit the packages so that the audience can apparently see the color of each ball. Announce that the balls will change places at command. "One, two, three, pass!" Unwrap rapidly so that the audience cannot see the colored papers.

You now announce that you will keep your promise by making the balls change places visibly, so that every one can see just how the trick is done. Give the red ball to the assistant on the right and the black ball to the one on the left, and request them to hold the balls between the fingers in order that every one can plainly see them. When placing the balls in their hands you whisper in their ears that at the command of "One, two, three, pass!" they will oblige by changing places. Of course, the assistants will enter into the spirit of the hoax, and at the command will obliging change places. "You see, ladies and gentlemen," concludes the conjurer, amid hearty laughter, "the experiment has been eminently successful. The red ball and the black ball have changed places before your very eyes."

As a rule a practical joke on the part of a performer is in very poor taste; but the climax just described is an exception to the rule. It never fails to put an audience into good humor, and to amuse is as much the province of the prestidigitator as to mystify.

CHAPTER XVIII

MISCELLANEOUS TRICKS.

THE FOUR PAPER BALLS AND PLATES.

An excellent after-dinner experiment based on the principle of the cups and balls. The performer lays four small plates in a row on the table, after which he makes four pellets of bread or tissue paper, about the size of hazel nuts. A ball is placed in front of each plate. Exhibiting both hands empty, the performer takes a pellet between the tips of the fingers and the thumb of the right hand, picks up a plate with the same hand and turns it over, leaving the pellet beneath the plate. A second pellet is placed under a second plate in the same way. A third pellet is apparently placed under the third plate, but is actually retained between the finger tips, the back of hand, of course, being toward the audience. The right hand immediately picks up the fourth plate and the left hand takes up the remaining ball. Place plate over the fourth ball, also leaving the palmed ball under the plate. If neatly done, the spectators will believe that there is a ball under each plate. The exact distribution of the balls, however, is as follows: A ball under plate No. 4; a ball under plate No. 3; nothing under plate No. 2; and two balls under plate No. 1. For convenience of explanation let us assume that the plates are numbered 1, 2, 3 and 4, from left to right.

The idea is to cause all the balls to appear eventually under plate No. 1. In order to accomplish this, turn over plate No. 4 with right hand and take the ball in the left hand in position for the tourniquet, or "French drop." Make the pass, apparently taking the ball in the right hand, and then apparently pass the ball through plate No. 1. Lift up plate No. 1 with the right hand, immediately transferring it to the left, thus concealing the ball in that hand. The audience sees two balls on the table, one supposedly having passed through the plate. Repeat the operation with the ball under plate No. 3. As there is no ball under plate No. 2, inform the audience that you will do the trick invisibly. Pretend to remove the ball through the plate, calling attention to the fact that you are holding an invisible ball, and then apparently pass it under plate No. 1, lifting up this plate and plate No. 2 simultaneously. The clever feature of this trick is that only four pellets are used which obviates the necessity of getting rid of the duplicate ball at the conclusion of the trick. In this respect the experiment resembles the trick of "The Sympathetic Coins," described in a previous chapter.*

THE FLYING SALT.

A startling and puzzling sleight-of-hand trick of the after-dinner variety, depending upon a very simple move, which, however, demands a great deal of practice before the trick can be presented with the proper illusory effect. The performer shakes a small quantity of salt into his left hand and then pours it onto a spectator's palm. The salt is now poured back into the performer's left hand, from which it mysteriously disappears, to be discovered later in the right hand.

The pouring of the salt on the spectator's palm really has nothing to do with the trick, but it creates what in military science is known as diversion. When the salt is returned to the performer's left hand he throws it up the right sleeve, using exactly the movement that is known in conjuring parlance as sleeving a coin. Adroitly done, the sleight is perfect, but it requires a great deal of practice. The moment the salt is sleeved the left hand is closed and extended slightly upward from the shoulder. The right hand, having been shown empty, is dropped to the performer's side. The salt, naturally, falls in this hand, which is also closed and extended. "One, two, three!" says the performer, and the left fingers are slowly opened. The salt has disappeared, and is discovered in the right hand.

---

* See Chapter 13, page 251.

The Art of Magic

THE CIGARETTE PAPER TRICK.

This is one of the oldest as well as the most mystifying of impromptu tricks. For some reason or other, the writers on magic have not considered it of sufficient importance to be included in their treatises; and, therefore, we shall present several new and subtle artifices that will be found useful in accomplishing the effect. We shall first explain what we consider the best method of working this charming trick.

The conjurer requests one of the spectators to lend him a cigarette paper and to take one himself. Explaining that the assistant shall imitate every movement, the conjurer tears the paper in half, puts the two halves together, and tears them in four. He rolls the small pieces into a ball, blows on it, and then, unrolling it, shows that the paper has been magically mended. The assistant follows each movement; but, of course, when he unrolls the pellet the pieces fall to the floor, which invariably causes a hearty laugh. "You rolled the pieces in the wrong direction," explains the conjurer. "You should have rolled them east to west instead of from west to east. I will do the trick again so that you may see how it is done." He repeats the trick, apparently explaining the method, but in reality the audience is more mystified after the explanation than before.

The reader is, of course, familiar with the conventional method of performing the trick. The conjurer has a duplicate cigarette paper balled and concealed between the tips of the first and second fingers of the right hand. The torn pieces are rolled into a ball, and this ball is exchanged for the duplicate. This exchange is simplicity itself. When the torn paper is rolled into a ball the latter is pressed against the duplicate ball, the two being held as one between the first finger and thumb. The spectators see that the hand is otherwise empty and never suspect that the pellet is really composed of two balls. The duplicate ball, which is on top, is now unrolled, and in doing so you put your fingers to your lips to moisten them — a perfectly natural movement — leaving the ball of torn

321

paper in the mouth. This movement should be done slowly and naturally. As in this part of the trick the attention of the spectators is divided between you and the assistant, you may safely pocket the pieces if you prefer. In fact, you should work this part of the trick so as to get a good deal of fun out of the assistant rather than to mystify the audience. The mystification comes later.

In the second part of the experiment you pretend to explain the trick. "It is really done by exchanging the torn pieces for a whole piece of paper," you assure the audience. While saying this you palm a ball of paper between the tips of the first and second fingers as before. Take a sheet of cigarette paper and crumple it loosely into a sort of ball and place it openly in the palm. Take a second sheet of cigarette paper and hold it between the thumb and the first and second fingers so that it conceals the palmed ball. "Ladies and gentlemen," you begin, "you will readily understand — being rational people — that the torn cigarette paper is not really mended by any supernatural means. Being rational people, you also know that the trick is accomplished by sleight of hand. If you will give me your attention for a few moments I will expose the necessary sleights — which are extremely simple — so that any of you will be able to perform the trick after a little practice. As you doubtless have guessed by this time, the trick is an example of what is technically known as palming. You will observe that one ball of paper is in my palm. Of course, in performing the trick the palm is turned away from the audience (suiting the action to the word) and all you see is the sheet of paper held between the fingers. I will now tear this sheet into four pieces (doing so) and roll them into a little ball (doing so). And now we reach the crucial moment, so to speak, in our little experiment. The ball of torn pieces must be exchanged for the whole ball in the palm. Of course, this exchange must be made adroitly, so that no one will observe the movement. And here is where the quickness of the hand deceives the eye. (Of course, this is not so, for the hand cannot move so rapidly

The Art of Magic

that the eye cannot follow it, but the explanation comes in very appropriately at this point, and it will be readily believed). I will illustrate how the exchange is made. (Make a sweeping movement of the arm, during which the ball of torn pieces is rolled behind the fingers and the duplicate ball rolled to the finger tips. The ball in the palm is not disturbed.) "During that movement, as you no doubt observed, the torn pieces were placed in the palm (indicating the palmed ball) and the whole ball is at the tips of the fingers. It takes some practice to make the movement neatly, but you can master it if you have the patience. Rome was not built in a day, and magicians cannot hope to attain perfection in an hour. After exchanging the balls, you unroll the one between the fingers. (Unroll the ball as before, getting rid of the torn pieces in the mouth). There, you see, the paper is restored. It really isn't so wonderful when you know how. (Here the performer pretends to hear some one asking what is done with the pieces in the palm). A lady in the rear of the room wants to know what is done with the ball of torn paper in the palm. Quite right. I had forgotten all about the torn pieces. Of course, they must be disposed of or the trick wouldn't be very effective. There are various ways of disposing of the pieces. Some conjurers drop the ball to the floor; others conceal it in their pocket; while others swallow it. Any one of these methods is good, but I have one of my own that I consider more effective. I simply take the pieces between the finger and thumb of the left hand (doing so); I blow on the ball (doing so), and unroll it in this way (doing so), and, you see, the pieces are magically joined together. Now that you understand how the trick is done, please don't give the secret away."

As a general rule the conjurer should be on his guard against explaining, or even attempting to explain, how a trick is done; for it is most unwise to give an audience even a hint of such things as palming or exchanging articles. But as the effect in this case is so bewildering, and as at the conclusion of the trick the spectators are no wiser than they were at the

The Art of Magic

beginning, the rule may safely be disregarded. Performed in this way, the cigarette paper trick is one of the most effective of impromptu effects.

There are many other ways of performing this charming illusion, and every performer of ability has his own favorite method of concealing the duplicate ball. Mr. Downs, for instance, conceals the ball under his finger ring, and, after the exchange, gets rid of the pieces in the same place. Mr. Hilliard carries a box of cork-tipped cigarettes for this trick. In the cork tip of each cigarette is concealed a pellet that may subsequently be exchanged for the torn pieces. Before rolling this whole paper into a ball Mr. Hillard burns a hole through the center with a lighted cigarette. Before presenting the trick he lights a cigarette — the ball in the cork tip does not interfere with smoking — and, holding the borrowed piece of cigarette paper between the thumb and fingers of each hand, requests some one to burn a hole through the paper with the lighted cigarette. The paper is held so that the spectator has no choice but to burn through the center, although the performer airily announces that the utmost freedom of choice is granted. The performer, of course, hands his own cigarette to the person invited to mark the paper, and in doing so the ball is abstracted from the cork tip and concealed between the tips of the second and first fingers of the right hand. The marked paper is now torn in pieces and magically restored, the hole in the paper adding largely to the effect. Another clever method of performing the trick is to affix, with a small pellet of wax, the duplicate ball on the nail of the right thumb. If this method is adopted the trick may be performed with both palms constantly exposed to the audience, the ball of torn pieces eventually being stuck to the thumb nail. This is a particularly neat and subtle method. In performing the trick at close quarters, with the spectators standing around, and it is not feasible to get rid of the pieces by "servanteing" them in the mouth, a bold and successful method is to slap one of the spectators on the shoulder, exclaiming, "How's that for a trick, old fellow!" As the hand strikes the

The Art of Magic

shoulder the pellet of torn pieces is allowed to drop behind the spectator's back to the floor.

THE TORN BANK NOTE.

This trick is an elaboration, or rather a variant, of the torn and restored piece of cigarette paper, and though worked on the same principle is even more startling in effect. The manipulation is more difficult than the cigarette paper trick, and requires patience and practice in order to make it a complete illusion. The effect is as follows: A banknote is borrowed, and the performer proceeds to tear it into a number of pieces. These are rolled into a ball, and after a mystic pass or two the pellet is unrolled and the banknote is found to have been magically restored. The performer offers to repeat the trick, and does so with even more startling effect.

The acute reader has already guessed that two bills are used; and the acute reader is half right. A duplicate bill is used for the second demonstration, but in the first part of the experiment *one banknote only is used*. We shall endeavor to explain the modus operandi as clearly as possible, although recognizing fully the dificulty of adequately explaining the first part of the trick.

The performer has a banknote of his own — say a dollar bill — loosely crumpled into a ball and concealed under a fold of the sleeve at the left elbow. He borrows a dollar bill, selecting a note that is neither too old or too new — a bill of medium freshness and stiffness, and resembling as closely as possible the duplicate bill. The borrowed bill must not be frayed or torn on the edges, however, or the denouement may be a disaster.

Having borrowed the proper banknote the performer holds it in the left hand, taking especial pains to show that his hands are otherwise empty, although he does not verbally call attention to this fact. The banknote must be held in the left hand precisely as follows The note is held at the upper edge, the face of the bill toward the performer, between the first joints of the thumb and the first finger. If properly held the tip of the thumb should exactly cover the letter "S" in the word "States," and the tip of the first finger will cover the final "E" in the word "Certificate" on the back of the bill. The upper left hand corner of the bill will be wedged in the crotch of the thumb. The right hand now grasps the bill at the opposite upper edge, between the thumb and the first finger. In order to attain the exact position, the tip of the right thumb should cover the words "States" and "America," on the front of the bill, while the first joint of the first finger completely covers the word "Silver" on the back of the bill. If the student will follow these directions with a banknote in his hand, he will instantly ascertain the exact position.

The right fingers now make a quick, sweeping movement toward the palm of the left hand, the upper edge of the bill slipping between the thumb and first finger, producing a noise that is an exact imitation of the tearing of paper. The movement must be quickly made, and the thumb and the finger should press rather tightly on the bill. At first the student will be loath to exert sufficient pressure, fearing to tear the bill; but if the upper edge of the bill is neither torn nor frayed there is no danger of such an accident. The paper used for banknotes is tough and strong. After the right hand makes the swoop to the palm of the left, the right end of the bill lies naturally along the fleshy part of the left thumb extending toward the wrist. The second, third and little fingers of the left hand hold it in this position. Properly done the noise and appearance of the folded bill produce a startling illusion and the spectator who loaned the banknote will be willing to take his oath that his property will have to be sent to the treasury department for redemption.

The performer does not pause long enough for the spectators to cogitate on the matter, however. The right hand is held as if containing a part of the bill — that is to say, the back is toward the audience and the tip of the thumb presses tightly against the bunched tips of the four fingers, imitating as closely as possible the action of holding a piece of the banknote. The right hand now apparently places the torn pieces of banknote

The Art of Magic

on the supposed half in the left hand, and it is on the naturalness of this movement that much of the illusion depends. The fingers of the left hand are opened, of course, so as to receive the torn half. The student should practice this movement in front of a mirror until he is able to deceive himself into the belief that he really places the torn half of the banknote into the left hand.

At this stage of the trick the banknote is folded in two. The right hand does not pause after apparently placing the torn piece into the left, but immediately grasps the doubled bill at the upper right hand corner, and repeats the "tearing" movement. This is accomplished in the same manner as before except in this instance the student has but half the surface to operate on. Accordingly the right thumb and forefinger clip the bill at the lower right hand corner, and move as before toward the left palm, producing the tearing noise. The second and third fingers of the left hand immediately close on the triangularly folded bill, which leaves but a small portion of the banknote exposed in the left hand. The effect is that you have actually quartered the bill. As before, the right hand simulates the action of holding a portion of the mutilated bill, and the same motion of apparently placing the torn portion onto the pieces in the left hand is repeated, this time the fingers of the right hand coming down on the folded bill with a smart slap, the noise assisting materially in the illusion. The banknote is now bunched in a sort of ball. A portion of the ball is grasped between the thumb and tips of the first and second fingers of the right hand, and the bill is twisted back and forth, the performer apparently exerting much strength to tear the bunch of supposed pieces. Finally, after an extra strong tug and wrench, the right hand flies away from the left, the tightly pressing fingers and thumb producing a sound as of tearing. The supposedly torn portion in the right hand is immediately slapped upon the bunch held between the left thumb and first and second fingers, and the two supposed portions are rolled together in a ball. This ball, which is about the size of a marble, is now held in the left hand between the thumb and tips of the fingers. If the movements have been neatly and smartly done the audience will be convinced that the ball is composed of the fragments of a once perfect bill, and will extend their sympathy to the unfortunate owner, who all this time has not made up his mind whether to take the matter as a joke or to demand his money back. The denouement is the same as in the cigarette paper trick. The performer makes two or three mystic passes over the pellet, breathes on it, and unrolls it in a restored condition, during which operation he takes especial pains to show that no duplicate bill is concealed in his hands.

The trick, however, is not finished. "Perhaps all of you didn't see how it was done," remarks the performer. "I will do it again." He repeats the trick exactly as described — that is to say, the first three tearing movements. The banknote is now bunched in the fingers of the left hand. The fingers of the left hand, still holding the bill, grasp the right sleeve at the bend of the elbow and pull the sleeve up. The right hand does the same for the left sleeve, and at the same time obtaining possession of the duplicate bill, which is placed *behind* the larger bunch in the left hand. Both bills are squeezed together so as to appear as one. The right hand grasps the duplicate bill and the left hand holds the borrowed bill. The performer now operates on the bunched bill, working the fingers back and forth making it appear as if he were exerting every ounce of strength in his hands. In reality the two bills are pressed tightly together. Suddenly, with a movement as if twisting the bill in two, the fingers are wrenched apart, the right hand carrying away the duplicate bill and the left hand holding the borrowed bill, the rubbing of one ball against the other producing a loud tearing noise. The tightly bunched condition of the banknotes and their jagged edges absolutely convince the spectators that you have destroyed the bill. You now apparently roll the two bills into one, really palming the duplicate bill in the right hand. Hand the other bill to a spectator, request him to breathe on the pellet and to unroll it. During this operation all eyes are nat-

The Art of Magic

urally on the spectator, which gives the performer ample opportunity to get rid of the duplicate bill. We have been somewhat prolix in describing this trick, but as it is really a very effective sleight of hand experiment we wished to make every detail clear to the reader, for upon the strict attention to detail depends the success of the trick. Mr. Francis Warner performs this trick very successfully.

THE BILL AND LEMON TRICK.

Another effective impromptu trick, which naturally follows the experiment just described. The effect is as follows: A borrowed banknote—any denomination—is marked with the initials of the owner and wrapped in a handkerchief. A borrowed and examined lemon is placed under a tumbler. The banknote is commanded to leave the handkerchief, and is found inside the lemon.

The only property required for this trick is an ordinary handkerchief, in one corner of which is sewn a tightly rolled piece of paper to represent a tightly folded banknote. This handkerchief is carried in any convenient pocket. Borrow a lemon, or allow a lemon of your own to be examined, and while the examination is going on borrow a banknote. Request the lender to mark the note with his initials, and while he is thus engaged take back the lemon, and with the thumb-nail cut through the skin at one end. This small slit will allow you to poke your forefinger into the lemon. Care should be exercised not to make the hole too large. Request the spectator to fold the bill in half; to fold it again in half; to fold this quarter in half; to fold this eighth in half; to fold this piece again in half, and roll it up, when it will resemble the size and shape of the paper concealed in the corner of the handkerchief.

While holding the lemon in the left hand (the end with the hole toward the palm), take out the handkerchief, show it on both sides, and throw it over the left palm — covering both the hand and the lemon.

The handkerchief should be arranged so that the right hand

The Art of Magic

corner (the one nearest the body) is the one that conceals the folded piece of paper. Taking the folded and rolled banknote from the spectator, the performer apparently places it in the center of the handkerchief, in reality, however, folding in the corner of the handkerchief containing the piece of paper. While the right hand is under the handkerchief, the borrowed banknote is pushed well into the lemon. In actual practice these two separate movements blend into one and occupy but a fraction of a second. The handkerchief is immediately handed to some one to hold, and as the spectator grasps what he thinks is the borrowed banknote, no suspicion is aroused. No one will ever dream that the lemon has been tampered with. Indeed, nine hundred and ninety-nine persons in a thousand would make an affidavit to the effect that the lemon was never out of their sight for an instant. The lemon is now placed on the table and covered with a tumbler. The performer takes hold of one corner of the handkerchief, requesting the spectator to drop the banknote at the word "three." "One, two three!" The bill disappears; the performer divides the lemon in half, and, separating the two halves, the banknote is discovered sticking in the upper half. This half is handed to a spectator, who removes and identifies the banknote. For obvious reasons the other half of the lemon is not handed for examination. It is either pocketed, thrown on the table, or, if the trick is being worked in a saloon or cafe, carelessly tossed into a cuspidor. As a matter of fact — which the reader will soon prove to his own satisfaction — no one ever thinks of examining the second half of the fruit.

There is another method of doing the trick which, while just as effective, is not quite so clean in workmanship. In this method two lemons are employed. One has a slit in the side, near the center. This lemon is in the right coat pocket at the beginning of the trick. An unprepared lemon is shown and then placed in the same pocket. A bill is borrowed and apparently wrapped in a handkerchief, as described in first method. Hand the handkerchief to some one to hold, and take the faked lemon

The Art of Magic

out of the pocket, at the same time inserting the bill. Lay the lemon on the table — slit side away from audience — and vanish the bill. Cut the lemon, beginning on side opposite slit and finishing with knife in slit. Allow spectator to remove top half and take out bill. The only advantage — if such it may be called — that this method has over the first one, is that both halves of the lemon may be examined.

THE RING ON THE WAND.

A very old and very well known conjuring trick consists of magically passing a borrowed ring onto the center of a wand or stick, both ends of which are held by a spectator. We shall not insult the intelligence of the reader by explaining the modus operandi, but shall describe an entirely new method of accomplishing the same effect, which is one of the ingenious specialties of Mr. Elbert Adams. This is the first time, we believe, that this method has been explained in print.

The effect is as follows: The performer borrows a ring, selecting one that is as distinctive in design as possible, so that there shall be no suspicion of a duplicate ring being used. Holding the ring in the left hand the performer requests a spectator to hold the wand at both ends. The ring in the left hand is now passed — visibly — onto the center of the wand.

The salient feature of this method is that the borrowed ring is not wrapped in a handkerchief, nor does it leave the performer's hand for an instant. This statement is true in a double sense. Two rings are really employed, and the means by which the exchange is made is decidedly ingenious. The performer holds the wand in the right hand, near the lower end. On this end of the wand, held in place by the curled third and fourth fingers, is the duplicate ring — an ordinary gold band ring, or a brass one if the performer is desirious of practicing economy. The borrowed ring is received in the left hand. The conjurer looks at it critically. "I guess it's big enough to go on the wand," he says, and, naturally enough, drops it over the top of the wand. The ring slides down the wand and falls off the lower end into the left hand. At least this is the way it appears to the audience. In reality the borrowed ring is retained by the curled first and second fingers of the right hand which open slightly to receive it. At the same instant the pressure of the third and fourth fingers relaxes, permitting the duplicate ring to fall into the left hand, which is held below the wand for this purpose. The release of the duplicate ring must be exactly timed, and there must be no bungling or hesitation. Neatly done the keenest observer cannot detect the substitution, but if there be so much as an instant's hesitation the performer may as well pass on to some other experiment. Consequently, this maneuver should be thoroughly practiced before the trick is presented to the public.

The conclusion of the trick needs no detailed explanation. The performer holds the substitute ring in his left hand, in such a manner that only a small portion of the band is visible. If the substitute closely resembles the borrowed ring, then the entire ring may be exhibited at the finger tips, but if the borrowed ring is of peculiar design, or if set with a stone, it should be held so that a small part only of the metal is visible. The wand, with the borrowed ring on one end, is in the right hand. Request a spectator to hold one end of the stick. When he takes hold of it move the borrowed ring to the center — of course, under cover of the right hand — and request him to hold the other end. Show the ring in the left hand count "one, two, three." At the word "three" make a throwing movement with the left hand, palming the substitute ring, and at the same instant removing the right hand from the wand with a jerk, which causes the borrowed ring to spin on the stick. Cleverly performed the illusion is all that can be desired by the most exacting artist in sleight of hand.

THE MYSTERIOUS MATCH.

This is merely an interlude, but may be introduced to good effect in any trick which requires the use of matches — say, the flag in the candle. In effect a match is lighted and held at the

The Art of Magic

tips of the fingers of the right hand, which is extended from the body as far as possible. The performer bends the left arm and blows smartly down the left sleeve, and at the same instant the flame of the match is extinguished. The right hand does not move nor is there any visible manipulation of the fingers.

The lighted match is held between the first and second fingers, near the tips, the back of hand to audience, the match extending at right angles from the fingers. A small portion of the end of the match — say a quarter of an inch — extends from the inside of the fingers. To extinguish the flame the right thumb smartly snaps this end. A few trials will give the reader a better idea of the exact position of the match than a page of print. Apropos of matches we may explain a device invented by L'Homme Masque for lighting magically a candle or cigarette. It consists of a miniature socket soldered to a finger ring. This socket is just large enough to accommodate a small piece of wax match. The method of working the apparatus is obvious.

THE INEXHAUSTIBLE HAT.

Tricks with hats are favorites both with magicians and their audiences; and undoubtedly the use of the hat as a storehouse of surprises will never go out of fashion among the conjuring fraternity. We have omitted hat tricks from this volume for two reasons, viz., lack of space and because the subject has been exhaustively treated in the standard works on conjuring. We depart from our purpose in this item, however, in order to add a decided novelty to the old, old trick known as the "Inexhaustible Hat." The ingenuity of various performers has greatly increased the number and variety of articles puroduced from the "dicer" or the "stovepipe." The modern magician is not content to produce playing cards, ribbons, handkerchiefs and such small articles as celluloid goblets, folding lanterns and spring flowers, but he must produce real lanterns of brass and glass, alarm clocks by the dozen, kitchen utensils, and last but not least, inflated balloons. This production is unquestionably the most brilliant of all hat tricks. Howard Thurston in-

The Art of Magic

troduced the trick into this country, inflating the balloons with a gas that carried the globes to the dome of the theater. The method used by Mr. Thurston was ingenious and scientific, but the apparatus was decidedly cumbersome and impractical for anything but stage work. The interior arrangement of the hat was mechanically intricate, and the balloons were inflated by gas drawn from a tank in the wings. The gas was forced through a tube under the stage, to which the performer made connection by means of a heel plate. A rubber tube passed up the performer's trousers, thence up his back and down his sleeve, and was connected at will with the inflating apparatus inside the hat.

The balloon trick immediately "caught on," as the saying is; and the ingenuity of American performers simplified the modus operandi, so that now the pretty trick can be presented in the drawing-room as easily as on the stage. The simplest, safest and best of the many methods of inflating the balloons is as follows: Take a small glass medicine vial, about two inches long and three-quarters of an inch in diameter. Fill this flask with a solution of tartaric acid and cork it with a rubber stopper. Place a small quantity of bicarbonate of soda inside the baloon, and in its mouth insert the small flask half ways, tying a string around the balloon to hold the bottle the firmly in place. A half dozen balloons arranged in this way are loaded into a hat — preferably an opera hat — and to produce them it is necessary only to pull out the rubber stopper, leaving the cork inside the balloon. The tartaric acid mixing with the soda produces a gas which inflates the balloon. Instead of tartaric acid the small bottle may be filled with commercial sulphuric acid, but the conjurer must use extreme caution in handling this chemical or damaged clothes or severely burned hands will be the result. The exact amount of chemicals used in this trick must be determined by experiment, for their strength often varies.

Apropos of the "Inexhaustible Hat," we may mention a novel feature from the programme of the late Harry Stork. This is the production of piping hot fried oysters from a bor-

The Art of Magic

rowed hat. The secret is simple. The oysters — each impaled on a toothpick — are enclosed in a rubber bag which retains the heat for about an hour. If a longer time must elapse before producing them the oysters may be kept warm on a hot tin back of the scenes until the performer is ready for them.

THE MYSTERIOUS KNOT.

The effect of this sleight is as follows: The performer lays a silk handkerchief across the palm of his hand. He tosses the silk into the air and lo! a knot mysteriously forms itself near the center.

So much for the effect. The secret is sleight of hand pure and simple. The handkerchief is twisted ropewise and the middle laid across the outstretched fingers of the right hand (palm up), the two ends hanging down equidistant on each side of the hand. The handkerchief is held in this manner for a moment in order to impress upon the audience the fact that the silk is free from preparation, although nothing is said to this effect. Now for the knot. Close the fingers over the handkerchief, at the same time turning the hand over. The hand should be turned over with a generous sweep of the arm so that the force of the movement will cause the right tip of the handkerchief to fly up and fall over the top of the hand. The handkerchief should fall across the knuckles, when it will be found that by slightly revolving the hand to the right the tip may be clipped between the second and third fingers. Clutch this end of the handkerchief and with a smart downward movement of the arm allow the handkerchief to drop off the hand, which forms a single loose knot. Snap the handkerchief by the end clipped between the second and third fingers, and the knot is tightened. The instant this is done the handkerchief is tossed into the air. In actual performance the various movements melt into one. Deftly done all that the spectators see is that the performer tosses the handkerchief into the air and that a knot mysteriously appears near the center. In order to achieve this charming effect, however, a good deal of practice is necessary, for the movements must

The Art of Magic

be deliberate rather than hurried; and there must not be any hesitation between the downward movement of the hand, when the knot is tied, and the upward movement by which the handkerchief is flung into the air. A slight turn of the body toward the right will materially assist in concealing the movements of the right hand.

THE VANISHING KNOT.

This is a specialty of Harry Houdini. In effect a knot, tied in a handkerchief, mysteriously vanishes at the command of the performer.

Hold an end of the handkerchief between the thumb and first finger of each hand, about three inches from the tip — the natural position for tying an ordinary knot. Now lay the right end across the left, and tie the two ends together — that is to say, you apparently do so. This is what you really do: When the two ends are crossed, the right over the left, the two ends are clipped, at the point of intersection, between the tip of the right thumb and the first finger. A sweeping movement of the right end back and down, when it is grasped by the tips of the left first and second fingers and brought up *in front*. The movement is simply the reverse of actually tying the right end around the left. The student should first tie a genuine knot, closely noting the movements of the hands and fingers, and these movements should be faithfully imitated in tying the fake knot. Deftly done the keenest eye cannot detect that the right end of the handkerchief is doubled behind the left end instead of going around in front. Holding the handkerchief tightly at the point where the ends are apparently tied, the performer requests one of the spectators to tie the second part of the knot, telling him to pull the ends as tight as possible. Cover the knot with the loose part of the handkerchief, and hand it to some one to hold. Grasp one end of the handkerchief, request the spectator to breathe on the knots, and at the word "three" to release his hold. He does so, the performer whips the handkerchief into the air, and the knot has disappeared.

The Art of Magic

THE MYSTIC TIE.

Ths is a favorite feat of the street fakir and the itinerant conjurer who charms at the county fair or harangues the crowds that flock in front of the medicine tent. Cleverly performed it is a very mystifying trick, and, although the principle — the feke loop used in "My Grandmother's Necklace" — is as old as the hills, the trick is puzzling even to many who are initiated in the mysterious of magic.

Two pieces of cord are passed for examination and when returned are placed around the performer's neck and the ends tied together with three or four solid knots. The performer instantly releases himself without untying the knots.

The cords, which are about five feet in length, may be offered for examination. When returned the performer shows them separately, one in each hand. They are then laid side by side across the second finger of the right hand, the four ends being allowed to hang down. As the right hand is moved toward the neck, the first finger separates the cords so that one is looped over the other as in the old trick of the tapes and balls, known to the profession as "My Grandmother's Necklace." This "twist," as it may be called, is made while the arm is in motion, the larger movement concealing the shorter one. At the conclusion of the "twist" the cords are held at the juncture between the first finger and thumb. In encircling the neck with the cords the loop, or point of juncture, is slipped under the collar of the vest. Now tie the ends of the cords into three or four knots. Put the hands to where cords are knotted and with the right hand grasp the upper cords, while the left hand seizes the lower ones. A slight tug on the cord and the neck is released, while a solid loop, composed of the doubled cord, remains in the hands. It is this last effect that makes the trick mysterious.

Here is another method of doing the trick. Use about five feet of cotton sash cord, one-quarter of an inch thick, and really pass the cord around the neck. Tie five or six knots close to the neck and request a spectator to tie the two ends to a chair or

The Art of Magic

post. The ends of the rope may be sealed if desired. A screen is placed before the performer, who in a few seconds releases himself without disturbing the knots either at the neck or where the ends are tied to the chair.

The secret is absurdly simple. It is impossible to tie a hard knot in cotton sash cord. Consequently the performer merely has to slip the knots along the cord toward the chair, for which reason there should be sufficient slack between the knots at the neck and the knots on the chair. The manipulation will not consume a minute. As soon as the loop about the neck is enlarged sufficiently, the head is slipped out and the knots worked back to their former position.

The effect of this trick will be enhanced if, after the neck is tied to a chair or post, the performer allows his hands to be secured behind his back either with tape or rope. If the reader is adept at opening handcuffs he could make the trick more mystifying by allowing his wrists to be manacled behind his back.

THE JACOBY ROPE TIE.

This is the king of all rope ties, and the most mysterious release ever invented. The secret has been well kept, and this is the first time, so far as we know, that the trick has been presented in a book. The author is certain that if this volume contained nothing else of value the reader would feel that he had received full value for his money in the following explanation.

The performer takes two strong cords or tapes (tapes are preferable in a drawing-room performance), each about two yards long. He places the middle of one cord on the extended wrist of the right hand, so that the ends hang down. The cord is now tied around the wrist by a committee from the audience, the knot coming on the inside of the wrist. As many knots may be tied as the committee desire, and the knots may be sewed or sealed with wax. The other wrist is then tied in the same manner. The performer now places the left hand, as far as he can reach, under his right armpit; then places the right arm

The Art of Magic

over the left elbow, extending the right hand under the left armpit. The cords hanging down from each wrist are brought together at the performer's back and tied into a secure knot, which may also be sealed. The performer seats himself on a chair (preferably a Vienna bentwood chair, or one with a straight rail at the top), and the double tapes are tied to the top rail of the chair near the post on the right side. The ends are either sealed to a card or tied to a bunch of keys. The method of tying the performer bears a slight resemblance to a straight jacket, and the performer may enhance the effect by calling attention to this fact, and also to the utter impossibility of his moving any portion of the arms or hands. The rest of the body is now tied to the chair — that is to say, the waist and the feet are securely fastened. These last ties have no significance whatever, as the performer desires the use of his arms only. A screen is now placed around the performer (Jacoby was carried into a cabinet), or he can be left on one side of a double parlor closed from view by a portierre. As soon as this is done, the performer leans back a little, sitting as far toward the front of the chair as possible. He now pushes the left hand as far as he can under the right armpit. This allows the right arm a little play, and with the right thumb he seizes the double cord extending from the right wrist and lifts it over his elbow and head. He now sits around a little toward the right and claps his hands together several times. Then he quickly seizes the double cord with the right thumb and lifts it back again over his head and arm, assuming his former position. The committee may now examine everything. A borrowed watch or ring (a watch has a better effect) is now laid upon the performer's right knee, and the cabinet is again closed, or the portierre drawn, as the case may be. The performer now brings his right arm over as before and sits around to the right. He pushes the ring, or the ring of the watch, over the loop formed by the double cord hanging between the right wrist and the rail of the chair, and seizing the loop by the right hand pushes it (without twisting it) under the tie around the left wrist from

The Art of Magic

the rear out (that is, from the cuff toward the fingers); and he then pulls the loop over the tips of the fingers. Drawing it entirely over the left hand, thence passing it under the tie on wrist (upper part) and pulls it back over the left hand again. Then he brings the double cord hanging from the right wrist to the front again, passing it over the head and left elbow, thus assuming the exact position in which he was tied. If the directions have been carefully followed the ring or watch will be tied in a knot at the back of the chair. The committee now make an examination, and the members are requested to remove the ring, a task they will soon give up. To remove the ring from the cords, a reverse process is employed. The directions may seem complicated at first reading; but if each move is followed with the materials in hand (an assistant doing the tying and reading the description), the knack of the Jacoby rope tie will soon be acquired.

The Jacoby rope tie may be used for almost all the so-called spiritualistic tests, such as "spirit" writing on slates, cutting out paper patterns, driving nails into a board, playing musical instruments, ringing bells, thumping a tambourine. Jacoby's final test was to invite one of the audience to sit in the cabinet with him. The spectator was blindfolded, and when the curtains were thrust aside again the spectator's vest was discovered turned inside out.

We earnestly advise the amateur magician or drawing-room performer to present the Jacoby rope tie as a genuine feat of magic rather than a spiritualistic test. The performer should have a duplicate set of tapes concealed on his person. Before being tied the performer may force a card, which is shuffled into the pack. After the performer is tied the pack is laid on the right knee, and the watch or ring laid on top of the pack. When the curtain is drawn the performer releases his arms, finds the drawn card, which he places between his teeth, allowing pack to fall to the floor, and manipulates the ring or watch onto the tapes as already described.

The Art of Magic

THE ROPE TIE PAR EXCELLENCE.

This rope tie we believe to be the strongest and best in the business, and like all other good tricks the modus operandi is simplicity itself. We are indebted to Mr. W. G. Edwards for this particular method of working the trick. The performer hands for examination a fifty-foot line, preferably a new clothes line, and offers himself to be bound up in any manner the audience sees fit, stipulating, however, that they commence at one end of the rope and finish at the other. This is one of the chief points of the trick, for we believe it is almost impossible for any person to tie you tight with this amount of line. While the committee from the audience are tying you slightly contract the muscles. Do this in such a manner that it will not be noticed by your audience, but rather contract the muscles of that part of the body that the rope is being fastened to. By the expansion of the lungs, and stiffening of the limbs the rope can be kept apparently tight. Stand as stiff as possible, place the hands or arms wherever required, allow them to be tied together at the sides, behind the back, or in front. They have to use one end of the rope, and threading it through each knot, loop, etc., will soon tire them and they will commence the winding of the rope around the body.

As soon as the rope is all wound and tied around you, request that you be carried to your cabinet, or behind a screen. Now comes the work of releasing yourself, which, after two or three attempts, you will be able to accomplish in the incredulously short time of two minutes. To commence with, draw in the breath, and shrink the body as much as possible. This allows you to see any slack loops, or looseness in the coils, etc. Nine cases out of ten you can release your hands first. No matter if you cannot, shake the loose coils around on your body, and begin to work them loose. Free the hands as soon as possible, or one hand. If the rope is around your neck release yourself here, and remove your coat (never be tied without it). This move practically places you in a position to remove the balance of the rope that is attached to your body, legs, etc. Mr. Ed-

The Art of Magic

wards takes only a few seconds to release himself, and rarely has to untie a knot. As before stated, the secret is this, it is *impossible* for any person to tie you in a standing position with fifty feet of any kind of rope so tight that you cannot "wriggle" out of it.

You should experience no difficulty in quickly releasing yourself on the first attempt, but for those who follow the strenuous side of the magical business and have a liking for this class of work, this release will be an easy matter and accomplished in a short time.

A good plan to work in connection with this "tie" is to force one of the hands to be tied first. This is accomplished by having a common slip knot in one end of the rope. Present the wrist to be tied first, then if bothered at all in trying to release yourself, get possession of a small sharp knife from your person, and cut the rope at the slip knot, and so have one free hand to work with. As soon as the rope is off and clear make a duplicate knot in the end of the rope and conceal the small piece of rope you have cut from the wrist about your clothing.

ESCAPE FROM A PAPER CYLINDER.

This particular method is, we believe, the invention of Mr. W. Russell, an exceedingly clever magician, who has given one or two "good things" to the profession since interested in magic.

The performer brings forward, and has examined, a large paper cylinder open at both ends, also half a dozen shoe strings, and a stick of sealing wax. The cylinder, which is made of stout wrapping paper, is then marked in any manner the audience see fit, and the performer is assisted into it and both ends tied with the shoe strings and the knots sealed.

The performer in his paper prison is then carried into his cabinet or behind a screen, and in a few minutes appears carrying the paper cylinder which is again examined without his means of exit being discovered.

To effect the escape the performer has concealed in his clothing a pocket knife with one of the blades ground down as

The Art of Magic

thin as possible, also a razor like edge. As soon as he is in his cabinet he gets possession of this knife and placing one of the mouths of the cylinder flat upon the floor feels for the strings and makes a clean cut about three-quarters of an inch long in the paper and also through one of the strings. This enables him to pull the other portion of the strings to the opening thus formed and sever them, allowing him to make his escape. He now quickly folds up the mouth of the cylinder in exactly the same shape as at first, and ties it with duplicate strings in the same manner as the committee from the audience did. He now procures from his pocket small bottle of alcohol and a cork with a piece of lamp wick threaded through it. The cork is removed from the bottle and the cork with wick inserted and lighted. A similar piece of sealing wax is now brought into play and the knots sealed as before, the complete operation lasting only a few minutes. Care must be taken to cover the cut in the paper with one of the folds, or better still, seal at this place.

THE GIANT MEMORY.

This feat depends upon a novel adaptation of the mnemonic system and has an excellent effect upon an audience blessed with more than the average intelligence. The performer hands a die to a spectator and requests that he throw it. We shall suppose for the sake of illustration that he throws 3. "Remember the number you threw," says the performer, who then hands the die to a second person, who, let us say throws 4. A third person throws 6. When eight or ten or even fifteen persons have thrown the die the performer tells each one his number.

In order to accomplish this effect the student has recourse to an ingenious system of mnemotechny. He imagines that all the persons throwing the number 1 wear silk hats; those throwing 2 wear a derby hat; those throwing 3 wear a straw hat; those throwing 4 wear a cap; those throwing 5 wear a full dress suit; and those throwing 6 a bathrobe. Of course any other series of pictures will accomplish the object as well as those enumerated, and the reader may easily arrange his own mnemonic code.

The Art of Magic

In taking the die out of the thrower's hand the performer looks fixedly in his face and fancies him with the hat or garment the number requires. When that same person, later on, asks the performer to name his number, the performer will remember the number by its association with the mental picture.

THE TRANCE VISION (First Method).

The performer distributes several blank cards and an equal number of envelopes with them. Each person is requested to write a question on the card, seal it in an envelope and hand it to the performer. The latter turns around for an instant and then hands the envelope back unbroken and in no way tampered with, and at the same time correctly answers the question written on the card. He repeats this with the other envelopes.

We are indebted to Mr. Henry Hardin for the secret of this ingenious trick. The performer has in his pocket a small electric light—the kind known as the pocket flashlight. In the act of turning around, or, preferably, in returning to his table, he takes the lamp out and, holding the envelope flat before him, presses the lens of the flashlight against the under side of the envelope. By pressing on the stud, which turns on the light, he is enabled to read the contents.

This trick is susceptible to development, and by means of the electric flashlight, the conjurer may treat his friends to a novel and mystifying effect which, in the parlance of the spiritualistic profession, is known as a "dark seance." In this form of entertainment each member of the audience writes a question on a small white card, addressing the missive to a spirit friend, and signing his or her own name. Each card is then sealed in an envelope, and sealing wax may be used as an extra precaution. The envelopes are collected on a tray and deposited on the conjurer's lap. The lights are put out, and the spectators sit in a circle holding one another's hands. The conjurer reads each question and answers it to the best of his ability.

The effect is little short of stunning, but the secret is simple. The small electric flashlight is employed. The conjurer has a

The Art of Magic

large hood or sack made of rubber cloth, or of any material impervious to light. This hood must be long enough to cover the upper portion of the person, including the head and hands. This sack, of course, is secreted in the pocket of the performer, or somewhere on his person. After the envelopes are collected and the lights extinguished the performer takes out the sack and places it over his head and the upper part of the body. Under cover of the hood the flashlight enables the conjurer to read the questions with perfect ease, and the effect of the answers depends upon the performer's ability and imagination. This is considered a very fine piece of spiritualistic work, and there is no reason why it should not be added to the repertoire of the parlor conjurer.

THE TRANCE VISION (Second Method.)

In this description the author takes pleasure in presenting Yank Hoe's original method of reading sealed questions. Twelve envelopes and the same number of cards are passed around, and twelve spectators write on the cards and seal them in envelopes. These are collected on a plate or small Japanese tray. Under this plate is an envelope containing a blank card, and in returning to the stage or to the table, this feke envelope is added to the stack, while one of the genuine envelopes is palmed. The performer hands plate and envelopes to his assistant and retires to rear of stage or drawing-room, and, picking up a handkerchief, wipes his hands. During this short trip, however, he has deftly removed the card from its envelope. The card is palmed in left hand and the envelope is disposed of in some convenient pocket, or is laid on a table in the act of replacing the handkerchief. Advancing toward the audience the performer takes an envelope from the tray held by assistant, places the billet to his forehead and apparently reads the contents. In reality, however, he reads the card in his palm. When the spectator who wrote the question acknowledges the authorship, the performer tears open the envelope, takes out the card, exchanges it for the one in his palm (the one just read) and hands the latter to the spectator. The other envelopes are read in the same manner. The last envelope, of course, contains the blank card, and this is simply exchanged for the written one.

This is by all odds the most perfect method of reading sealed envelopes, and obviates the necessity of having a confederate in the audience to write a pre-arranged sentence on one of the cards. So far as we are aware this is the first time that the explanation has appeared in print. We have explained the trick exactly as it was presented by the celebrated Yank Hoe and Omeni, his wife, when they were in the United States, in 1891. The drawing-room performer, however, will be able to present the trick without the services of an assistant.

Students desirous of making a stud yof this branch of magic art should procure Mr. David Abbott's book "Behind the Scenes with the Mediums."

THE QUICK OR THE DEAD.

Another mystifying and subtle experiment in mental magic. The performer hands five slips of paper to the spectators, requesting four persons to write the names of living celebrities and one person to write the name of a dead person. Each person folds his paper into a billet and all are mixed together on the table. The performer selects the paper on which the name of the dead person is written, and, holding the billet to his forehead, reads the name.

We shall first explain how the performer is enabled to select the slip bearing the dead name. Take a sheet of paper six inches by four and tear off from one end a strip about an inch in width. This strip, of course, will have a more or less jagged edge. The top edge, however, will be smooth. Hand this strip to a spectator and request him to write the name of a dead person. Now tear off another strip about an inch wide. Both edges of this strip will be jagged. Tear off three more strips of the same width, and *throw away* the remaining part of the sheet. These four strips will have jagged edges, and it is on these that the names of the living celebrities are written. The papers are now folded into billet shape and mixed together on the table. Owing to the

The Art of Magic

fact that one edge of the billet containing the dead name is jagged and the other edge smooth, the performer has no difficulty in distinguishing it from the billets on which the names of the live persons are written, for both edges of the latter are jagged or uneven. The reading of the name will present no difficulty. A pad containing impression paper may be used. A more subtle method is to use an envelope containing a letter. A small piece of impression paper is affixed inside the envelope and the missive is used as a pad for the convenience of the spectator. Other envelopes — of course unprepared — are handed to the other spectators. All the performer has to do in order to get a knowledge of the name is to turn his back and slip out the letter, on which the name is transferred. This is an excellent impromptu experiment.

In conclusion we can do no better service to the amateur than to epitomize the advice and counsel of the best magicians in the following DON'TS:

Don't address your audience too often as "ladies and gentlemen;" take it for granted that they are.

Don't try to be funny unless you are naturally.

Don't perpetrate "puns" or "wheezes." They are the lowest form of wit.

Don't verbally draw attention to the fact that your hands are empty. Give your audience credit for some intelligence.

Don't (if you are a professional) tell the manager how you "packed 'em in" at Squeedunk. He wants to know what you can do in his house.

Don't tell every one you meet that you are the inventor of the back hand palm—because you are not.

Don't cumber your programme with such expressions as "Marvelous Digital Dexterity" or "Magic, Mirth and Mystery." They have been used before.

Don't programme yourself as "Professor." You are an entertainer, not a pedagogue.

Don't speak of your work as a "swindle." Magic is an Art.

The Art of Magic

Don't think that because you are a magician you don't have to know anything else.

Don't prate too much of palming, and
DON'T EXPOSE!

L 'ENVOI.

The pleasant task is ended. The pen is laid aside not without a sigh of regret for the subject is as interesting as it is inexhaustible; and if the reader derives as much pleasure and satisfaction from a perusal of these pages as the author and editor has experienced in writing them, then the labor has not all been in vain. And we hope that the book will prove profitable as well as entertaining, and that at some future day we may renew our acquaintance with the reader in a further exploitation of "THE ART OF MAGIC."

THE END.

INDEX

CHAPTER I.

FLOURISHES AND FANCY SLEIGHTS WITH CARDS.

	PAGE
The Card Fan	19
Card Balancing	23
To Tear a Pack of Cards	24
The Fan and Ruffle	26
The Downs Fan	27
Springing the Cards	28
Second Method	30
Third Method	32
The One-Hand Drop	32
Second Method	33
The Cards on the Arm	34
A Series of Fancy Flourishes	35
The Flower of Cards	36
Throwing Cards	37
Cards from the Mouth	38

CHAPTER II.

CARD TRICKS WITH UNPREPARED CARDS AND NOT REQUIRING SLEIGHT OF HAND.

Novel Card Discovery	40
Second Method	41
Third Method	42
Fourth Method	42
New Methods of Concluding Card Tricks	43
Second Method	43
Third Method	44
The Reversed Card	46
The Piano Trick	47
The Transposed Cards	49

INDEX

CHAPTER III.

CARD TRICKS INVOLVING SLEIGHT OF HAND.

	PAGE
The Transfixed Pack	52
Second Method	55
Everywhere and Nowhere	55
Everywhere and Nowhere; new method	63
The General Card; T. Nelson Downs' Method	71
The Flying Card	77

CHAPTER IV.

SLEIGHT OF HAND WITH CARDS (Continued).

The Princess Card Trick	80
Second Method	82
The Prince's Card Trick	84
The Twenty Card Trick	85
A Comedy of Errors	87
The Siamese Aces	89
The Card in the Pocket	92
Houdini's Torn Card Trick	94
Barrington's Torn Card Trick	96
A Card Discovered by Sense of Touch	98
The Flying Cards	99
Second Method	107

CHAPTER V.

SLEIGHT OF HAND WITH CARDS (Continued).

The Cards up the Sleeve	111
Second Method	114
The Dissolved Card	124
The Mysterious Card	126
The Card and Hat	127
The Stabbed Card	127
The Great Poker Trick	128
Another Poker Trick	130
The Disappearing Queen	133
The Card Through the Handkerchief	136
The Card in the Watch	140
Second Method	141

INDEX

CHAPTER VI.
CARD TRICKS BASED ON A NEW AND ORIGINAL SYSTEM OF LOCATING A CHOSEN CARD.

	PAGE
Chosen Card Appears in Any Part of the Deck	142
Second Method	150
Third Method	150
Fourth Method	152
Fifth Method	154
Sixth Method	155
The Ubiquitous Cards	157
Second Method	162

CHAPTER VII.
CLAIRVOYANCE WITH CARDS.

First Method	165
Second Method	165
Third Method	166

CHAPTER VIII
A SERIES OF CARD TRICKS BASED ON A NEW AND ORIGINAL SYSTEM.

The Irregularities of Scroll Designed Cards	169
Mind-reading with Cards	171
Divination Extraordinary	173
The Transfixed Card	174
The Magician's Will Power	176
Prophecy Down-to-Date	178

CHAPTER IX.
THE RISING CARDS.

The Tattlings of Toto	184
DeKolta's Rising Cards	191
DeKolta's New Rising Cards	194
The Rising Cards in Swinging Houlette	198
The Thurston Rising Cards	202
Resurrection of the Cards	207

INDEX

CHAPTER X.
THE FOUR ACE TRICK.

	PAGE
First Method	213
Second Method	215
Third Method	216
Fourth Method	217
Fifth Method	218
Sixth Method	219
Seventh Method	221

CHAPTER XI.
CARD TRICKS WITH APPARATUS AND IN COMBINATION WITH OTHER OBJECTS.

Card, Orange and Candle	225
The Card in the Frame	229
The Valladon Cards on Glass	235

CHAPTER XII.
FANCY FLOURISHES WITH COINS, USEFUL SLEIGHTS AND ADDITIONS TO THE MISER'S DREAM.

An Illusive Coin Pass	243
The Hilliard Pass	245
The Coin Roll	246
The Coin Through the Knee	248
The Traveling Coin	249
Down's Latest Method for "The Miser's Dream"	249

CHAPTER XIII.
COIN TRICKS WITH AND WITHOUT APPARATUS.

The Sympathetic Coins	251
The Coin Through the Hat	255
The Expansion of Texture	256
The Bewitched Nickel	260
The Disappearing Dollars	261
The Free and Unlimited Coinage of Silver	262
Coin, Glass and Cone	263

INDEX

	PAGE
The Trained Half-Dollar	266
The New Flying Coin	267
The Coin Through the Hat	267
The Transmutation of Metal	268
Subtraction of Money	270
Every Man His Own Mint	270
New Coin Catching	271
A New Coin Combination	271
The Downs Coin Wand	273
The New Coin Wand	275
A New Coin Spider	276

CHAPTER XIV.

A COIN ACT AND A COIN LADDER.

A Coin Act and a Coin Ladder	278
The Coin Easel	282

CHAPTER XV.

TRICKS OF THE TRADE.

Tricks of the Trade	289

CHAPTER XVI.

TRICKS WITH EGGS.

To Balance an Egg on a Table	294
Egg Changed into Confetti	295
A New Idea in the Vanishing of an Egg	296
The Eggs from the Mouth	296
The Conjurer as Chicken Fancier	297
Japanese Egg Trick	298
The Latest Egg, Handkerchief and Glass Trick	300
"Eggsample"	304

CHAPTER XVII.

TRICKS WITH BALLS.

The Four-Ball Trick, with Novel Passes	305
Passing Four Solid Balls from Hand to Hand	310
Color Change with Four Solid Balls	313
The Traveling Balls	314

INDEX

CHAPTER XVIII.

MISCELLANEOUS TRICKS.

	PAGE
The Four Paper Balls and Plates	319
The Flying Salt	320
The Cigarette Paper Trick	321
The Torn Bank Note	325
The Bill and Lemon Trick	329
The Ring on the Wand	331
The Mysterious Match	332
The Inexhaustible Hat	333
The Mysterious Knot	335
The Vanishing Knot	336
The Mystic Tie	337
The Jacoby Rope Tie	338
The Rope Tie par excellence	341
Escape from a Paper Cylinder	342
The Giant Memory	343
The Trance Vision	344
Second Method	345
The Quick or the Dead	346
Don'ts	347
L'Envoi	348